Language an

Rachelle Vessey

Language and Canadian Media

Representations, Ideologies, Policies

palgrave
macmillan

Rachelle Vessey
Newcastle University
Newcastle Upon Tyne
United Kingdom

ISBN 978-1-137-53000-4 ISBN 978-1-137-53001-1 (eBook)
DOI 10.1057/978-1-137-53001-1

Library of Congress Control Number: 2016936505

Cover illustration: © PhotosIndia.com LLC / Alamy Stock Photo

Printed on acid-free paper

This Palgrave Macmillan imprint is published by Springer Nature
The registered company is Macmillan Publishers Ltd. London

Acknowledgements

Some material from Chap. 3 was originally published as "Vessey, R. (2015). Corpus approaches to language ideology. *Applied Linguistics,* by permission of Oxford University Press". http://applij.oxfordjournals.org/

Material from Chap. 5 was originally published in the following article:

Vessey, R. (2013). Too much French? Not enough French? The Vancouver Olympics and a very Canadian language ideological debate. *Multilingua, 32*(5), 659–682. http://www.degruyter.com/view/j/mult

Some material from Chap. 7 was originally published in articles in the following articles:

Vessey, R. (forthcoming 2016). Language ideologies in social media: the case of Pastagate. *Journal of Language and Politics, 15*(2). https://benjamins.com/#catalog/journals/jlp/main

Vessey, R. (2015). Food fight: moral panic in news and social media concerning 'Pastagate'. *Journal of Multicultural Discourses, 10*(2), 253–271. www.tandfonline.com

Contents

List of Figures

List of Tables

1

Introduction

> The Internet, new media and social media have become a way of life for many Canadians. These new forms of communication are affecting the lives of Anglophone and Francophone Canadians, who are using them in many areas. These new tools are both instant and accessible. The use of these new technologies is spreading quickly, but are Canadians' language rights being respected? (Canadian Standing Senate Committee 2012)

In 2011, the Canadian Standing Senate Committee on Official Languages undertook a study of Internet use and social media in Canada and observed that although the Internet and new and social media present opportunities for the French language (e.g. web initiatives to promote French and those who speak it), the Internet remains English-dominant (Senate Committee 2012: 102). Notably, the report stressed the need to expand the presence of French in the digital world (Senate Committee 2012: 103). While recommendations focussed primarily on the potential for action within the government and civil service, the Committee also stressed the importance of the private sector and the significant role of financial incentives in encouraging growth (Senate Committee 2012: 103).

R. Vessey, *Language and Canadian Media*,
DOI 10.1057/978-1-137-53001-1_1

Such recommendations allude to the powers of the nation-state and their role-effecting change in language issues. Although the Canadian government has been widely successful in effecting linguistic change in offline environments, the media have consistently posed challenges to the Canadian nation-state model. In particular, the emergence of new and social media that are transnational and "superdiverse" raises questions about the extent to which a government can continue to enforce language policies—and thus protect language rights—in an increasingly mediatised world. Moreover, viral news stories that present specific languages and language groups in a negative light indicate that the *presence* of a language in online spaces is not always the issue; rather, the issue is sometimes the extent to which explicit or implicit *representations* of these languages and speakers contribute to discourses about—and the uptake of—language policies.

Viral news stories that focus on languages and language groups highlight the provocative nature of language issues in Canada—and in particular official language issues. Although English and French are both the official languages of the country, they are not spoken in equal numbers from coast to coast, nor do they share a history of equality. While open debates about the two languages are not everyday affairs, beliefs about the two languages are embedded and naturalised in day-to-day life in Canada; they arguably underpin Canadians' very understanding of the country and, to some extent, their place within it. News stories, online commentary, and social media data can show how beliefs about languages become manifested and openly contested, but examinations of large-scale data sets can also show us the more mundane ways in which language ideologies are part of everyday Canadian discourse.

The theoretical framework of "language ideologies" is useful for explaining how language, identity, nationhood, and the state become interconnected in the social imaginary and represented in discourse. If beliefs about languages—or language ideologies—differ between French speakers and English speakers, then debates over the country's official languages may be inevitable. Moreover, since the vast majority (83 %) of Canadians are not fluent in both official languages (Statistics Canada 2011), most English and French speakers do not have full access to alternative perspectives voiced in the other language. Thus, if different language ideologies circulate within linguistic communities, then these may perpetuate the historic isolation of and misunderstandings between English- and French-speaking Canadians. It is the objective of this book to examine and compare language ideologies in English and French media data in order to identify how they contribute to language policymaking and the adoption of language policies on the ground.

This introductory chapter supplies some of the ideas presented in this book by exploring the role of language ideologies in the media. It begins by outlining previous research on language ideologies before turning to their study in news media. Although there has been less research on language ideologies in new and social media, an overview of scholarship in this emerging field will be provided. Having reviewed the state-of-the-art, the chapter will then turn to the research questions guiding the book, before concluding with an overview of the chapters.

1.1 An Introduction to Language Ideologies and the Media

Although the use of languages in media is certainly important for respecting language rights, there is also the question of *how* languages are being used, by whom, and for what purposes. More specifically, it is crucial to understand how languages are being represented—or misrepresented—in different media because such representations can have implications for the uptake of language policies and, thus, the respect of language rights. Even though representations of languages can be explicit (e.g. "English is practical"; "French is romantic"), they can also be implicit and take shape in incremental, banal ways. Whether explicit or implicit, representations of languages tend to be based on fundamental beliefs about and understandings of languages ingrained in a society and taken to be commonsense. In this book, such beliefs and understandings about languages are referred to as "language ideologies" (Woolard 1998). These are:

> Set[s] of beliefs on languages or a particular language shared by members of a community [...] These beliefs come to be so well established that their

> origin is often forgotten by speakers, and are therefore socially reproduced and end up being 'naturalized', or perceived as natural or as common sense, thereby masking the social construction processes at work. (Boudreau and Dubois 2007: 104)

Language ideologies include understandings of the role language does or should play in society, and these may involve beliefs about the kind or variety of language that is or should be spoken in (certain sectors of) society.

Language ideologies have been a topic of research for linguists since the 1970s (e.g. Silverstein 1979) and were largely defined by the publication of the edited collection *Language Ideologies: Practice and Theory* (Schieffelin et al. 1998). However, not all research that concerns beliefs about language in society has used the term "language ideology". For example, research on language attitudes, motivation, folk linguistics, language planning, prestige, standards, aesthetics, and language awareness all deal to a certain extent with beliefs about language (see Ager 2001; Coupland and Jaworski 2004: 23; Preston 2002; Ricento 2005; Ruiz 1984; Woolard 1998: 4). Talk about language, or "metalanguage", tends to express these beliefs, and metalanguage is studied across various disciplines (Kelly-Holmes and Milani 2011: 468). Jaworski et al. (2004a: 4) describe metalanguage in terms of what are often evaluative understandings and beliefs, referring to "[l]anguage in the context of linguistic representations and evaluations". Metalanguage may involve expressions of how language works, what it is normally like, what various ways of speaking may imply or connote, and what language ought to be like (Jaworski et al. 2004b: 3; Silverstein 1998: 136; Spitulnik 1998: 163). When metalanguage is used to make sense of the "reality of language", it tends to become ideological (Jaworski et al. 2004b: 3; Preston 2004: 87–89). However, since beliefs about and understandings of languages are not always explicitly stated (i.e. with metalanguage), the language ideologies framework is preferred here (cf. Johnson and Ensslin 2007: 7).

According to Woolard (1998: 3), language ideologies are "[r]epresentations, *whether explicit or implicit*, that construe the intersection of language and human beings in a social world" (emphasis added). Language ideologies may be implicit if, for example, they are naturalised and do not require articulation, or they may become explicit in "linguistic representations" (e.g. Boudreau 2008) or "language ideological debates" (Blommaert 1999a). Thus, "[i]deology is variously discovered in linguistic practice itself; in explicit talk about language, that is, metalinguistic or metapragmatic *discourse*; and in the regimentation of language use through more implicit metapragmatics" (Woolard 1998: 9). Language ideologies may concern linkages between such diverse categories as spelling and grammar with other categories such as nation, gender, authenticity, knowledge, power, and tradition. The linkages between language (or language features) and social categories are the result of what Silverstein (2003) calls the "orders of indexicality". Indexicality involves signs that either naturally or as a result of social construction point to some property common to a group (Squires 2010: 459). However, the orders of indexicality, as used by Silverstein, focus specifically on linguistic features and how strata of social meanings come to be indexed by these linguistic features: "'indexical order' is the concept necessary to showing us how to relate the micro-social to the macro-social frames of analysis of any sociolinguistic phenomenon" (Silverstein 2003: 193).

When a feature is noticed and correlated with a specific speech community, this is the first-order index (what Silverstein calls the *n*th order). When this order becomes metapragmatically linked to an entire speech group, this is a second-order index (what Silverstein calls the *n*th + 1 order). When these features are "objectified and metadiscursively linked to stereotypic personae", a third-order index (or *n*th + 1 + 1 order) is established (see discussion in Squires 2010: 460). The idea is that meaning is transferred from one level onto another level where two things are clearly less connected (Silverstein 2003: 194). Since dialects, accents, and lexicogrammar tend to be interpreted as indexical signals, readers and listeners ascribe meaning to these indexical signals through socially held orders of indexicality. The meaning attributed to indexical signals tends to be evaluative because communication is achieved because of—or fails as the result of—standards, norms, and expectations (Blommaert 2005b: 393). Since meanings, and thus evaluations, of indexes are not precise or fixed, the range of potential meanings is what Eckert (2008: 454) calls an "indexical field", which she defines as a "constellation of ideologically related meanings, any one of which can be activated in the situated use of the variable".

It is as a result of these indexical processes that beliefs about language become transferred onto speakers and language communities; such transfers can have real and important impacts on social life. For example, language ideologies can contribute to the value attributed to a language, which can impact on its perceived worth (or "misrecognition" of worth, see Blackledge 2005: 34; Bourdieu 1977; Spitulnik 1998: 163). Here, this will be referred to as the "commodification" of language; that is, the process of changing a language into a valuable commodity (Heller 2003). The belief that one language is more valuable than another, or that one language has any real marketable value at all, has a crucial effect on the function of a language in society (Bourdieu 1977: 30). Some language varieties come to be valued more than others because of attributions of social, moral, and political value to that language, and because of constructed links between languages and categories of people (Blackledge 2005: vii; Irvine 1998: 61; Woolard 1998: 19).

Throughout history, language has been associated with communities of speakers, their ethnicity, their culture, and their territory. These associations often evolve into nation-states with distinctive and defended language varieties; nation-internal coherence has been fostered by asserting the distinctiveness of the "national language" in opposition with other nations' (often closely related) languages. At the same time, "similar" language varieties have been used as the rationale for uniting speaker communities together as a single nation, wherein a single dialect is privileged over the others to encourage linguistic and social assimilation (see e.g. Kasuya 2001; Lo Bianco 2005). Nation-states have played an important role in the management of language ideologies by mediating between international/transnational models of language and national/local models and providing infrastructure (e.g. media, education, culture) for the (re)production of language regimes (Blommaert 2005b: 396–397). Of course, the increasingly globalised world has also had profound effects on communities, nations, and the language(s) that they speak.

One central way that globalisation has impacted on local communities is through the increased prestige of English as the "international" language. In today's world, English is the international language of the global market and fluency in English is often considered an invaluable asset (or symbolic resource, see Bourdieu 1977; see also Bolton and Kachru 2006; Heller 2003; Oakes and Warren 2007: 63; Ricento 2005: 352–353). This commodification of English has tended to have rather significant effects on communities that speak other languages. In fact, the growth and expansion of English has sometimes been at the expense (i.e. diminishment, "death" or "genocide", see Skutnabb-Kangas 2006) of minority languages, their speakers, and their cultures (May 2008). In reaction, there has been a growing movement to protect minority languages (see e.g. discussion in Duchêne and Heller 2007). In addition to commodifying English, globalisation has also had the reverse effect of encouraging communities to rediscover their roots as "legitimate" sources of identity and culture, and to "act locally", in part, by speaking and marketing their authentic, local language (Budach et al. 2003; Coupland 2003; da Silva et al. 2007; Heller 2003; Jaffe 2007: 149; King and Wicks 2009; Oakes and Warren 2007: 5, 17).

In this globalised context, languages and language varieties can be perceived as valuable in two overarching ways: language may be perceived as having a core or "intrinsic" value if it is seen as a cultural asset in a particular social group; and language may have an "instrumental" value that enables individuals to achieve specific goals (Ager 2001: 2–10; Gardner and Lambert 1959: 267; Oakes and Warren 2007: 34, 91; Robichaud and De Schutter 2012; cf. Kulyk 2010: 84 on the "ideology of understanding"). According to Garvin's (1993) conceptual framework of language standardisation, in locations where a language has predominantly instrumental value, individual fluency in a standard language is highly prized. In contrast, if a language tends to have predominantly intrinsic value, then expectations for individual fluency in a standard language may be lower. Garvin cites English-speaking countries as examples of places where the instrumental attachment to language dominates (Garvin 1993: 51; Yavorska 2010: 167). However, intrinsic and instrumental values are not necessarily mutually exclusive; languages that maintain a long-lasting and secure place in society arguably need both.

The respective value of different languages is not a natural fact; neither are the linkages between linguistic categories and social categories intrinsic. Rather, these beliefs, values, and understandings exist because they are part of and contribute to social practice. In other words, language ideologies affect our way of behaving and interacting in society. These are not abstract considerations of opinion or manipulation of the "truth"; language ideologies are organised and lived through practices, expectations, and understandings of human nature and the world (Williams 1973: 7). In other words, no language ideology is real or unreal, "right" or "wrong", "true" or "false"—ideology simply refers to lived experience that, because it is lived, "become[s] coextensive with itself" (Eagleton 2007: 58; see also Charland 1987: 143; Eagleton 2007: 13; Gal 1998: 321; van Dijk 1998: 24–29, 2006: 117). One way that language ideologies become "co-extensive" with lived reality is through the ways in which individuals speak about issues in society. While no single discussion in and of itself would necessarily have an impact on society, when ideologies become embedded in overarching ways of speaking that are shared throughout a community, these can help to (re)institute these ideologies in social life. In this book, "ways of speaking" will be referred to as "discourse".

In its most basic form, "discourse" refers to language above the sentence level; this is meaning that is not reducible to single words or phrases, but meaning that exists because of the complex links that exist among what is said, what has been said previously, and expectations of what will be said in the future. While texts are examples of people "doing" (i.e. communicating) what they think, pragmatic reasons prevent individuals from expressing all that they know and think. As a result, texts tend to be intertextual, drawing on the words, phrases, patterns, and even ideas that have been used by others. Meaning is achieved because of access to shared understandings of words and phrases and their uses in society. Thus, discourses are inherently social; they exist because of the complex ways through which meaning is conveyed in social contexts. Social groups that share common ways of expressing meanings can be called "discourse communities" (Swales 1990); these are composed of "individuals who share the same social practices" and thus who must, most of the time, "understand one another correctly" (Eagleton 2007: 13). However, just as most individuals belong to more than one social group, so too they are part of more than one discourse community and produce and consume more than one discourse.

Discourse is central to the study of language ideologies because, as Eagleton (2007: 9) remarks, "ideology is a matter of 'discourse' rather than 'language'". While texts only reflect the "tip of the [ideological] iceberg" (van Dijk 1998: 28), they tend to be created within discourse communities and contain at least some ideological discourse. Drawing on a common discourse, texts share commonalities in terms of language patterns, logical assumptions, and underlying ideologies. Thus, by examining individual texts, we can look at inventories of communication; by examining texts specific to social groups, we can start to conceive of a group's ideological discourse. Studying language ideologies therefore means, at least to a certain extent, the study of the social groups and their ways of communicating. Language ideologies contribute to transforming the beliefs and values of social groups into reality, but such transformations depend on the communication channels available to the groups in question (cf. Johnson 1999). As we will see in the next section, the media plays an important role in the dissemination of language ideologies across groups and spaces, thus contributing to the reification of commonsense notions in society—including those related to language issues.

1.2 Language Ideologies and News Media

Language ideologies have been central to the evolution of the media, beginning with the printing press, which arguably played a major role in the creation and diffusion of language ideologies. With the printing press and the rise of literacy, many groups of people found that they could understand and relate to each other despite geographic expanse and perhaps localised differences. In other words, since they could read and understand the same language and material, this facilitated the creation of a shared—albeit imagined—identity (Anderson 1983). Still today, many populations are convinced they belong to a unique community largely because they read, listen to, and watch the same material in a common language. A "nation" can be understood—at least in part—as a body of people sharing beliefs about and understandings of a language and believing themselves connected due to this shared language. The consequence of the connection between language and nation is that nations have tended to be conceptualised as monolingual and linguistically homogeneous. As Androutsopoulos (2007: 207–208) remarks, this intensified with the emergence of the mass media: "The mass media contributed to the constitution of national languages and gave rise to the linguistic ideal of public discourse in the monolingual nation-state: a language as homogeneous as the nation it represents." As a result, the belief in a singular, homogeneous national language emerged as a supposed indicator of national legitimacy.

The printing press was instrumental in the development of the news media. The news media became a particularly well-known site in the study of language ideology not least because they are powerful sites of ideological discourse production in society more generally. The mass media are social institutions that impact on the communication flow in society (Leitner 1997: 188) and thus have power over how individuals access information and communicate with each other. They also impact *which* information is disseminated to the public, how this information is presented, and at what point this information is released (Baker 2010: 141; Jaffe 2007: 166–167). According to Cotter (2001: 423), journalists "manipulate" temporal elements, and as a result they are not "stenographers or transcribers; they are storytellers and interpreters". However, since not all interpretations are explicit, they can involve hidden relations of power (Fairclough 1989: 49).

The news media, as producers and distributors of the information, directly affect the discursive representation, construction, and reproduction of society (see Bell 1998: 64–65; DiGiacomo 1999: 105; Fowler; 1991: 4; Machin and van Leeuwen 2007: 1–24). This is achieved, on the one hand, by manipulating the focus of the public eye on events that are deemed relevant, important, or "newsworthy", and on the other hand, simply by being a highly visible information source that has the capacity to distribute and publicise information over a vast geography (Bednarek 2006: 18; Conboy 2007: 30; Cotter 2010: 80; Fowler 1991: 13; Spitulnik 1998: 165). The capacity to distribute and publicise is particularly potent if a news agency forms part of a chain or conglomerate. When individuals or corporations own a number of newspapers and/or other media establishments (e.g. TV, radio), then competition for alternate sources of information is reduced (Bell 1991; Pritchard et al. 2005: 293; Soderlund and Hildebrandt 2005: 33).

When information is conveyed in the media, the impact is significant because it is considered authoritative, reproduced en masse, and widely distributed. The power of the news media is thus in part the result of its systematic tendencies and cumulative effect. As Fairclough (1989: 54) explains, "[a] single text on its own is quite insignificant: the effects of media power are cumulative, working through the repetition of particular ways of handling causality and agency, particular ways of positioning the reader, and so forth". As a result, the media has a more important function than that of an individual speaker or text. As Fowler (1991: 124) explains, "[t]he articulation of ideology in the language of the news fulfils, cumulatively and through daily iteration, a background function of reproducing the beliefs and paradigms of the community generally". Media discourse is designed for mass audiences, with a target audience or readership in mind; as a result, the communicative strategies deployed in the news are oriented and motivated by opportunities of reception and the chance of profit (see Bell 1991: 38; Bourdieu 1977: 654).

Within this news media system, journalists report news that is relevant to the "community of coverage" (Cotter 2010: 26). This includes not only people who are readers or listeners but also those who live in the media outlet's geographical region, or those who have exposure to it. The news is a discursive product that emerges from processes within the journalistic discourse community; this community includes not only journalists but also editors and news executives (Bell 1991: 38). Since these individuals tend to live and work in their inhabitant or geographic community, the ties between the journalist community and the community of coverage can be quite strong (Cotter 2010: 34). As a result, in order to produce news that appeals to the community of coverage, a newspaper tends to carry specific stories that are presented in such a way as to make the news relevant to and coherent with its community of coverage (Cotter 2010: 46; Fletcher 1998).

Sometimes it is clear which stories and perspectives are relevant to a community; however, other times journalists must deduce or assume. At these times, journalists presuppose a "prototypical image" or an "ideal" recipient (Fairclough 1989: 49; Leitner 1997: 189), appealing to what Bakhtin (1981) called the "superaddressee": an invisible but responsive and understanding third party existing above all individual participants in a dialogue. In other words:

> With a greater or lesser degree of awareness, every utterance is also constituted by another kind of listener, a supreme one "whose absolutely just responsive understanding is presumed, either in some metaphysical distance or in distant historical time" [...] This superaddressee would actively and sympathetically respond to the utterance and understand it in "just the right way". (Morson and Emerson 1990: 135)

The journalists adopt norms in such a way as to appeal not only to immediately identifiable addressees but also to an overarching, generalisable audience (see also Blommaert 2005a: 73, 2007: 118). This generalisation of public opinion arguably leads journalists to adopt the "vox populi", that is, the (presumed or assumed) voice and/or perspective of the community's dominant group (Fairclough 1989: 51; Karim 1993; Leitner 1997: 194).

By adopting dominant norms, the media appeal to, produce, and reproduce the discourse of the status quo wherein one social group dominates (Conboy 2007: 24; Cotter 2010: 187; Fowler 1991: 23). News discourse, although inherently intertextual (continuously drawing on the language of other people), thus continues to emphasise the language of the dominant group (Bakhtin 1981; Catenaccio et al. 2011: 1845). In this way, the news media are not solely responsible for the ideologies they may contain; rather, they can be taken as an example of ideological discourse that is already in circulation in society. Thus, although the news media are a powerful site of ideological discourse production, members of the journalistic discourse community are not authority figures in isolation from society; rather, they interact with the "community of coverage", which includes participants active in the media process (Bell 1991; Cotter 2001: 422; Eagleton 2007: 34; Gal 1998: 321; Jaffe 2007: 159; Robinson 1998: 4).

Despite the power of the news media, recipient uptake of the news is not prescribed or predictable, and the effects of media discourse can be equally uncertain. Leitner (1997: 189) explains that "[i]t is recipients that expose themselves to or withdraw from media output, they decode adequately or misconstrue content, they reinforce messages or alternatively nullify their effect". Audiences have the possibility—and indeed the power—to resist media discourse. The meanings contained in the news, then, are "a product of negotiation between readers and texts" (Garrett and Bell 1998: 2). The process of recipient uptake also involves the choice of information source. Although newspaper readership, for instance, is often restricted by newspaper availability (e.g. Canada is dominated by "one-newspaper-towns"), when there is a choice between newspapers, readers are drawn to papers that report stories in a way that is designed to evoke a particular response. The newspaper's "audience design" thus tends to accommodate addressees and their interests by reporting the "familiar and culturally similar" (Kariel and Rosenvall 1983: 431; see also Gagnon 2006: 80). Also, by including letters to the editor in the newspaper, the newspaper includes in a more visible way the discourse of its readers. Although many letters may be published in online editions of newspapers, only a small number of letters can be published in print versions. As a result, the selection of which letters to publish can have ideological implications (Richardson 2007: 151).

Nevertheless, it is important not to attribute undue causal power to the media as a distributor and disseminator of ideology (see, e.g. Eagleton 2007: 34). Some researchers argue that the study of ideology in the media may simply support a researcher's own "ideological frame" or bias about what may be present in the text. Bell (1998: 65), for example, warns that overeagerness to get to the "real meat" of ideological detective work can lead researchers to draw erroneous conclusions. Also, the search for ideology in the media often presumes clear, definable relations between linguistic choices and specific ideologies, attributing to individuals (i.e. reporters and editors) a far more deliberate ideological intervention than is likely (Cotter 2001: 421; see also Bell 1991: 214).

Another criticism of the study of ideology in the news media is that most analysts do not contextualise media language as the "outcome of a discourse process" (Cotter 2010: 4). Journalists, for example, report, write, edit, and produce text within the context of their discourse community (Catenaccio et al. 2011; Cotter 2001: 428; Sauvageau 2001: 38). Through socialisation in the community, journalists learn the ideological values and norms that underlie the news discourse, which include categorisations concerning how the world works and the beliefs that structure it (Conboy 2007: 30). Cotter (2010: 4) argues that a lack of understanding of the "normative routines of daily journalism" compromises linguistically oriented research into media language and discourse, since "everyday practice [...] shapes the language of the news". Journalists produce language within the context of membership in the journalistic discourse community; they are also not alone in the production of the news, since they work alongside editors and within institutional contexts (Bell 1991: 33–50).

In summary, the media does not so much produce but establish and reproduce ideas and values that are already present in society (Fowler 1991; Leitner 1997); news media also cannot be presumed to have a direct—or indeed any—impact on readers (Cotter 2010: 131; Johnson and Ensslin 2007: 9). Nevertheless, the news media remain an important site for the study of ideological discourse, in part because of the interweaving of the journalistic community and the community of coverage. Media discourse is not necessarily more ideological than any other discourse; all discourse is, to a certain extent, ideological, but media discourse has a more important function than that of an individual speaker or text. As Fowler (1991: 124) explains, "[t]he articulation of ideology in the language of the news fulfils, cumulatively and through daily iteration, a background function of reproducing the beliefs and paradigms of the community generally". In particular, the news media are an important site for the study of systematic beliefs and paradigms of the community that concern language (Delveroudi and Moschonas 2003: 6; Horner 2007: 144; Johnson and Ensslin 2007: 13; Pujolar 2007: 121; Spitulnik 1998).

News media are important in the study of language ideologies in three main ways. First, news texts are written by members of journalistic communities who have a "very self-conscious relationship to language" (Cotter 2010: 187). As Cotter (2010) has shown in detail, journalists' language attitudes tend to be conservative, prescriptive, and mainstream, and journalists tend to adhere to the "ideology of the standard" (Milroy 2001), believing that there is a singular "best practice" and that "optional variability" should be suppressed (see also Cameron 1995: 53). Also, Cotter (2010) explains, "meta-talk" (cf. metalanguage, above) is a part of everyday practice, and such talk is often evaluative and based on notions of correctness. Since journalistic communities interconnect with the communities of coverage, "commonsense" beliefs about language tend to be shared between these two communities. In other words, since most members of the public and most journalists are not linguists, the conclusions of both tend to embody "lay" notions of language (Cotter 2010: 190).

Together, journalistic attitudes and meta-talk help to shape the "prescriptive imperative" (Cotter 2010) of news language. Thus, news media are a particularly useful site for the study of standard language ideologies.

Second, the importance of linguistic "correctness" to news discourse is not simply a matter of journalistic preference: it is often required by the news outlet. The use of correct language is believed to contribute to accurate, clear, and precise reporting (Cotter 2010: 195), and this is often mandated in style guides and explicit and implicit standardisation policies (Cameron 1995: 45; Richardson 2007: 97). These guidelines and policies help to institute the fact that news texts tend to "embody a particular ideology of orthography, syntax, and usage" (DiGiacomo 1999: 105). These tendencies have important implications for the community of coverage; despite audience design meaning that the language of many news outlets aligns with the language of the community of coverage (Bell 1991), readers often come to expect the language of the news to be correct and to be a reliable sample of standard language. Indeed, well-respected newspapers are often a source of (what is seen to be) educated language usage for lexicographers and grammarians. Cameron (1995: 55) explains, "Thus when a *Times* editor or writer of the future goes to the dictionary for guidance, he or she may well be looking at a description of acceptable usage that is based on the usage of *The Times*."

Finally, the news media are an important site for the study of language ideologies because the news media tend to be a site where language issues are discussed (e.g. Cameron 1995; DiGiacomo 1999; Johnson and Ensslin 2007). These metalinguistic discussions do not necessarily rely on the voices of "experts" (e.g. Cameron 1995: 229–236; Cotter 2010: 220–229; Johnson 2001; Johnson and Ensslin 2007; Wallace and Wray 2002), but rather draw on the opinions of public figures (e.g. political leaders, representatives of civil society) who serve as "ideological brokers" (Blommaert 1999b) and even the general public through the ways in which the community of coverage engages with the news. Johnson and Ensslin (2007: 14) suggest that the media play an important role in helping to perform and refashion language issues into existence; this is because language ideologies pertain to the concern related to discourses *about* language—whether explicit or implicit—because "language is a fluid, discursive construct—an 'emergent property of social interaction'"

(Pennycook 2004: 7). Crucially, the media function at the centre of a matrix between the local and the global, between the personal and the private, and between the official and the popular spheres. It is because of these junctures that the media prove to be such a valuable site for the study of language ideologies.

1.3 Language Ideologies in New and Social Media

Of course, media do not only consist of news media. Media, Johnson and Ensslin (2007: 11) explain, consist of "any tools and techniques employable by intelligent mammals to carry out, consciously or unconsciously, an unlimited range of highly specific signifying practices". The participatory nature of Web 2.0 has changed the ways in which people communicate; the interaction between producers and consumers of mediatised language is much more complex than was previously the case with the journalistic community and the community of coverage in the news media (Androutsopoulos 2009: 286; Busch 2006: 207). Nevertheless—and despite increasingly multimodal affordances—new media still rely on language for communication. As such, writers, speakers, reporters, producers, and interlocutors more generally rely on normative understandings of language, vocabulary, and even style in order to communicate effectively (cf. Wright 2004: 2). Also, language issues continue to be an important topic of discussion online (Barton and Lee 2013).

In this book, new and social media refer to modes of communication that rely on technologies, and in particular the Internet, to promote and/or facilitate communication and interaction. These include, for example, instant messaging, email, Facebook, and Twitter. These media are used by and facilitate communication between individuals, groups, grassroots movements, businesses, corporations, NGOs, and heads of states alike; they also exist in a variety of languages at local, national, and supranational levels. New and social media do not only serve the purpose of interaction but also exist for informational purposes as individuals—and indeed news agencies and corporations—capitalise on the expanded possibilities of disseminating information to a wider public. These media have increasingly allowed for grassroots news reporting (including e.g. citizen journalism; Cotter 2010: 46), which again shifts understandings of the nature of "media language" from one associated with the newsroom and formalised institutional positions (e.g. reporters) to everyday people and their individual linguistic repertoires. In other words, media language is increasingly produced not within institutions but rather by and for individuals. Indeed, because new and social media have become integrated into communication in a range of different contexts, today, it is difficult to identify communication that is *not* mediated (cf. Barton and Lee 2013: 7).

In the past, media—and particularly news media—contributed to the formation and maintenance of social groups and even nation-states through the use of and meta-talk about standard and national languages. However, it is less clear what role language ideologies have in transnational social media (cf. Androutsopoulos 2013; Kelly Holmes and Milani 2011). While more traditional media such as newspapers have been the mainstay of, for example, the ideology of the standard (i.e. beliefs in prescriptive, normative language use; Milroy 2001), in "superdiverse" forums such as social media, the role of language ideologies is less clear. Social media normalise complex patterns of social relations and interactions across traditional boundaries; they also feature plurality, heterogeneity, and polycentricity in language use, communication, dissemination of information, and mediation of cultural practices (Leppänen et al. 2013). Accordingly, social media provide contexts for discussions about language in which traditional offline categories such as "speech community", "official language minority", and indeed "nation state" have questionable relevance (Gee 2005; Tagg 2015).

In such diverse, boundary-free environments, language ideologies could play any number of different roles, especially because of the variety of contextual factors affecting the interpretation of online messages (Kelsey and Bennett 2014). However, English continues to be a major player online and its role as a hegemonic medium of ideological transmission should not be underestimated. Thus, in new and social media, it remains unclear whether and how beliefs about language are manifested and the role they play in communication. It is the objective of this book to account for not only the ways in which language ideologies permeate news media but also their role in new and social media.

1.4 Research Questions

In summary, although there has been increasing research on the role of language ideologies in news media, there is less research on language ideologies in new and social media and little comparison of the language ideologies across these media types. There is also a notable gap in *comparative* research on ideologies in different cultures and languages. Most studies on language ideologies have tended to focus on monolingual media data and not comparable media data in different languages. This gap is in keeping with research in other areas wherein monolingualism prevails. Accordingly, this book aims to fill these gaps by examining the role of language ideologies in Canadian news, new and social media, and the increasingly diversified way in which such ideologies come to impact upon the "offline" Canadian nation-state. More specifically, because Canada has two official languages, this book examines English-medium and French-medium data and compares and contrasts the language ideologies therein. The research questions guiding this book are as follows:

1. How do the French and English Canadian media discursively represent (i.e. construct, construe, or allude to) languages and language issues?
2. Which language ideologies predominate in English and which predominate in French?
3. To what extent do the language ideologies that underpin traditional news media also exist in new and social media?

To answer these questions, the book covers a range of different data types and case studies that are contained within separate chapters.

1.5 Overview of Chapters

Chapters 2 and 3 provide some of the foundations for the book. Chapter 2 consists of an overview of relevant literature, including a brief history of language in Canada and a history of Canadian media including newspapers and new and social media. The chapter also highlights dominant theoretical and methodological frameworks that have been used in previous media research. Chapter 3 expands on this last point by exploring the methods that have traditionally been used to study language ideologies in the media and then explaining the precise approaches that were used in the analyses undertaken in the case studies in the later chapters.

Chapters 4, 5, 6, and 7 all consist of case studies of research on language ideologies in Canadian media. Chapter 4 is a study of English and French Canadian print newspapers from 2009 and, because there were no salient "language ideological debates" during this time period, provides a general overview of some of the language ideologies that exist in Canadian media. In separate sections, the chapter covers language ideologies in English and French Canadian newspapers and suggests some of the main differences between these. In Chap. 5, the focus moves from print newspapers to online newspapers, and in this case the issue is a "language ideological debate" about the use of English and French in the 2010 Vancouver Olympics opening ceremonies. In addition to the online newspaper data, the case study also draws on online news and commentary as data.

Chapter 6 presents findings from another case study, which examines the ways in which language ideologies are embedded in English and French Canadian Twitter. Data for this chapter consist of five different corpora: the Twitter accounts of Canada's three current main political party leaders and tweets containing Canadian politics hashtags (#polcan and #cdnpoli). Finally, Chap. 7 presents findings on a case study about a language ideological debate known as "Pastagate". Combining data from Twitter, online news, and news commentary, this chapter tackles the issue of finding commonalities across language ideologies in different media (news, commentary, and Twitter), different languages (English and French), and from different countries (Canada, the USA, the UK, and France). The findings from all chapters are drawn together in Chap. 8, which also returns to and addresses the research questions that were presented here.

References

Ager, D. (2001). *Motivation in language planning and language policy*. Clevedon: Multilingual Matters.

Anderson, B. (1983). *Imagined communities: Reflections on the origin and spread of nationalism*. London: Verso.

Androutsopoulos, J. (2007). Bilingualism in the mass media and on the internet. In M. Heller (Ed.), *Bilingualism: A social approach* (pp. 207–230). New York: Palgrave.

Androutsopoulos, J. (2009). Policing practices in heteroglossic mediascapes: A commentary on interfaces. *Language Policy, 8*, 285–290.

Androutsopoulos, J. (2013). Participatory culture and metalinguistic discourse. In D. Tannen & A. M. Trester (Eds.), *Discourse 2.0: Language and new media* (pp. 47–71). Washington, DC: Georgetown University Press.

Baker, P. (2010). *Sociolinguistics and corpus linguistics*. Edinburgh: Edinburgh University Press.

Bakhtin, M. (1981). *The diaglossic imagination* (Holquist, M. Ed., trans.: Emerson, C., & Holquist, M.). Austin: University of Texas Press.

Barton, D., & Lee, C. (2013). *Language Online: Investigating digital texts and practices*. London: Routledge.

Bednarek, M. (2006). *Evaluation in media discourse. Analysis of a newspaper corpus*. London: Continuum.

Bell, A. (1991). *The language of news media*. Oxford: Blackwell.

Bell, A. (1998). The discourse structure of news stories. In A. Bell & P. Garrett (Eds.), *Approaches to media discourse* (pp. 64–104). Oxford: Blackwell.

Blackledge, A. (2005). *Discourse and power in a multilingual world*. Amsterdam: John Benjamins.

Blommaert, J. (Ed.). (1999a). *Language ideological debates*. Berlin: Mouton de Gruyter.

Blommaert, J. (1999b). The debate is open. In J. Blommaert (Ed.), *Language ideological debates* (pp. 1–38). Berlin: Mouton de Gruyter.

Blommaert, J. (2005a). *Discourse: A critical introduction*. Cambridge: Cambridge University Press.

Blommaert, J. (2005b). Situating language rights: English and Swahili in Tanzania revisited. *Journal of Sociolinguistics, 9*(3), 390–417.

Blommaert, J. (2007). Sociolinguistics and discourse analysis: Orders of indexicality and polycentricity. *Journal of Multicultural Discourses, 2*(2), 115–130.

Bolton, K., & Kachru, B. B. (Eds.). (2006). *World Englishes*. Abingdon: Routledge.

Boudreau, A. (2008). Le français parlé en Acadie: idéologies, représentations et pratiques. In *La langue française dans sa diversité* (pp. 59–74). Government of Quebec. Available http://www.spl.gouv.qc.ca/fileadmin/medias/pdf/actes_colloque_langue_francaise_2008.pdf

Boudreau, A., & Dubois, L. (2007). *Français, acadien, acadjonne*: Competing discourses on language preservation along the shores of the Baie Sainte-Marie.

In M. Heller & A. Duchêne (Eds.), *Discourses of endangerment: Ideology and interest in the defence of languages* (pp. 99–120). London: Continuum.

Bourdieu, P. (1977). The economics of linguistics exchanges. *Social Sciences Information, 16*(6), 645–668.

Budach, G., Roy, S., & Heller, M. (2003). Community and commodity in French Ontario. *Language in Society, 32*(5), 603–627.

Busch, B. (2006). Changing media spaces: The transformative power of heteroglossic practices. In C. Mar-Molinero & P. Stevenson (Eds.), *Language ideologies, policies and practices: Language and the future of Europe* (pp. 206–219). Basingstoke: Palgrave Macmillan.

Cameron, D. (1995). *Verbal hygiene*. London: Routledge.

Canadian Standing Senate Committee on Official Languages. (2012). *Internet, new media and social media: Respect for language rights!* Available http://www.parl.gc.ca/Content/SEN/Committee/411/OLLO/rep/rep05oct12-e.pdf

Catenaccio, P., Cotter, C., de Smedt, M., Garzone, G., Jacobs, G., Macgilchrist, F., Lams, L., Perrin, D., Richardson, J. E., van Hout, T., & van Praet, E. (2011). Towards a linguistics of news production. *Journal of Pragmatics, 43*, 1843–1852.

Charland, M. (1987). Constitutive rhetoric: The case of the *peuple québécois. Quarterly Journal of Speech, 73*, 133–150.

Conboy, M. (2007). *The language of the news*. Abingdon: Routledge.

Cotter, C. (2001). Discourse and media. In D. Schiffrin, D. Tannen, & H. E. Hamilton (Eds.), *The handbook of discourse analysis* (pp. 416–436). Oxford: Blackwell Publishers.

Cotter, C. (2010). *News talk: Investigating the language of journalism*. Cambridge: Cambridge University Press.

Coupland, N. (2003). Sociolinguistic authenticities. *Journal of Sociolinguistics, 7*(4), 417–431.

Coupland, N., & Jaworski, A. (2004). Sociolinguistic perspectives on metalanguage: Reflexivity, evaluation and ideology. In A. Jaworski, N. Coupland, & D. Galasiński (Eds.), *Metalanguage: Social and ideological perspectives* (pp. 15–52). Berlin: Mouton de Gruyter.

da Silva, E., McLaughlin, M., & Richards, M. (2007). Bilingualism and the globalized new economy: The commodification of language and identity. In M. Heller (Ed.), *Bilingualism: A social approach* (pp. 183–206). New York: Palgrave.

Delveroudi, R., & Moschonas, S. A. (2003). Le purisme de la langue et la langue du purism. *Philologie im Netz, 24*, 1–23.

DiGiacomo, S. M. (1999). Language ideological debates in an Olympic city: Barcelona 1992–1996. In J. Blommaert (Ed.), *Language ideological debates* (pp. 105–142). Berlin: Mouton de Gruyter.

Duchêne, A., & Heller, M. (Eds.). (2007). *Discourses of endangerment: Ideology and interest in the defence of languages.* London: Continuum.

Eagleton, T. (2007). *Ideology. An introduction.* (New and updated ed.). London: Verso.

Eckert, P. (2008). Variation and the indexical field. *Journal of Sociolinguistics, 12*(4), 453–476.

Fairclough, N. (1989). *Language and power.* Essex: Longman.

Fletcher, F. J. (1998). Media and political identity: Canada and Quebec in the era of globalization. *Canadian Journal of Communication, 23*(3). Retrieved from http://www.cjc-online.ca/index.php/journal/article/view/1049/955

Fowler, R. (1991). *Language in the news: Discourse and ideology in the press.* London: Routledge.

Gagnon, C. (2006). Language plurality as power struggle, or: Translating politics in Canada. *Target, 18*(1), 69–90.

Gal, S. (1998). Multiplicity and contention among language ideologies: A commentary. In B. B. Schieffelin, K. A. Woolard, & P. V. Kroskrity (Eds.), *Language ideologies. Practice and theory* (pp. 317–332). Oxford: Oxford University Press.

Gardner, R. C., & Lambert, W. E. (1959). Motivational variables in second-language acquisition. *Canadian Journal of Psychology, 13*(4), 266–273.

Garrett, P., & Bell, A. (1998). Media and discourse: A critical overview. In A. Bell & P. Garrett (Eds.), *Approaches to media discourse* (pp. 1–20). Oxford: Blackwell.

Garvin, P. (1993). A conceptual framework for the study of language standardization. *International Journal of the Sociology of Language, 100*(101), 37–54.

Gee, J. P. (2005). Semiotic social spaces and affinity spaces: From the age of mythology to today's schools. In D. Barton & K. Tusting (Eds.), *Beyond communities of practice* (pp. 214–232). Cambridge: CUP.

Heller, M. (2003). Globalization, the new economy, and the commodification of language and identity. *Journal of Sociolinguistics, 7*(4), 473–492.

Horner, K. (2007). Global challenges to nationalist ideologies: Language and education in the Luxembourg press. In S. Johnson & A. Ensslin (Eds.), *Language in the media: Representations, identities, ideologies* (pp. 130–148). London: Continuum.

Irvine, J. T. (1998). Ideologies of honorific language. In B. B. Schieffelin, K. A. Woolard, & P. V. Kroskrity (Eds.), *Language ideologies. Practice and theory* (pp. 51–67). Oxford: Oxford University Press.

Jaffe, A. (2007). Corsican on the airwaves: Media discourse in a context of minority language shift. In S. Johnson & A. Ensslin (Eds.), *Language in the media: Representations, identities, ideologies* (pp. 149–172). London: Continuum.

Jaworski, A., Coupland, N., & Galasiński, D. (Eds.). (2004a). *Metalanguage: Social and ideological perspectives*. Berlin: Mouton de Gruyter.

Jaworski, A., Coupland, N., & Galasiński, D. (2004b). Metalanguage: Why now? In A. Jaworski, N. Coupland, & D. Galasiński (Eds.), *Metalanguage: Social and ideological perspectives* (pp. 3–10). Berlin: Mouton de Gruyter.

Johnson, S. (1999). *From linguistic molehills to social mountains? Introducing moral panics about language* (Lancaster University Centre for Language in Social Life Working Papers Series 105). http://www.ling.lancs.ac.uk/pubs/clsl/clsl105.pdf. Accessed 4 Dec 2014.

Johnson, S. (2001). Who's misunderstanding whom? Sociolinguistics, public debate and the media. *Journal of Sociolinguistics, 5*(4), 591–610.

Johnson, S., & Ensslin, A. (2007). Language in the media: Theory and practice. In S. Johnson & A. Ensslin (Eds.), *Language in the media: Representations, identities, ideologies* (pp. 3–23). London: Continuum.

Kariel, H. G., & Rosenvall, L. A. (1983). Cultural affinity displayed in Canadian daily newspapers. *Journalism Quarterly, 60*(3), 431–436.

Karim, K. H. (1993). Construction, deconstructions, and reconstructions: Competing Canadian discourses on ethnocultural terminology. *Canadian Journal of Communication, 18*(2). Retrieved from http://www.cjc-online.ca/index.php/journal/article/viewArticle/744/650

Kasuya, K. (2001). Discourses of linguistic dominance: A historical consideration of French language ideology. *International Review of Education, 47*(3–4), 235–251.

Kelly-Holmes, H., & Milani, T. M. (2011). Thematising multilingualism in the media. *Journal of Language and Politics, 10*(4), 467–489.

Kelsey, D., & Bennett, L. (2014). Discipline and resistance on social media: Discourse, power and context in the Paul Chambers 'Twitter joke trial'. *Discourse, Context & Media, 3*(1), 37–45.

King, R., & Wicks, J. (2009). "Aren't we proud of our language?" Authenticity, commodification, and the Nissan Bonavista television commercial. *Journal of English Linguistics, 37*(3), 262–283.

Kulyk, V. (2010). Ideologies of language use in post-Soviet Ukrainian media. *International Journal of the Sociology of Language, 201*(1), 79–104.

Leitner, G. (1997). The sociolinguistics of communication media. In F. Coulmas (Ed.), *The handbook of sociolinguistics* (pp. 187–204). Oxford: Blackwell.

Leppänen, S., Kytölä, S., Jousmäki, H., Peuronen, S., & Westinen, E. (2013). Entextualization and resemiotization as resources for identification in social media. In P. Seargeant & C. Tagg (Eds.), *The language of social media* (pp. 112–138). Houndsmills: Palgrave Macmillan.

Lo Bianco, J. (2005). Globalisation and national communities of communication. *Language Problems and Language Planning, 29*(2), 109–133.

Machin, D., & van Leeuwen, T. (2007). *Global media discourse: A critical introduction.* Abingdon: Routledge.

May, S. (2008). *Language and minority rights: Ethnicity, nationalism and the politics of language.* New York: Routledge.

Milroy, J. (2001). Language ideologies and the consequences of standardization. *Journal of Sociolinguistics, 5*(4), 530–555.

Morson, G., & Emerson, C. (1990). *Mikhail Bakhtin: Creation of a prosaics.* Palo Alro: Stanford University Press.

Oakes, L., & Warren, J. (2007). *Language, citizenship and identity in Quebec.* Basingstoke/England/New York: Palgrave Macmillan.

Preston, D. R. (2002). Language with an attitude. In J. K. Chambers, P. Trudgill, & N. Schilling-Estes (Eds.), *The handbook of language variation and change* (pp. 40–66). Oxford: Blackwell.

Preston, D. R. (2004). Folk metalanguage. In A. Jaworski, N. Coupland, & D. Galasiński (Eds.), *Metalanguage: Social and ideological perspectives* (pp. 75–104). Berlin: Mouton de Gruyter.

Pritchard, D., Brewer, P. R., & Sauvageau, F. (2005). Changes in Canadian journalists' views about social and political roles of the news media: A panel study, 1996–2003. *Canadian Journal of Political Science, 38*(2), 287–306.

Pujolar, J. (2007). The future of Catalan: Language endangerment and nationalist discourses in Catalonia. In M. Heller & A. Duchêne (Eds.), *Discourses of endangerment: Ideology and interest in the defence of languages* (pp. 121–148). London: Continuum.

Ricento, T. (2005). Problems with the 'language-as-resource' discourse in the promotion of heritage languages in the U.S.A. *Journal of Sociolinguistics, 9*(3), 348–368.

Richardson, J. E. (2007). *Analysing newspapers: An approach from critical discourse analysis.* Basingstoke: Palgrave.

Robichaud, D., & De Schutter, H. (2012). Language is just a tool! On the instrumental approach to language. In B. Spolsky (Ed.), *The Cambridge handbook of language policy* (pp. 124–146). Cambridge: Cambridge University Press.

Robinson, G. (1998). *Constructing the Quebec referendum: French and English media voices.* Toronto: University of Toronto Press.

Ruiz, R. (1984). Orientations in language planning. *NABE (The Journal for the National Association for Bilingual Education), 8*(2), 15–34.

Sauvageau, F. (2001). Would the real journalists please stand up! In J.-P. Baillargeon (Ed.), *The handing down of culture, smaller societies, and globalization* (pp. 35–42). Toronto: Grubstreet Books.

Schieffelin, B. B., Woolard, K. A. & Kroskrity, P. A. (Eds.) (1998). Language ideologies. *Practice and theory* (pp. 285–316). Oxford: Oxford University Press.

Silverstein, M. (1979). Language structure and linguistic ideology. In P. Clyne, W. Hanks, & C. Hofbauer (Eds.), *The elements: A parasession on linguistic units and levels* (pp. 193–247). Chicago: Chicago Linguistic Society.

Silverstein, M. (1998). The uses and utility of ideology: A commentary. In B. B. Schieffelin, K. A. Woolard, & P. V. Kroskrity (Eds.), *Language ideologies. Practice and theory* (pp. 123–148). Oxford: Oxford University Press.

Silverstein, M. (2003). Indexical order and the dialectics of sociolinguistic life. *Language & Communication, 23*(3–4), 193–229.

Skutnabb-Kangas, T. (2006). Language policy and linguistic human rights. In T. Ricento (Ed.), *An introduction to language policy* (pp. 273–291). Malden: Blackwell Publishing.

Soderlund, W. C., & Hildebrandt, K. (2005). The relationship between the press and democratic politics. In K. Hildebrandt & W. C. Soderlund (Eds.), *Canadian newspaper ownership in the era of convergence rediscovering social responsibility* (pp. 1–10). Edmonton: University of Alberta Press.

Spitulnik, D. (1998). Mediating unity and diversity: The production of language ideologies in Zambian broadcasting. In B. B. Schieffelin, K. A. Woolard, & P. V. Kroskrity (Eds.), *Language ideologies. Practice and theory* (pp. 163–188). Oxford: Oxford University Press.

Squires, L. (2010). Enregistering internet language. *Language in Society, 39*(4), 457–492.

Statistics Canada. (2011). *Canada at a glance.* Available http://www.statcan.gc.ca/pub/12-581-x/12-581-x2012000-eng.pdf

Swales, J. (1990). *Genre analysis: English in academic and research settings.* Cambridge: University of Cambridge Press.

Tagg, C. (2015). Exploring digital communication: Language in action. Abingdon: Routledge.

Van Dijk, T. A. (1998). Opinions and ideologies in the press. In A. Bell & P. Garrett (Eds.), *Approaches to media discourse* (pp. 21–63). Oxford: Blackwell.

Van Dijk, T. A. (2006). Ideology and discourse analysis. *Journal of Political Ideologies, 11*(2), 115–140.

Wallace, M., & Wray, A. (2002). The fall and rise of linguists in education policy-making: From "common sense" to common ground. *Language Policy, 1*(1), 75–98.

Williams, R. (1973). Base and superstructure in Marxist cultural theory. *New Left Review, 82*, 1–14. Retrieved from http://www.newleftreview.org/?getpdf=NLR08101&pdflang=en

Woolard, K. A. (1998). Introduction: Language ideology as a field of inquiry. In B. B. Schieffelin, K. A. Woolard, & P. V. Kroskrity (Eds.), *Language ideologies. Practice and theory* (pp. 3–50). Oxford: Oxford University Press.

Wright, S. (2004). *Language policy and language planning: From nationalism to globalisation*. Basingstoke: Palgrave Macmillan.

Yavorska, G. (2010). The impact of ideologies on the standardization of modern Ukrainian. *International Journal of the Sociology of Language, 201*, 163–197.

2

The Media in Canada

While Chap. 1 explored the ways in which the media have played an important role uniting people into nations across the globe, in Canada the media have played a particularly unique role in creating connections between the diverse areas and people of Canada—and across the two official languages. Vipond (2012: 12) remarks that networks of communication, fostered by the mass media, have been central to "both the material and mythological definition of Canada". This chapter examines how Canada has been defined by and through the media, and in particular how language ideologies have been embedded in this history. More specifically, the chapter explores the evolution of Canadian media concomitant with Canadian language politics and the so-called two solitudes. The discussion begins with a brief history of radio and newspapers in Canada before turning to the status quo of new and social media.

R. Vessey, *Language and Canadian Media*,
DOI 10.1057/978-1-137-53001-1_2

2.1 Brief History of Language in Canada

There is a Canadian cliché, drawn from a novel by Hugh MacLennan (1945), that Canada is composed of "two solitudes", one of English speakers, and the other of French speakers. This, Heller (1999: 143) explains, refers to

> the seemingly insurmountable obstacles which keep Canada's two major linguistic groups apart. And not just apart; alone, isolated one from the other, unable to share the other's experience, and hence incapable of understanding the other's point of view.

Even today, this phrase continues to be used to evoke the incongruity of Canada's two dominant linguistic groups, which dates from the European colonisation of North America.

Canada was home to numerous indigenous groups prior to the arrival and establishment of permanent European settlements in the sixteenth and seventeenth centuries. The French were the first Europeans to set roots down on Canadian soil, establishing communities in areas of what is now Atlantic Canada and Quebec. The settlers of these communities inhabited the area for so long that when France ceded the majority of its claims to North America to Britain in the Treaty of Paris in 1763, many communities had little real attachment to France. Despite their mother tongue, many felt more connected to North America than to the land of their European forefathers (see e.g. Allaire 2007: 30; Bouchard 2002: 59–63; Conlogue 2002: 50; Landry and Lang 2001: 66–71). As a result, many French speakers chose to stay in Canada even after the territory was officially passed over to the British. Others, unfortunately, did not have a choice and were effectively abandoned by France when the territory was ceded to Britain. A predominantly English-speaking Britain thus came into possession of a vast territory that was inhabited by a majority of French speakers until the 1830s (Bouchard 2002: 79). Although increasing numbers of British colonialists, and later, other immigrants, came to occupy the land, the historical population of French speakers continued to flourish and continued to comprise a sizeable proportion of the Canadian population.

The French-speaking population was concentrated in the territory of what is now Quebec and disparate regions of Acadia (now Atlantic Canada). However, French speakers migrated away from these original heartlands, and pockets of French-speaking communities spread across the country. In fact, a "French belt" of communities extended from the St Lawrence River, down the Great Lakes of Ontario, and into the USA (Conrick and Regan 2007: 13). In the meantime, immigrants to Canada arrived in increasing numbers and tended to adopt the English language and assimilate into the English-speaking community, leaving French speakers largely apart, marginalised, and distinct from the rest of Canada (Conrick and Regan 2007: 19–20). Fearing that Canada would follow the USA in a quest for independence, and that this would be spearheaded by French speakers' discontent with British rule, Britain introduced the Quebec Act in 1774. This allowed the province to maintain its historic civil law code, system of land tenure, and Catholic tradition, all of which were diametrically opposed to the rest of Canada (Bouchard 2002: 59; Fraser 2006: 15).

The separation of the populations continued thus well into the twentieth century. Indeed, although Canada modernised, progress was not uniform or consistent across the various sectors of its population. French speakers and indigenous groups notably continued to live as they had throughout the previous centuries. A change in the pattern only emerged when, in Quebec, French speakers were forced to move from the country into more urban areas because of a population boom that resulted in decreased availability of farming land (Bouchard 2002: 72). The move of French speakers to urban areas resulted in large numbers of youths who were able to attain higher education. This unprecedented access to education gave rise to a generation of French speakers who began to bear witness to fundamental discrepancies in Canadian society (see Oakes and Warren 2007: 9). Educated and freed from the commitment to agricultural work, they were nevertheless generally obliged to work for English-speaking industrialists who controlled the economy across Canada—including in Quebec, where the vast majority of the population did not speak English (see e.g. Fraser 2006: 21). French speakers were therefore dominated by English speakers, even in the territory where they formed the sizeable majority (Conrick and Regan 2007: 35). An increasing awareness of the status quo amongst the new, educated French-speaking middle class resulted in general uprisings across Quebec in the 1960s and 1970s that came to be known as the Quiet Revolution (*la Révolution tranquille*).

The Quiet Revolution led to a number of sociopolitical changes in Quebec and across Canada. In Quebec, the elected conservative *Union Nationale* government fell and subsequent government parties sought to equalise the power structure of Quebec society. Government changes to the social landscape included the nationalisation of the power corporation (Hydro-Québec) and language policies that, above all, made French the official language of the province (see e.g. Ignatieff 1994: 113; Oakes and Warren 2007: 84–91). The success and popularity of these changes, alongside a newfound recognition of difference from the rest of the country, fostered a national movement wherein the plausibility of forming a separate, distinct, French-speaking nation-state became possible. This national movement, primarily linguistic and cultural in essence, was at the basis a reinterpretation and reformulation of the historic French Canadian nation (Oakes and Warren 2007: 26–32). However, the nationalist movement was also territorial and defined according to the provincial boundaries of Quebec. As a result, French speakers living outside Quebec were, for the most part, not included in the nationalist movement. New categories of belonging evolved: from what were once known as "the French Canadian nation" and "French Canadians" categorically emerged the Quebec nation and the *Québécois* (see e.g. Pelletier 2003: 38), French Ontario and French Ontarians (*franco-Ontariens*), French Manitoba and French Manitobans (*franco-Manitobains*), and so on (Bouthillier 1997: 117). Charland (1987: 134) notes that with the renaming of Quebec, a "national identity for a new type of political subject was born, a subject whose existence would be presented as justification for the constitution of a new state". In other words, the new identity label "Québécois" emphasised an allegiance to an emerging Quebec nation-state, which was an alternative to the label "French Canadian" that presupposed allegiance to Canada (McRoberts 1997: 183; Robinson 1998: 28).

Quebec's nationalist movement resulted in Canada becoming indexed by language and geography with new and ideological categories of belonging. Indeed, the link between language and community—if not nation—has become largely essentialised to the extent that identity labels in Canada tend to be linguistic (see Giampapa 2001; Heller 1999: 144; Karim 1993; Labelle and Salée 2001; Patrick 2007: 44). According to Karim (1993), it is common to use a "tripartite linguistic distinction" in Canada to distinguish between identity categories: francophones (French speakers), anglophones (English speakers), and allophones (those whose first language is neither English nor French) (see also Bouthillier 1997: 83–84, 117). In the most recent Census, Statistics Canada has moved away from this simplistic tripartite distinction (Marian Scott 2012), which notably does not include First Nations and aboriginal peoples and is a simplistic way of conceptualising Canada's diverse population of 33.5 million. The categories are, though, indicative of the ways social groups in Canada have tended to be indexed by language (Molinaro 2005: 98).

The rise of Quebec nationalism and its related secessionist movement forced the Canadian federal government to make major adjustments to the political landscape. Then Prime Minister Pierre Trudeau made it his priority to stem the tide of nationalism flowing from Quebec and to make Quebec an integral part of a pan-Canadian nation. Indeed, in his view, nationalism is passionate, emotional, and irrational behaviour that contrasts with "cold, unemotional rationality" (Trudeau 1968: 202–203, emphasis in original):

> nationalism cannot provide the answer [...] It is possible that nationalism may still have a role to play in backward societies where the *status quo* is upheld by irrational and brutal forces; in such circumstances, *because there is no other way*, perhaps the nationalist passions will still be found useful to unleash revolutions, upset colonialism, and lay the foundations of welfare states.

While in office, some of Trudeau's most notable initiatives included the reformulation of new Canadian linguistic, and later cultural, policies. French and English were made the official languages of the federal government in a move to show how French speakers in Quebec, along with minority French speakers in the rest of Canada, could, like their English-speaking counterparts, communicate with their elected representatives (see Webber 1994: 58). Later, the multiculturalism policy (Canadian Multiculturalism Act, R.S.C. 1985, c. 24 (fourth Supp.)) made all cultures equal in Canada; in other words, "multiculturalism" was made the official culture rather than any single culture. The idea was to show privilege to no single community over any other. In the words of Trudeau himself (1968: 5), "Canada must become a truly bilingual country in which the linguistic majority stops behaving as if it held special and exclusive rights, and accepts the country's federal nature with all its implications". Society was to be de-stratified according to language and culture, and instead, individuals were to be equal. Not showing privilege also meant not recognising any particular status for Quebec (see Vipond 1996).

Quebec is not the only province that is home to French speakers; minority French-speaking communities exist in other provinces, including Manitoba, Saskatchewan, Ontario, and the Atlantic provinces (Nova Scotia, New Brunswick, Prince Edward Island, and to some extent Newfoundland and Labrador). Faced with English majorities, though, these minority French speakers have struggled throughout history (see e.g. Bouchard 2002; Hayday 2005; MacMillan 1998: 45). Although the Royal Commission on Bilingualism and Biculturalism (commonly known as the "B&B Commission") made recommendations, based on in-depth research, to protect French speakers, many of these were not adopted at either federal or provincial levels (see e.g. Innis 1973; Fraser 2006; Haque 2012; Hayday 2005). Ontario, for instance, resisted pressure to declare itself officially bilingual despite a sizeable and historic French-speaking population, and Quebec went the other direction, declaring French the official language despite a substantial population of English speakers. However, New Brunswick and the National Capital Region of Ottawa (Ontario) and Gatineau (Quebec) were made officially bilingual. Indeed, reactions to the Commission varied from province to province, and in some cases these provincial differences can be attributed to the subjectivity of individual provinces' own historic relationship with French-speaking minorities. In sum, there are fundamental political and historical divides in Canada that tend to be marked by language.

Simon (1992: 159) has argued that social categories based on class in the UK and race in the USA are comparable to social categories based on language in Canada. Language marks a national divide by serving as both the medium and the message (i.e. the subject) in ideological debates in Canada. Language is a distinctive feature of Quebec, the home to and representative of the majority of Canada's French speakers; Quebec continues to seek recognition of its distinctiveness and autonomy over both its internal and international affairs, particularly with regard to language. Other Canadian provinces are English-dominant; many have adopted policies that tend to either condone or condemn French speakers. For example, while a policy of bilingualism in New Brunswick supports the minority French-speaking community, Ontario's resistance to a policy of official bilingualism arguably avoids the recognition of French speakers as a historical founding people of the province (for a discussion of alternative Ontarian language legislation, see Boileau 2011).

Each province has a unique historical, political, and cultural relationship with language. While most Canadian provinces are English-dominant, many have sizeable French minorities (e.g. Ontario, 4 % of the population or 499,000 people are mother tongue French speakers; New Brunswick, 31 % of the population or 238,090 people are mother tongue French speakers), and still others, like Nova Scotia and Manitoba, have historic French-speaking populations (Statistics Canada 2011). Quebec is also home to a large and active English-speaking minority. Thus, the population of Canada consists of a web of historically founded relationships that tend to be indexed by language. Not only are there province-internal dynamics specific to different language communities, there are also dynamics between French-speaking minorities and French-dominant Quebec and dynamics between English-dominant provinces and Quebec (see Fig. 2.1).

Since it has been illustrated how Canadians have, throughout history, been indexed by language, it is a logical assumption that not only have understandings about language been the basis of relationships between Canadians, but also the relationships between Canadians have informed, produced, and reified beliefs about language. Canada consists of an immense territory, a dispersed population, and a complex history; and beliefs about language are not uniform across the country. Canada remains, therefore, fragmented not only by colonial history and disparate geography, but also by abstract, fundamental, and systematic

Fig. 2.1 Map of Canada (*Modified from*: St Catharines Downtown [computer file]. (no date). St Catharines, Ontario: Brock university map, Data & GIS library. Available: Brock university map, Data & GIS library controlled access http://www.brocku.ca/maplibrary/maps/outline/local/stcathDT.jpg. Accessed 21 September 2015)

understandings about languages, and their role in society. This context has been uniquely affected by the development and evolution of media.

2.2 From the Public Broadcaster to Commercial Enterprises

From its inception, the media in Canada have been obliged to serve separate majority language populations. The Canadian Radio Broadcasting Act of 1932 created the national public broadcaster, the Canadian Radio Broadcasting Commission (CRBC), which would later evolve into the

Canadian Broadcasting Corporation (CBC-Société Radio Canada). In the beginning, there were attempts to air both languages on the national CRBC radio service. As Vipond (2012: 50) explains:

> the government believed broadcasting was unique in its ability to facilitate nationwide communication. Whereas newspapers were local, magazines middle-class, and movies purely entertainment, radio could be used not only for entertainment but also for information and propaganda, reaching into the living rooms of all classes in all parts of the country.

More generally, the view seemed to be that there was only one radio audience in Canada made up of two different language groups: English speakers and French speakers (Fletcher 1998; Raboy 1991). According to Vipond (2008: 320), "the CRBC seemed to be claiming the authority to define Canada linguistically and culturally". As a powerful national institution, the CRBC could be used to create an "imagined community" (Anderson 1983) of a bilingual pan-Canadian nation (see Charland 1986; Hayday 2009; Raboy 1991). In other words, the idea was that with a bilingual national broadcaster, individual listeners would come to appreciate the different language communities sharing the territory.

However, the CRBC was unable to simply create national unity without resistance. Bilingual broadcasts were met with "absolute, militant" opposition from English Canada (Raboy 1991). According to Vipond (2008: 332), English Canadians argued that CRBC bilingual programming was being "forced" and "foisted" upon them, "rammed down their throats" and "thrust into [their] homes". In fact, when the CRBC included French content, it led many Canadian listeners to turn to American English-language stations (Vipond 2008: 332). As a result of the public and political pressure, and to avoid American influence, the CRBC moved away from French and bilingual programming on the national networks (Vipond 2008: 342). According to Raboy (1991), this was actually welcomed by French Canadians, who had feared marginalisation within a single service that was only nominally bilingual.

By World War II (WWII), the divide between English and French branches of the CRBC was complete. It became obvious, however, during the conscription crisis of 1942 when French Canadians resisted conscription to WWII, that media power still lay in the hands of the English-speaking majority. By order of the federal government, the CBC denied the Quebec-based *Ligue pour la défense du Canada*, who spearheaded the "No" campaign, access to its stations. As a result, despite the divide between the English and French branches of the radio, the national public broadcaster came to be seen as an "oppressive agent of centralised federalism", controlled by English speakers (Raboy 1991). It is clear, then, that the CBC as the federal, national broadcaster was designed to contribute to Canadian unity.

Historically, this mandate has meant working against the Quebec nationalist movement. Indeed, when it became apparent to the federal government in 1964 that the nationalist movement in Quebec was spreading and increasingly radical, one action taken in the House of Commons was the announcement of new policy measures in which the CBC played a central role. Secretary of State Maurice Lamontagne declared the CBC "one of Canada's most vital and essential institutions" which was assigned the crucial task of "becom[ing] a living and daily testimony of Canadian identity, a faithful reflection of our two main cultures and a powerful element of understanding, moderation and unity in our country" (cited in Raboy 1991). The national public broadcaster was therefore attributed considerable power by the federal government (Conlogue 2002: 26; Fletcher 1998; Smith 1998). Today, unlike the CBC, most Canadian media are privately owned and need not support federal Canada, even if they are required to operate within it.

During the Quiet Revolution, French speakers gained control of their own media; since then, media services in Canada have become to some extent polarised as each official language community manages its own media. Because they work within and produce news products for their respective communities, the English and French Canadian media reflect different views and interests (see Conlogue 2002: 7; de Mer 2008: 33; Gagnon 2006: 81; la Presse Canadienne 2012). Smith (1998: 22) makes the following observations about Canada's dual broadcasting:

> Operating separate English and French broadcasting systems potentially conflicts with creating unity. Not only can the systems be captured by groups that disagree on what the situation is and what information they

> should provide, but each language also organizes conception and perception in fundamentally different ways. These differences can cause and reinforce disagreements and impede consensus.

The private media, then, may contain language ideologies that are not evident in the Canadian public media outlet, the CBC-SRC. Since the English and French communities have unique histories (see Sect. 2.1), this polarisation may mean that the English and French Canadian media represent languages and language issues differently according to community beliefs.

Canadian media products are designed to be appropriate for and acceptable to specific communities, or "media audiences". According to Fletcher (1998), Canada contains two distinct media audiences, one French-speaking and one English-speaking. Since news is produced for specific communities (see Chap. 1), if communities are distinct from one another then it follows that the news may be different as well. This means not only that the media tend to avoid "regular in-depth coverage of the other linguistic community" (Pritchard and Sauvageau 1999: 300; see also la Presse Canadienne 2012; Saul 1997: 163–164), but also that the media texts may contain ideologies specific to the home community. This is because journalists often tend to be members of their home communities and journalism influences community beliefs (see Chap. 1). This is particularly the case in Quebec, where French-speaking journalists form an integral part of the intelligentsia (Fletcher 1998). It follows, then, that the news may be designed differently in English and French to suit the communities' needs and value systems (de Mer 2008: 16, 105–109; Pritchard and Sauvageau 1999: 291).

Another important difference between the English and French Canadian media is that journalists work in largely separate professional worlds. English and French Canadian journalists tend to belong to different professional communities, which may influence, shape, and socialise individuals into a specific ideology (Cotter 2010: 34–36; van Dijk 2006: 122–123). There are two main journalist associations in Canada: the Canadian Association of Journalists (CAJ) and *La fédération professionelle des journalistes du Québec* (FPJQ), both of which are monolingual. Fraser (2007) remarks that the CAJ and the FPJQ have run along "parallel tracks, with amicable but distant relations", and more French-speaking Canadian journalists are members of the FPJQ than English-language journalists are members of the CAJ. Membership numbers are important because Pritchard et al. (2005: 302) have found that the FPJQ "actively socializes journalists to the profession and its ideology", which may result in "greater solidarity among francophone journalists, perhaps leading to a greater constancy in their professional values".

Another example of working within different professional worlds arises from an extensive survey, which found that most journalists do not engage with the other language media: although 85 % of francophone journalists claim to speak English, only 41 % read English Canadian newspapers, whereas only 14 % of anglophone journalists claim to speak French, and only 5 % read francophone newspapers (Pritchard and Sauvageau 1999: 292). Oakes and Warren (2007: 166) cite the example of a 2002 "newspaper swap" undertaken by two Quebec journalists, one from Montreal's anglophone daily *The Gazette* and the other from francophone daily *La Presse*. They remark that interest in such a media swap arises from the "polarised newspaper ecology" in Montreal (2007: 166). Indeed, the polarisation would seem to extend much wider than this single city: the aforementioned survey of Canadian journalists has suggested that French- and English-speaking journalists are uninterested in each other's work, media, and even culture (Pritchard and Sauvageau 1999). Although these trends certainly may have changed in the past 15 years, they nevertheless indicate the extent to which Canadian media have tended to exist in "two solitudes".

Finally, English and French Canadian media may be affected by the major stakeholders in Canadian media outlets. Canada has one of the most consolidated media systems in the developed world, and "an unrivalled scale of cross-media ownership" wherein left-of-centre political orientations are remarkably few (Winseck 2002: 799; see also Beaty and Sullivan 2010: 16; Karim 2008: 59; Soderlund and Hildebrandt 2005c; Soderlund and Romanow 2005: 11). Prior to 2010, when near bankruptcy forced the dismantling of CanWest into separate television and newspaper holdings, for a decade the company had owned 13 major papers (accounting for over 30 % of total daily circulation) and the Global TV network (Vipond 2012: 72). Still today, Postmedia (the newspaper arm of the former CanWest conglomerate) holdings include some of the most widely circulated English-language dailies in Canada: the *National Post*, *The Province* (Vancouver), *The Vancouver Sun*, *Edmonton Journal*, *Calgary Herald*, *Ottawa Citizen*, and *Montreal Gazette*. Similarly, the Quebecor/Sun Media group owns 37 papers with 24 % of circulation, including the widely circulated English-language *Sun* tabloids (published in Toronto, Calgary, Ottawa, Edmonton, and Winnipeg) and the tabloids *Journal de Montréal* and *Journal de Québec,* the former of which has the highest circulation in Quebec. Torstar owns four papers, including the *Toronto Star*, which is the most widely circulated paper in the country, the *Metro* free daily newspapers (published in Toronto, Ottawa, Winnipeg, Calgary, Edmonton, and Vancouver), and *Sing Tao*, Canada's most widely read Chinese-language newspaper (daily editions in Toronto, Vancouver, and Calgary). Finally, the Power Corporation owns seven French-language papers, including the most widely read French-language broadsheet, *La Presse*. In other words, four groups control 76 % of English and French newspaper circulation in Canada, and ownership is sometimes divided along language lines.

Although there is no consensus as to whether ownership or concentration of ownership affects newspaper content (Pritchard et al. 2005: 293; Vipond 2012), cases have been noted wherein media ownership has affected the employment of individuals with notable national views. Aldridge (2001: 615), for example, cites how an editor-in-chief at *The Gazette* (Montreal) lost her job because of disagreements over Quebec sovereignty with the proprietor of the newspaper, Conrad Black. Although it is debatable how much power conglomerates exercise over news content and perspective, the fact that most English Canadian newspapers are owned by a small number of shareholders and the largest French Canadian newspapers are owned by different shareholders, means that the potential for polarisation is great (on media ownership, see Fletcher 1998; Fraser 2007; Pritchard and Sauvageau 1999; Raboy 1991; Soderlund and Hildebrandt 2005a; Young 2001: 650).

In sum, the French and English Canadian private media may contain different content because of community differences, professional worlds, and media ownership. Indeed, numerous studies have found important differences between the content of the French and English Canadian media (e.g. Elkin 1975; Fletcher 1998; Fraser 2007; Halford et al. 1983; Hayday 2005: 60; Kariel and Rosenvall 1983; Raboy 1991; Robinson 1998; Siegel 1979; Taras 1993).

2.3 Newspapers in Canada

Local daily newspapers were established early in Canadian history. The first newspaper, the Halifax *Gazette,* was established in Nova Scotia in 1752, and was soon followed by the bilingual Quebec *Gazette* in 1764. These local productions provided a unique service that could not be fulfilled by traditional colonial imports: the provision of current and relevant local commercial and official information (Vipond 2012).

By 1885, transnational transportation via the new railway system improved the speed of circulation of goods, people, and ideas; this also increased to the circulation of newspapers, which contributed to the economic, political, and cultural integration of the Canadian population (Charland 1986). Literacy in Canada rose from approximately 70 % in 1850 to 90 % in 1900 and 95 % in 1921 (Vipond 2012). Although these figures were slightly lower in the French Canadian population, they indicate nonetheless the growing importance of the written word for Canadians. By 1911, there were 143 daily newspapers in Canada and by the 1920s Canada was home to a strong indigenous newspaper industry, all of which was privately owned (Vipond 2012).

Notably, the English Canadian newspaper system has been strongly influenced by the USA. The popular dailies that emerged in the late nineteenth century in Montreal, Toronto, Ottawa, and Hamilton tended to follow an American formula in being independent from party politics and adopting a more informal language style. Even today, newspapers save by sharing editorial costs and importing editorial material from the USA. According to Vipond (2012), the Canadian Press buys almost all of its foreign news from the Associated Press and then rewrites it for Canadian consumption. However, Quebec's distinctive language has historically encouraged "more indigenous cultural development and offered some protection from the tidal wave of American popular culture pouring into Canada" (Vipond 2012: 51).

Newspapers Canada, the advocacy group for publishers of daily newspapers in Canada, divides newspapers in the country according to five geographic areas: Atlantic Canada (the provinces of Newfoundland and Labrador, Nova Scotia, New Brunswick, and Prince Edward Island), Ontario (the province of Ontario), the Prairies (the provinces of Manitoba, Saskatchewan, and Alberta), British Columbia and the Yukon (the province of British Columbia and the Yukon Territory), and Quebec (the province of Quebec). The newspapers with the highest circulation figures from each of area of Canada can be seen in Tables 2.1 and 2.2, where an additional category of "national newspapers" has been added. These tables indicate changes in circulation figures over the past five years and the marked differences across regions and languages. Notably, the 2014 figures include both print and digital circulation, which are much higher than the print circulation figures alone, which are in decline.

The high circulation figures in Ontario reflect the fact that it is the most populous province in Canada (12.85 million inhabitants; 38 % of Canada's population; see Statistics Canada 2011), and that population is still growing, with a considerable population of French speakers (499,000 people mother tongue French speakers). In contrast, the comparatively low circulation figures across the four Atlantic provinces reflect the sparse population (2.3 million inhabitants across four provinces) and low population growth (Statistics Canada 2011). Circulation figures also reflect the number of dailies published: while populous Ontario publishes 43 daily newspapers (including both national papers), sparsely populated Atlantic Canada publishes only 13 (see Table 2.3).

The different circulation figures in French correlate with the unique demographics of French speakers across Canada. Only 21.2 % of the Canadian population speaks French as a first language (7.1 million people), and 87 % of this population lives in the province of Quebec. The remaining large populations of French mother tongue speakers live in New Brunswick and Ontario, hence the existence of French dailies in these areas. In other words, the French-speaking population of Canada is significantly smaller than the English-speaking population, and French speakers are predominantly concentrated in Quebec. As a result, the vast majority of the French Canadian newspapers are published in Quebec,

Table 2.1 English Canadian daily newspapers with highest circulation

			2009 data		2014 data (print/digital)	
Area	Paper title	Origin	Weekly total	Ave. Daily	Weekly total	Ave. Daily
Atlantic Canada	*The Telegram*	St John's, NL	181,646	25,949	198,815	33,136
	Moncton Times & Transcript	Moncton, NB	223,311	37,219	173,328	28,888
	Chronicle Herald	Halifax, NS	752,397	107,485	548,938	91,490
Ontario	*Hamilton Spectator*	Hamilton, ON	573,663	95,611	686,450	114,408
	London Free Press	London, ON	455,939	65,134	417,901	69,650
	Ottawa Citizen	Ottawa, ON	900,197	128,600	626,272	104,379
	The Toronto Star	Toronto, ON	2,349,760	335,680	2,397,691	342,527
	The Toronto Sun	Toronto, ON	1,162,864	166,123	967,574	138,225
Prairies	*Winnipeg Free Press*	Winnipeg, MB	889,457	127,065	663,431	110,572
	Winnipeg Sun	Winnipeg, MB	226,829	32,404	375,876	53,697
	Saskatoon Star Phoenix	Saskatoon, SK	335,990	55,998	261,691	43,615
	Calgary Herald	Calgary, AB	852,599	121,800	680,009	113,335
	Edmonton Journal	Edmonton, AB	839,365	119,909	597,789	99,631
	The Edmonton Sun	Edmonton, AB	401,207	57,315	286,693	40,956
BC and Yukon	*Vancouver Province*	Vancouver, BC	995,027	165,838	760,874	126,812
	Vancouver Sun	Vancouver, BC	1,060,139	176,690	970,710	161,785
	Victoria Times-Colonist	Victoria, BC	488,988	69,855	330,301	55,050
	Whitehorse Star	Whitehorse, YK	11,335	2,267	8,993	1,799

(continued)

Table 2.1 (continued)

Area	Paper title	Origin	2009 data Weekly total	2009 data Ave. Daily	2014 data (print/digital) Weekly total	2014 data (print/digital) Ave. Daily
Quebec	*The Gazette*	Montreal, QC	1,057,294	151,042	547,445	91,241
	The Record	Sherbrooke, QC	22,865	4,573	21,715	4,343
National papers	*The Globe and Mail*	Toronto, ON	1,996,582	332,764	2,149,124	358,187
	The National Post	Don Mills, ON	1,182,206	197,034	1,097,080	182,847

Source: Newspapers Canada

Table 2.2 French Canadian daily newspapers with highest circulation

Area	Paper title	Origin	2009 data Weekly total	2009 data Ave. Daily	2014 data (print/digital) Weekly total	2014 data (print/digital) Ave. Daily
Quebec	*La Presse*	Montreal, QC	1,504,674	214,953	1,734,445	289,074
	Le Nouvelliste	Trois Rivières, QC	257,234	42,872	256,565	42,761
	Le Soleil	Québec, QC	610,173	87,168	553,309	79,044
	Le Devoir	Montreal, QC	175,308	29,218	214,263	35,710
	Le Journal de Montréal	Montreal, QC	1,577,987	225,427	1,633,726	233,389
	Le Journal de Québec	Quebec, QC	617,781	88,254	1,055,490	150,784
Atlantic Canada	*L'Acadie Nouvelle*	Caraquet, NB	120,912	20,300	108,612	18,102
Ontario	*Ottawa LeDroit*	Ottawa, ON	215,579	35,930	205,136	34,189
Prairies	(No data available)					
BC and Yukon	(No data available)					

Source: Newspapers Canada

Table 2.3 Regions of Canada with circulation figures in English and French

Area	Circulation figures (average per day)		Circulation figures (weekly total)		Number of English papers published		Number of French papers published	
	2009	2014 (print/ digital)	2009	2014 (print/ digital)	2009	2014	2009	2014
Atlantic Canada	316,901	313,620	2,032,159	1,837,796	12	12	1	1
Quebec	921,892	1,321,755	6,322,671	8,094,237	2	2	9	11
Ontario	1,857,474[a]	2,272,915	11,890,127[a]	13,640,603	37[a]	42	1	1
Prairies	703,950	781,558	4,479,186	4,688,396	17	19	0	0
BC & Yukon	495,020	622,170	3,036,963	3,504,405	17	16	0	0

[a]Including two national papers

thus skewing the data towards this geographic area, rather than across the entire country. These demographics are reflected in the circulation figures: although Quebec has the highest newspaper circulation figures in Canada after Ontario, two of the seven newspapers published are in English, thus changing the composition of the readership in comparison with all other areas of Canada. These circulation figures all indicate the widely different demographics of French and English speakers and the effects on circulation figures.

One final important point is that while there are two national English newspapers with high circulation figures (*Globe and Mail* and *National Post*), no pan-Canadian newspaper exists in French. However, within Quebec, *La Presse* and *Le Devoir* are sometimes considered to be the "national" newspapers in terms of their scope and alignment with Quebec nationalism or a pan-Canadian perspective (see e.g. Gagnon 2003: 78; Ignatieff 1994: 120–121; Oakes and Warren 2007: 158; Soroka 2002).

Notably, nearly all newspapers belong to sizeable news conglomerates and many are the only daily newspaper in the city in which they are produced. Here, details about a sample of the aforementioned newspapers will be provided; these are the newspapers that are used as data in Chap. 4 and these were selected as data because each was among the most widely circulated newspaper from the regions of Canada in 2009.[1] Each newspaper is presented according to its status and ownership in 2009, when the data were collected.

In Atlantic Canada, the Halifax *Chronicle Herald* and its Sunday edition the *Sunday Herald* are published by Halifax Herald Limited and owned by Graham William Dennis. Although not classified as "independent" by Newspapers Canada (2009, 2013), its website claims that it is a paper "free of chain ownership" (*Chronicle Herald* 2010). The *Chronicle Herald* has been the only daily newspaper published in Halifax, the capital and most populous city of Nova Scotia, since the *Daily News* closed in 2008. Similarly, the *Times & Transcript* is the only daily newspaper published in Moncton, New Brunswick. The *Times & Transcript* is owned by Brunswick News Incorporated, a company that owns all other New Brunswick English-language daily newspapers. *L'Acadie Nouvelle* is an independently owned tabloid and the only French-language daily newspaper published in Atlantic Canada.

In Quebec, the *Gazette* is Canada's oldest continuously published newspaper (Newspapers Canada 2008) and the only English-language daily broadsheet published in the city of Montreal, the most populous city in Quebec. In 2009, it was owned by CanWest Publishing, one of the largest media stakeholders in Canada, which is also said to support the Conservative Party (Beaty and Sullivan 2010: 19); by 2013, the ownership had been changed to the Postmedia Network Inc. Notably, the *Gazette* has the largest English-speaking readership of Quebec dailies and it is argued to support Canadian (i.e. rather than Quebec) nationalism (Gagnon 2003: 78). The Sherbrooke *Record* is a tabloid owned by Glacier Ventures International Corporation in 2009 (now ALTA Newspaper Group/Glacier), and is the only English daily newspaper published in the city of Sherbrooke, Quebec. It is also the only other English-language daily published in the province. Quebec City's *Le Soleil* is a tabloid owned by Power Corporation of Canada and is one of two French-language tabloids published in the provincial capital, where no daily broadsheets are published.

[1] Only newspapers from different provinces (or, in the cases where regions consisted of a single province, cities) were considered and no free newspapers were included in the sample. Some newspaper data, such as the *Journal de Montréal* and the *Journal de Québec*, were unavailable.

In the province of Ontario, Canada's most populous province that also produces the most daily newspapers, the *Toronto Star*, owned by Torstar Corporation, is one of two daily newspapers published in the provincial capital and Canada's largest city. Other newspapers published in the Greater Toronto Area include the two national newspapers, which are discussed below. In Ottawa, the national capital, the *Ottawa Citizen* is the only English-language daily broadsheet and in 2009 was owned by CanWest Publishing (now the Postmedia Network Inc.). Ottawa's French-language tabloid *Le Droit* was owned by Gesca Incorporated in 2009 and is now also owned by the Power Corporation of Canada; it is the only French-language daily published in Ontario.

In the Prairies of Western Canada, the *Calgary Herald* is the only daily broadsheet published in Calgary, the most populous city in the province of Alberta; in 2009, it was also owned by CanWest publishing (now Postmedia Network Inc.). The *Winnipeg Free Press* is the only daily broadsheet published in Winnipeg, the capital and most populous city in Manitoba. It is owned by F.P. Canadian Newspapers Limited Partnership. No French-language dailies are published in the Canadian prairies. In Western Canada, the *Vancouver Sun* is the only daily broadsheet published in the most populous city of British Columbia and in 2009 it was owned by CanWest Publishing (now Postmedia Network Inc.). The *Whitehorse Star* is an independently owned tabloid and the only daily newspaper published in the Yukon Territory. No French-language dailies are published in British Columbia or the Yukon.

Apart from these provincial newspapers, there are four newspapers in Canada that are here considered "national" in the sense that they have a different scope and distribution from local papers (Cotter 2010: 121). First, in English, the *Globe and Mail* is published in Toronto and was owned by CTVglobemedia Incorporated in 2009 (it is now owned by Globe and Mail Inc.). When it was first acquired by Thomson Newspapers in 1980, substantial changes were made, notably a drop in Toronto-related material in order to make the newspaper "Canada's national newspaper" (Soderlund and Hildebrandt 2005b: 39). It remains today Canada's most widely read national newspaper and the Canadian newspaper with the highest circulation after the *Toronto Star*. The *Globe and Mail* is widely recognised as liberal and left wing in its political orientation and a supporter of Canadian federal nationalism (Gagnon 2003: 78; Pritchard et al. 2005: 291; Retzlaff and Gänzle 2008: 84).

Competing with the *Globe and Mail* is the *National Post*, another national newspaper published in the Greater Toronto Area. In 2009, the *National Post* was owned by CanWest Publishing (now Postmedia Network Inc.) and in 2009 was the eighth most widely read newspaper in Canada (by 2013, this ranking had slipped to ninth). The *National Post* is widely recognised as conservative in its ideology (Soderlund et al. 2002: 81). Although the two French-language "national" newspapers tend to be distributed only in Quebec, they are broadsheets with nationalist perspectives that are widely read in the province and beyond. The Montreal-based *Le Devoir* is labelled as "independent" by Newspapers Canada (2008), and targets a "small Francophone elite and promotes Quebec nationalism" (Gagnon 2003: 78). Montreal's *La Presse* is owned by Power Corporation and is the fourth most widely read newspaper in Canada and the most widely read broadsheet in Quebec. It is also said to support Canadian federal nationalism (Gagnon 2003: 78; Oakes and Warren 2007: 158; Soroka 2002).

In summary, then, this overview of newspapers in Canada suggests that the French and English Canadian newspapers may differ not only because of the aforementioned community differences, professional worlds, and media ownership, but also because of widely divergent availability of newspapers—and in particular newspapers in different languages—and the circulation figures of these newspapers in different regions of the country.

2.4 New and Social Media in Canada

Crucially, though, Canada has never been a country wholly reliant on newspapers. Over its history, Canada has constantly seen an influx of media from Britain, France, and especially the USA. In an era of mass media and electronic communication, it is clear that such international influences are increasing.

According to Vipond (2012), in 1996 less than 7 % of Canadians had access to the Internet; this rose to 45 % by 2001 and 62 % the following year. By 2009, 75 % of Canadian households were Internet subscribers and by 2010 Canadians spent an average of 18.1 hours per week online, up from 14.9 hours the year before (Ipsos Reid, cited in Vipond 2012: 87). However, Internet access depends on urban and rural contexts and household incomes: households with incomes of $85,000 or more had a 94 % usage rate in 2009 compared to only 5 % usage rate for low-income households of $30,000 or less. Notably, Vipond (2012: 87) and Chen and Smith (2011: 406) have remarked that francophones tend to have lower Internet and social media usage rates, which is attributed to the slower development of French-language services. Nevertheless, precise figures on access and communication trends using developing technology change so quickly that precise data are hard to come by and soon outdated. By the end of 2013, Canadians still tended to be heavy users of desktop Internet (third in usage internationally), but their engagement had started to shift towards mobile platforms. Three out of four mobile phone users in Canada use smartphones and between 2012 and 2013 there was a 23 % increase in users accessing social networking via smartphones on a daily basis. In 2009, the most common use of the Internet at home was email (93 % of users), followed by general browsing or surfing (78 %). However, the growing area of mobile content consumption mainly pertains to social networking, instant messaging, photo/video sharing, and local, world, and entertainment news (Duong and Lella 2014).

The use of social media, for example, Facebook and Twitter, continues to grow exponentially. Vipond (2012: 88) notes that in 2009, 27 % of respondents claimed to contribute online content through blogs, photos, or discussion groups, and 45 % of respondents claimed to use instant messaging. In late 2010, Facebook (a free online social network where registered users maintain profiles, upload photos and videos, and send private or public messages) was the number one website accessed by Canadians, receiving 11.5 % of all website visits. Although Small (2014: 93) notes that the number of Canadians using Facebook has stagnated, 50 % of Canadians surveyed in 2011 said that they had social networking profiles; of these, 86 % maintained Facebook profiles and 19 % had Twitter accounts (Ipsos 2011; cited in Giasson et al. 2014: 195). Nevertheless, it was not until 2009 that Facebook offered a version of Facebook tailored for French Canadians specifically; also, in 2008 only 12 % of the French Canadian population used Facebook, compared to

30 % in English-speaking Ontario and 25 % across Canada more broadly (Chen and Smith 2011: 406).

Twitter, an online social networking service that allows users to send and read short messages of 140 characters ("tweets"), is enjoying a huge increase in popularity in Canada. Although in 2009 less than 1 % of Canadians used Twitter, two years later that number had increased to almost 20 % (Ipsos 2011; cited in Small 2014: 91). The significance of Twitter is that, when not restricted to private accounts, tweets reach beyond the platform and are often reported in mainstream media (Small 2014: 98). Furthermore, since Twitter users can easily use the service to "follow" individuals and institutions, it is increasingly serving as a site for Canadians to obtain personalised news streams. It is estimated that over ten million Canadians enjoy a personalised news stream through social media such as Twitter (Small et al. 2014: 16). Furthermore, this news stream is increasingly believed to be a reliable source of information. A 2011 survey found that over 80 % of Canadians felt that mainstream media were reliable sources of information; by comparison, about 40 % trusted government information and 25 % felt that social media was trustworthy (Small et al. 2014: 15). Crucially, these opinions differ according to age groups, and younger Canadians are the population increasingly reliant on online media.

Everyday Canadians are not the only people using social media. Researchers (e.g. Chen and Smith 2011; Marland et al. 2014) have shown that new and social media are used by a wide range of institutions and politicians, too. Together, these media types have created new ways of communicating for Canadians, but research has not yet explored how language issues are embedded in Canadian new and social media. As Vipond (2012: 92) has noted, the Internet is impossible to regulate and the Canadian Radio-television and Telecommunications Commission (CRTC) announced as long ago as 1999 that it had no intention of trying. The global distribution capacity of new media thus opens Canada up to foreign content, which means that language issues and ideologies that were perhaps established in traditional national media may be confronted and even challenged in these international spheres.

Crucially, as the Standing Senate Committee (2012) has mentioned (see Chap. 1), the Internet remains English-dominant (even if the use of other languages is increasing; Crystal 2011: 78–91). Therefore, the dynamic is not only between the national and the international spheres, but also between a regulated national media sphere that must conform to official language policies and regulations and an international one that need not conform and that is driven by English as a common language (Mac Síthigh 2015).

2.5 Analyses of Canadian Media

Although there has been considerable research on Canadian news and new/social media, most of this research has focused on specific electoral and national issues and has tended to gloss over the subtle and inconspicuous features of Canadian media language. There has been a dearth of research focusing on language and the language and Canadian media, and the little research that has compared English and French is rather dated (for some exceptions, see de Mer 2008; Kuhn and Lick 2009; Young and Dugas 2011, 2012). Moreover, there has been little linguistic research on Canadian media (for exceptions, see Boudreau and Urbain 2014; Tagliamone and Denis 2008). Nevertheless, the state of the art suggests that differences in media content, language of use, and metalinguistic discussions may have implications for English and French speakers who read little and thus gain little understanding of the other linguistic community (e.g. Saul 1997: 163–164).

The little non-linguistic research that has compared French and English media has predominantly used content analysis, which is quantitative (although sometimes supplemented by interview or survey data) and does not account for the more nuanced differences that are perhaps at the heart of the national, ideological, and linguistic divide (Richardson 2007). As Fletcher (1998) notes:

> Standard content analysis, focusing on manifest content, has its uses, but it cannot capture the cultural differences that reinforce identity and, perhaps, exacerbate conflict. Nor can it capture the distressingly cynical interpretations of the motives of politicians or citizens from the other community that crop up from time to time in the French and English media. It seems clear that a new research agenda is needed.

There has been little discourse analysis of the Canadian media (for some exceptions, see Harding 2006; Greenberg and Hier 2001; Retzlaff and Gänzle 2008), and even less discourse analysis comparing English and French media data (some rare examples include Gagnon 2003; Kuhn and Lick 2009; see discussion in Roy 2009: 261). The few examples of discourse analyses of Canadian media that do exist draw on relatively small data samples.[2] Finally, although languages serve important functions in Canada, little research has attempted to account for differences between beliefs about language (i.e. language ideologies) in French- and English-speaking Canada. Fundamental differences between the development and evolutions of the English and French Canadian media suggest that they may serve as a rich site for comparative analysis.

To address these gaps, the next chapter overviews the methods that have been developed to analyse and compare language ideologies in English and French Canadian media using both corpus linguistics (to tackle large-scale data sets) and discourse analysis (to access the more subtle means of expression of language ideologies). These methods have been called "cross-linguistic corpus-assisted discourse studies" (Vessey 2013).

References

Aldridge, M. (2001). Lost expectations? Women journalists and the fall-out from the 'Toronto newspaper war'. *Media, Culture & Society, 23*, 607–624.

Allaire, G. (2007). From "Nouvelle-France" to "Francophonie canadienne": A historical survey. *International Journal of the Sociology of Language, 185*, 25–52.

Anderson, B. (1983). *Imagined communities: Reflections on the origin and spread of nationalism*. London: Verso.

Beaty, B., & Sullivan, R. (2010). Introduction: Contexts of popular culture. In B. Beaty, D. Briton, G. Filax, & R. Sullivan (Eds.), *How Canadians communicate III: Contexts of Canadian popular culture* (pp. 11–34). Edmonton: Athabasca University Press.

[2] One exception to this general trend is a large study on representations of climate change in English and French Canadian news media, which has used both quantitative and qualitative methods, including discourse analysis, on a large corpus of data (see DiFrancesco and Young 2010; Young and Dugas 2011, 2012).

Boileau, F. (2011). Les héritiers de la Loi sur les langues officielles. In J. Jedwab & R. Landry (Eds.), *Life after forty/Après quarante ans: Official languages policy in Canada/Les politiques de langue officielle au Canada* (pp. 121–130). Kingston: McGill-Queen's University Press.

Bouchard, C. (2002). *La langue et le nombril: Histoire d'une obsession québécoise*. Montreal: Fides.

Boudreau, A., & Urbain, É. (2014). La presse comme tribune d'un discours d'autorité sur la langue: représentations et idéologies linguistiques dans la presse acadienne, de la fondation du Moniteur Acadien aux Conventions nationales. *Francophonies d'Amérique, 35* (*Les journaux des communautés francophones minoritaires en Amérique du Nord*, Ed. D. Laporte), 23–46.

Bouthillier, G. (1997). *L'obsession ethnique*. Outremont: Lanctôt.

Canadian Standing Senate Committee on Official Languages. (2012). *Internet, new media and social media: Respect for language rights!* Available http://www.parl.gc.ca/Content/SEN/Committee/411/OLLO/rep/rep05oct12-e.pdf

Charland, M. (1986). Technological nationalism. *Canadian Journal of Political and Social Theory, 10*(1–2), 196–220.

Charland, M. (1987). Constitutive rhetoric: The case of the *peuple québécois*. *Quarterly Journal of Speech, 73*, 133–150.

Chen, P. J., & Smith, P. J. (2011). Digital media in the 2008 Canadian election. *Journal of Information Technology and Politics, 8*(4), 399–417.

Conlogue, R. (2002). *Impossible nation: The longing for homeland in Canada and Quebec*. Toronto: The Mercury Press.

Conrick, M., & Regan, V. (2007). *French in Canada: Language issues*. Oxford: Peter Lang.

Cotter, C. (2010). *News talk: Investigating the language of journalism*. Cambridge: Cambridge University Press.

Crystal, D. (2011). *Internet linguistics: A student guide*. London: Routledge.

De Mer, E. (2008). *Les differences de traitement des journalistes Canadiens anglais et Québécois francophones: Le cas de la mission militaire canadienne en Afghanistan* (Unpublished Masters Thesis. University of Ottawa). Retrieved from http://www.crej.ca/demer.pdf

DiFrancesco, D. A., & Young, N. (2010). Seeing climate change: The visual construction of global warming in Canadian national print media. *Cultural Geographies, 18*(4), 517–536.

Duong, K., & Lella, A. (2014). *Canada digital future in focus 2014*. Available http://cwta.ca/wordpress/wp-content/uploads/2011/08/2014-Canada-Digital-Future-in-Focus_FINAL.pdf

Elkin, F. (1975). Communications media and identity formation in Canada. In B. D. Singer (Ed.), *Communications in Canadian society* (2nd ed., pp. 229–243). Vancouver: Copp Clark Publishing.

Fletcher, F. J. (1998). Media and political identity: Canada and Quebec in the era of globalization. *Canadian Journal of Communication, 23*(3). Retrieved from http://www.cjc-online.ca/index.php/journal/article/view/1049/955

Fraser, G. (2006). *Sorry, I don't speak French. Confronting the Canadian crisis that won't go away*. Toronto: McClelland and Stewart.

Fraser, G. (2007). *The role of the media in bridging the French-English divide: Remarks to the Ottawa chapter of the Canadian Association of Journalists*. Ottawa, 24 Jan 2007. Office of the Commissioner of Official Languages. Retrieved from http://www.ocol-clo.gc.ca/html/speeches_discours_24012007_e.php

Gagnon, S. (2003). La construction discursive du concept de la souveraineté dans les medias canadiens lors du referendum de 1995. *Revue québécoise de linguistique, 32*(2), 97–116.

Gagnon, C. (2006). Language plurality as power struggle, or: Translating politics in Canada. *Target, 18*(1), 69–90.

Giampapa, F. (2001). Hyphenated identities: Italian-Canadian youth and the negotiation of ethnic identities in Toronto. *International Journal of Bilingualism, 5*(3), 279–315.

Giasson, T., Jansen, H., & Koop, R. (2014). Blogging, partisanship, and political participation in Canada. In A. Marland, T. Giasson, & T. A. Small (Eds.), *Political communication in Canada: Meet the press and tweet the rest* (pp. 194–211). Vancouver: UBC Press.

Greenberg, J., & Hier, S. (2001). Crisis, mobilization and collective problematization: "Illegal" Chinese migrants and the Canadian news media. *Journalism Studies, 2*(4), 563–583.

Halford, P. W., van den Hoven, A., Romanow, W. I., & Soderlund, W. C. (1983). A media tale of two cities: Quebec referendum coverage in Montreal and Toronto. *Canadian Journal of Communication, 9*(4), 1–31.

Haque, E. (2012). *Multiculturalism within a bilingual framework: Language, race, and belonging in Canada*. Toronto: University of Toronto Press.

Harding, R. (2006). Historical representations of aboriginal people in the Canadian news media. *Discourse & Society, 17*(2), 205–235.

Hayday, M. (2005). *Bilingual today, united tomorrow: Official languages in education and Canadian federalism*. Montreal/Kingston: McGill-Queen's University Press.

Hayday, M. (2009). Variety show as national identity: CBC television and Dominion Day Celebrations, 1958–1980. In G. Allen & D. J. Robinson

(Eds.), *Communicating in Canada's past: Essays in media history* (pp. 168–192). Toronto: University of Toronto Press.

Heller, M. (1999). Heated language in a cold climate. In J. Blommaert (Ed.), *Language ideological debates* (pp. 143–170). Berlin: Mouton de Gruyter.

Ignatieff, M. (1994). *Blood and belonging: Journeys into the new nationalism.* London: Vintage.

Innis, H. R. (1973). *Bilingualism and biculturalism. An abridged version of the Royal Commission report.* Toronto: McClelland and Stewart.

Kariel, H. G., & Rosenvall, L. A. (1983). Cultural affinity displayed in Canadian daily newspapers. *Journalism Quarterly, 60*(3), 431–436.

Karim, K. H. (1993). Construction, deconstructions, and reconstructions: Competing Canadian discourses on ethnocultural terminology. *Canadian Journal of Communication, 18*(2). Retrieved from http://www.cjc-online.ca/index.php/journal/article/viewArticle/744/650

Karim, K. H. (2008). Press, public sphere, and pluralism: Multiculturalism debates in Canadian English-language newspapers. *Canadian Ethnic Studies, 40*(1), 57–78.

Kuhn, J., & Lick, E. (2009). Advertising to Canada's official language groups: A comparative critical discourse analysis. *Semiotica, 176*(1/4), 165–176.

Labelle, M., & Salée, D. (2001). Immigrant and minority representations of citizenship in Quebec. In T. A. Aleinikoff & D. Klusmeyer (Eds.), *Citizenship today* (pp. 278–315). Washington, DC: Brookings Institution Press.

Landry, N., & Lang, N. (2001). *Histoire de l'Acadie*. Quebec: Septentrion.

La Presse Canadienne (2012, 15 October). La SRC serait trop centrée sur le Québec. *Le Devoir*. Available http://www.ledevoir.com/societe/medias/361421/la-src-serait-trop-centree-sur-le-quebec?utm_source=infolettre-2012-10-15

MacLennan, H. (1945). *Two solitudes.* Kingston/Montreal: McGill-Queen's University Press.

MacMillan, C. M. (1998). *The practice of language rights in Canada.* Toronto: University of Toronto Press.

Mac Síthigh, D. (2015). Because the computer speaks English? Language rights and digital media. *Journal of Media Law, 7*(1), 65–84

Marland, A., Giasson, T. & Small, T. A. (Eds.) (2014) Political communication in Canada: Meet the press and tweet the rest. Vancouver: UBC Press.

McRoberts, K. (1997). *Misconceiving Canada: The struggle for national unity.* Oxford: Oxford University Press.

Molinaro, I. (2005). Context and integration: The allophone communities in Québec. In I. Lockerbie, I. Molnaro, K. Larose, & L. Oakes (Eds.), *French as the common language in Québec: History, debates and positions* (pp. 67–116). Québec: Éditions Nota bene.

Newspapers Canada. (2008). *The scoop on daily newspapers in Canada.* Retrieved from http://www.newspaperscanada.ca/daily-newspaper-paid-circulation-data

Newspapers Canada. (2009). *Circulation data report.* Retrieved from http://www.newspaperscanada.ca/sites/default/files/2009CirculationDataReport_3.pdf

Newspapers Canada. (2013). *Daily newspaper circulation report.* http://www.newspaperscanada.ca/sites/default/files/2013%20Daily%20Newspapers%20Circulation%20Report%20FINAL.pdf. Accessed 7 Apr 2015.

Oakes, L., & Warren, J. (2007). *Language, citizenship and identity in Quebec.* Basingstoke/England/New York: Palgrave Macmillan.

Patrick, D. (2007). Indigenous language endangerment and the unfinished business of nation states. In M. Heller & A. Duchêne (Eds.), *Discourses of endangerment: Ideology and interest in the defence of languages* (pp. 35–56). London: Continuum.

Pelletier, R. (2003). Un divorce consommé. In S. Langlois & J. L. Roy (Eds.), *Briser les solitudes: Les francophonies canadiennes et québécoise* (pp. 31–42). Québec: Nota bene.

Pritchard, D., & Sauvageau, F. (1999). English and French and Generation X: The professional values of Canadian journalists. In H. Lazar & T. McIntosh (Eds.), *How Canadians connect* (pp. 283–306). Montreal/Kingston: McGill-Queen's University Press.

Pritchard, D., Brewer, P. R., & Sauvageau, F. (2005). Changes in Canadian journalists' views about social and political roles of the news media: A panel study, 1996–2003. *Canadian Journal of Political Science, 38*(2), 287–306.

Raboy, M. (1991). Canadian broadcasting, Canadian nationhood: Two concepts, two solitudes and great expectations. *Electronic Journal of Communication, 1*(2). Retrieved from http://www.cios.org/EJCPUBLIC/001/2/00123.HTML

Retzlaff, S., & Gänzle, S. (2008). Constructing the European Union in Canadian news. *Critical Approaches to Discourse Analysis Across Disciplines, 2*(2), 67–89.

Richardson, J. E. (2007). *Analysing newspapers: An approach from critical discourse analysis.* Basingstoke: Palgrave.

Robinson, G. (1998). *Constructing the Quebec referendum: French and English media voices.* Toronto: University of Toronto Press.

Roy, F. (2009). Recent trends in research on the history of the press in Quebec: Towards a cultural history. In G. Allen & D. J. Robinson (Eds.), *Communicating in Canada's Past: Essays in media history* (pp. 257–270). Toronto: University of Toronto Press.

Saul, J. R. (1997). *Reflections of a Siamese twin: Canada at the end of the twentieth century*. London: Penguin.

Scott, M. (2012, 26 October). Census 2011: StatsCan does away with 'francophone', 'anglophone' and 'allophone'. *The Gazette*. Available http://www.montrealgazette.com/news/Census+2011+StatsCan+does+away+with+francophone/7439307/story.html

Siegel, A. (1979). French and English broadcasting in Canada—A political evaluation. *Canadian Journal of Communication, 5*(3), 1–17.

Simon, S. (1992). The language of cultural difference: Figures of alterity in Canadian translation. In L. Venuti (Ed.), *Rethinking translation: Discourse, subjectivity, ideology* (pp. 159–176). London: Routledge.

Small, T. A. (2014). The not-so-social network: The use of Twitter by Canada's party leaders. In A. Marland, T. Giasson, & T. A. Small (Eds.), *Political communication in Canada: Meet the press and tweet the rest* (pp. 92–110). Vancouver: UBC Press.

Small, T. A., Giasson, T., & Marland, A. (2014). The triangulation of Canadian political communication. In A. Marland, T. Giasson, & T. A. Small (Eds.), *Political communication in Canada: Meet the press and tweet the rest* (pp. 3–22). Vancouver: UBC Press.

Smith, J. (1998). Media policy, national identity, and citizenry in changing democratic societies: The case of Canada. In J. Smith (Ed.), *Media policy, national identity and citizenry in changing democratic societies: The case of Canada* (pp. 3–32). Durham: Duke University.

Soderlund, W. C., & Hildebrandt, K. (2005a). *Canadian newspaper ownership in the era of convergence rediscovering social responsibility*. Edmonton: University of Alberta Press.

Soderlund, W. C., & Hildebrandt, K. (2005b). Chain ownership: Review and analysis of empirical studies. In W. C. Soderlund & K. Hildebrandt (Eds.), *Canadian newspaper ownership in the era of convergence: Rediscovering social responsibility* (pp. 31–44). Edmonton: University of Alberta Press.

Soderlund, W. C., & Hildebrandt, K. (2005c). The relationship between the press and democratic politics. In K. Hildebrandt & W. C. Soderlund (Eds.), *Canadian newspaper ownership in the era of convergence rediscovering social responsibility* (pp. 1–10). Edmonton: University of Alberta Press.

Soderlund, W. C., & Romanow, W. I. (2005). Failed attempts at regulation of newspaper ownership: The Davey committee and the Kent royal commission. In W. C. Soderlund & K. Hildebrandt (Eds.), *Canadian newspaper ownership in the era of convergence rediscovering social responsibility* (pp. 11–30). Edmonton: University of Alberta Press.

Soderlund, W. C., Lee, M. F., & Gecelovsky, P. (2002). Trends in Canadian newspaper coverage of international news, 1988–2000: Editors' assessments. *Canadian Journal of Communication, 27*, 73–87.

Soroka, S. N. (2002). *Agenda-setting dynamics in Canada*. Vancouver: University of British Columbia Press.

Statistics Canada. (2011). *Canada at a glance*. Available http://www.statcan.gc.ca/pub/12-581-x/12-581-x2012000-eng.pdf

Tagliamonte, S., & Denis, D. (2008). Linguistic ruin? LOL! Instant messaging and teen language. *American Speech, 83*(1), 2–34.

Taras, D. (1993). The mass media and political crisis: Reporting Canada's constitutional struggles. *Canadian Journal of Communication, 18*(2), 131–148.

The Chronicle Herald. (2010). *Our history*. Retrieved from http://thechronicle-herald.ca/services/aboutus.html

Trudeau, P. E. (1968). *Federalism and the French Canadians*. Toronto: Macmillan.

Van Dijk, T. A. (2006). Ideology and discourse analysis. *Journal of Political Ideologies, 11*(2), 115–140.

Vessey, R. (2013). Challenges in cross-linguistic corpus-assisted discourse studies. *Corpora, 8*(1), 1–26.

Vipond, R. C. (1996). Citizenship and the Charter of Rights: The two side of Pierre Trudeau. *International Journal of Canadian Studies, 14*, 179–192.

Vipond, M. (2008). One network or two? French-language programming on the Canadian Radio Broadcasting Commission, 1932–36. *The Canadian Historical Review, 89*(3), 319–343.

Vipond, M. (2012). *The mass media in Canada* (4th ed.). Toronto: James Lorimer and Company.

Webber, J. (1994). *Reimagining Canada: Language, culture, community, and the Canadian constitution*. Montreal/Kingston: McGill-Queen's University Press.

Winseck, D. (2002). Netscapes of power: Convergence, consolidation and power in the Canadian mediascape. *Media, Culture and Society, 24*, 795–819.

Young, D. (2001). Céline Dion, national unity and the English-language press in Canada. *Media, Culture & Society, 23*, 647–663.

Young, N., & Dugas, E. (2011). Representations of climate change in Canadian national print media: The banalization of global warming. *Canadian Review of Sociology/Revue canadienne de sociologie, 48*(1), 1–22.

Young, N., & Dugas, E. (2012). Comparing climate change coverage in Canadian English- and French-language print media: Environmental values, media cultures, and the narration of global warming. *Canadian Journal of Sociology/Cahiers canadiens de sociologie, 37*(1), 25–54.

3

Approaches to Language Ideology

The investigation of language ideologies is thorny because these are beliefs, values, and assumptions about language that take shape not only through explicit evaluation and judgements but also through more implicit means (van Dijk 1998: 29). Language ideologies cannot be deduced from singular examples, nor examples that are speciously argued to be representative of the discourse as a whole. The fact is that bias, evaluation, judgements, and assumptions must be shown to exist across numerous examples and in various forms in order to suggest the existence of ideological discourses. Furthermore, media discourse, like nearly all samples of discourse, is socially constructed as both a social product and a social practice (Fowler 1991: 8). The result of being embedded in social practice means that all discourse tends to be ideological to a certain extent. Media discourse is simply argued to be a particularly important example because of its (often) institutional and systematic functions. Following Fowler (1991: 8), it is not argued that media discourse is "biased" or "more ideological" than any other discourse. To the contrary, what is claimed about media discourse "can equally be claimed about *any* representational discourse [because] [a]nything that is said or written about the world is articulated from a particular ideological position" (Fowler 1991: 10). As a

R. Vessey, *Language and Canadian Media*,
DOI 10.1057/978-1-137-53001-1_3

result, it is not a coincidence that the media's words "intersect with our own" (Cotter 2001: 430), since the media serves to reflect and reinforce social norms, impacting agendas and identities (Cotter 2010: 2).

This chapter proceeds first by outlining the concept of language ideology as it evolved in the field of linguistic anthropology. Then, it turns to the important distinction between implicit and explicit manifestations of ideology and the corresponding theoretical and methodological issues, especially for studies of media language. Next, the chapter turns to some basic tenets of corpus linguistic theory and method and how these can be usefully applied to studies of language ideology. Following this, some of the main approaches in discourse analysis relevant to the study of language ideology are discussed. Finally, the chapter concludes with the specific procedure used in the analyses of this book.

3.1 Language Ideology: Theory and Method

As a field of study, "Language Ideology" (henceforth LI) refers to the body of work that emerged primarily from linguistic anthropologists in the USA, and in particular those associated with the work of Dell Hymes (Milani and Johnson 2008: 362; Schieffelin et al. 1998). The objective in LI research is to understand when and how links are forged between such apparently diverse categories as language, spelling, and grammar on the one hand, and nation, gender, simplicity, intentionality, authenticity, knowledge, development, power, and tradition on the other (Woolard 1998: 27). These categories, and the linkages between them, have real effects on the social world; therefore, the study of language ideologies consists of examinations of the broader sociopolitical contexts in which language ideologies are embedded in order to establish longer-term implications for social change (Milani and Johnson 2008: 373; Wassink and Dyer 2004: 5).

According to one of the earliest definitions, LI refers to "sets of beliefs about language articulated by users as a rationalization or justification of perceived language structure and use" (Silverstein 1979: 193). This definition and derivations of it are still often used by researchers in the field (e.g. Laihonen 2008: 669; Stewart 2012: 190; Wassink and Dyer 2004). However, some (e.g. Blommaert and Verschueren 1998) have argued that research should not be singularly focused on "articulated" or explicit manifestations of language ideologies. These researchers have argued that of equal importance are the implicit ("latent", "immanent") expressions of these ideologies (see discussion in Woolard 1998: 9–11). Thus, "[r]epresentations, *whether explicit or implicit*, that construe the intersection of language and human beings in a social world are what we mean by 'language ideology'" (Woolard 1998: 3; emphasis added). Language ideologies may be implicit if, for example, they are naturalised and do not require articulation, or they may become explicit in "linguistic representations" (e.g. Boudreau 2008), and in particular in "language ideological debates" (Blommaert 1999a).

Despite Woolard's inclusive discussion of the implicit and the explicit nature of language ideologies, she does note that the tension between these different sitings is a recurrent concern to researchers in the field (Woolard 1998: 6). For example, she notes that Blommaert and Verschueren (1998) posit the importance of naturalised, implicit, "unsaid" ideologies, whereas Briggs (1998) suggests that such an emphasis privileges the analyst's perspective and may contribute to the analyst's unintended collusion in reifying the perspective of only a sector of a community (Woolard 1998: 9). Debates about the "sitings" of LI have not been easily dismissed, and researchers (e.g. De Costa 2010: 220; Griswold 2011: 407) continue to highlight the distinction between implicitness and explicitness in LI research. Crucially, the distinction has implications not only in terms of theories and definitions (i.e. what LI *is*) but also in terms of methodological approach (i.e. how LI can be studied). In other words, it is only by establishing whether LI occurs in implicit or explicit forms that an appropriate methodology can be established to investigate these forms. Since the understanding in this book is that LI occurs in both implicit and explicit forms, it follows that the methodology applied here must account for both forms in the data.

To a large degree, the methods that LI researchers have tended to use are oriented towards the theory and methods of linguistic anthropology (see Milani and Johnson 2008). This is in line with the Hymesian origins of LI (e.g. Hymes 1974: 31), since theories of language ideologies emerged as a way of enriching and explaining ethnographic data (Woolard 1998: 14). However, the rich theorisation of LI has been increasingly used in disciplines beyond linguistic anthropology. For example, researchers in language and education policy have long been interested in the theories and literature of LI to explain and even to predict the effectiveness of language policy in society (Ricento 2006: 50). More recently, researchers in conversation analysis (Laihonen 2008), perceptual dialectology (Stewart 2012), and phonology (Wassink and Dyer 2004) have found the explanatory power of language ideologies to be useful in their own work. The theory and literature of LI have been applied to study subjects as diverse as the language of courtrooms (e.g. Eades 2012), debates over scripts to represent sign language (Hoffmann-Dilloway 2011), and the evaluation of language skills in call centres from New Brunswick to Pakistan and in-between (e.g. Dubois et al. 2006; Duchêne 2009; Rahman 2009). However, when LI is studied in fields where ethnographic data are not in use or appropriate, new methods should be adapted. This is sometimes the case in studies of media discourse.

As noted in Sect. 1.2, the media are an important source of language ideologies. Studies of news media often adopt a discourse approach (see e.g. Cotter 2001) and, similarly, discourse analysis has often had a part to play in LI research (e.g. Boudreau 2008; Milani and Johnson 2008; Woolard 1998: 7). In fact, Gal (2006: 388) describes LI as a kind of discourse analysis in which the study of metapragmatic assumptions about the relationship between words, speakers, and worlds provide explanatory power about the effectiveness of verbal action in the society. Milani and Johnson (2008: 365) explain that the traditions of LI and discourse analysis offer "important and potentially *complementary* theoretical and methodological frameworks" (emphasis in original). Indeed, some studies of news media have combined ethnographic and discursive approaches (e.g. Van Hout and Macgilchrist 2010), which suggests that LI work might fit in easily with discourse approaches to media language. However, discourse approaches to media language have also benefited from an infusion of corpus linguistics theory and methods in the form of "corpus-assisted discourse studies", or "CADS" (see e.g. Baker 2006; Partington 2010; Stubbs 2001). While CADS research has already tackled ideology in the media in different forms, there has been little corpus linguistic research on LI specifically. What little research does exist (e.g. Fitzsimmons-Doolan 2014; Subtirelu 2013) has tended to focus only on explicit rather than both explicit and implicit language ideologies. This chapter explores the importance of corpus linguistics and discourse analysis for the study of LI in both explicit and implicit forms in media discourse.

3.2 Methods

3.2.1 Corpus Linguistics

Corpus linguistics is an approach to the study of language with theories that attempt to explain the function of language in society according to attested data and a methodology with a set of ever-expanding tools for linguistic analysis that contribute to and enhance this theory. The foundation of corpus linguistics is the use of a principled collection of electronically stored and computer-readable texts known as a "corpus" or "corpora" (Baker et al. 2008: 274; Teubert 2007: 89). The compatibility of corpora with computer programs, which are capable of handling and sorting through substantial quantities of data, means that larger and more comprehensive samples tend to be used for analysis. Corpus linguists also tend to study real, naturally occurring data rather than artificially constructed examples; corpus linguistics research is thus by and large a study of language in society and can be considered inherently sociolinguistic (Partington 2009: 298; Stubbs 1996: 23, 2001: 221).

Sociolinguistic data is language that is both routine and creative, and language that is the product of discourse communities. Shared understanding is created within discourse communities by common discourses; these discourses rely on common understandings of words and phrases, and not only those that are obviously ideologically loaded but also those that are frequent or used in frequent combinations with one another (Stubbs 2003: 313). Many words are frequent in a community because they occur in frequent phrases, which are in turn frequent because they are conventional ways of expressing common meaning (Stubbs 2007: 100). Conventional ways of expressing common meaning are related to community-internal value systems, which determine and establish the extent to which meaning is implied or must be overtly stated. According to Stubbs (2001: 166), "[a] community's value system is built up and maintained, at least partly, by the recurrent use of particular phrasings in texts". Frequent phrases and patterns are vital to communities because they facilitate understandings of connected discourse and the attitudes, values, and even ideologies within this discourse (Stubbs 1996: 153–158, 2003: 306). In other words, the consideration of the function of frequent and repeated words and phrases provides researchers insight into the discourse and culture of specific communities. This reasoning is in line with the social theories of Bourdieu (e.g. 1991) and Giddens (1984), among others, who contend that routine and often mundane processes serve to reproduce culture through tradition and conventions (see Stubbs 2001: 241).

Corpus linguistics theory also builds on the work of John Sinclair (e.g. 1991, 1996), who theorised that meaning in language is not created by words used in isolation from one another, but rather from words used in combination. Meaning is often distributed across units larger than individual words, and thus words must be viewed in context (or "co-text") in order for meaning to be understood (Stubbs 2001: 100). This theory of meaning can be tested as never before using corpus linguistics. Corpus researchers are able to study previously unobservable phenomena that are revealed through frequent and statistically significant linguistic patterns. Complementing these majority patterns are considerations of low frequency or absence from the data sample, which have important implications too (Baker 2010: 125). The goal of corpus linguistics, then, is to develop a theory of meaning from corpus data; depending on the sample of data under investigation, the meaning may be general and widespread or specific to the community from which the data are drawn (Hunston 2002: 22; Stubbs 2001: 20). Thus, although corpus linguistics is often criticised for not having a unified social theory, or worse, for being "theory light" (see discussions in Hunston and Thompson 2006: 1–3; Stubbs 2006: 15, 2010: 21–22), it is argued here that corpus linguistics is in fact based on a considered rationale for authentic language use, understandings of frequency, and a recognition of meaning distributed across units of language. Together, these comprise the central theoretical underpinnings of corpus linguistics.

In order to determine what is meaningful within a corpus, there are a variety of computer programs that rely on fairly standardised procedures to establish salience. Although there is no single methodology for how to "do" corpus analysis (Hunston and Thompson 2006: 3), there are some dominant tools. The most common procedures include the three principal functions contained within WordSmith Tools (Mike Scott 2014), which is the corpus linguistics programme used here for analysis. These principal functions include WordList (a frequency tool), Concord (a concordancer), and KeyWord (a statistical significance ranking function). These will be discussed in the subsequent sections with relation to their usefulness in studies of LI.

WordList is a tool that allows researchers to view the frequency of all words within a corpus according to either the rank of frequency (most to least frequent, or vice versa) or alphabetical order. As mentioned, frequency is of primary importance in corpus linguistics, and it becomes meaningful when it is interpreted as typicality of speakers' tacit knowledge of discourse norms (Stubbs 2001: 61). Indeed, Gries (2008: 403) goes so far as to say that frequency data can reveal the "cognitive entrenchment"—that is, the extent to which a word is embedded in the minds of language users—of particular words within a community. It is argued that frequency indicates lexical choices that writers or speakers have made or avoided in their language use. Frequency is the most common statistic employed in corpus linguistics, and tends to be the first step of most corpus analyses (Archer 2009: 2; Gries 2008: 403). In studies of LI, frequent words and phrases may indicate the prominence of certain topics and ways of discussing them.

However, it is clear that frequency can be misleading (Sinclair 1996: 80). If researchers only examine the most frequent words in a corpus, they may overlook less frequent ones, which can be as significant to studies of LI as more frequent words. This is because ideology is not only evident from words that are clearly ideologically loaded or phrases that are plainly evaluative and repeated; ideology can also be present in assumptions in discourse, which may mean that words and phrases are elided and their frequency is thus affected. This is also one way in which implicit language ideologies might be approached for analysis. For instance, if a speaker assumes that language plays a central role in national identity, this may mean that the language is frequently under discussion, or it may mean that it is rarely discussed because it is presumed to be already within the minds of the interlocutors of that discourse community. The challenge of how to utilise frequency in corpus linguistics is not limited to studies of LI; numerous researchers (e.g. Baker 2009b, c; Davies 2009; Kirk 2009; Mautner 2009) have noted how, more generally, a single-minded focus on frequency may result in some findings being overlooked. For example, it may mean that frequent words are decontextualised (and thus misunderstood), or it may mean that analytical categories, based on what appear to be majority trends, are oversimplified and erroneously applied to the data (see Freake et al. 2011: 40; Williams 1977 as discussed in Phillips 1998: 215). Also, a single-minded focus specifically on high-frequency items may mean that lower-frequency items, or variation more generally, are overlooked (Mautner 2009: 44; Stubbs 2001: 29).

However, these potential problems with frequency can be avoided through good research practice. For instance, Stubbs (2001: 221) argues that unique or unusual occurrences, marked by low frequency, may only be described against the background of what is normal and expected according to higher-frequency scores; thus, frequency proves to be useful to establish both what is typical and atypical. Also, researchers can use dispersion plots (i.e. charts that present the distribution of an item according to its locations in the data) in order to establish consistency and typicality of categories as well as variation and minority trends (Baker 2010: 39; Gries 2008: 404–405). If an item occurs frequently only within a small number of texts, then it is not representative of trends across the entire corpus. Thus, dispersion plots can also be used to contextualise high- and low-frequency items. Low-frequency items can also be considered through tests of statistically significant absence ("negative keywords"; see e.g. Baker 2009c: 95), which can help to determine which words occur less often than predicted in comparison with other corpora. Finally, frequency can also be derived from individual lines of words in context (i.e. concordance lines), rather than from frequency lists, in order to establish the relevance of examples (Baker 2010: 42). This in-text contextualisation can also serve to establish the discourse function of specific words, and thus their significance with relation to research objectives (Baker 2009b: 6). This brings us to the next important tool in WordSmith Tools: Concord.

Concord is a concordancer that enables researchers to determine which words collocate with which other words, thus revealing semantic or discursive relationships. The tool has several different functions that show terms in context. For example, concordance lines display and organise the data according to search terms within their original "co-text" (i.e. the lexical content, or words surrounding a search term to the left and the right). These lines can be experimentally manipulated so that words within the co-text of individual lines are aligned and arranged in similar fashions (e.g. according to alphabetical order), making patterns more easily observable (Stubbs 2006: 18). Collocate lists also provide an option for viewing connections between search terms and other words. These lists show words that "collocate" with the search term, with what frequency, and in which positions with relation to the search term. In default settings, Concord considers items that occur within five words of a search term to be meaningful collocates, although this too can be manipulated by individual researchers. Indeed, some argue that the closer a word tends to be located to a search term, the stronger the relationship is between the words (e.g. Milizia and Spinzi 2008: 335; Stubbs 2001: 29). Another component of the Concord tool is the clusters function. This enables researchers to see which words tend to cluster together in fixed or semi-fixed patterns, revealing phraseology and multiword phrases that function as single semantic units (Archer 2009: 6; Greaves 2009; Milizia and Spinzi 2008: 323).

The relationship between words and the meanings that result from their combination is of central interest to corpus linguists. Numerous theories have emerged to account for the relationship between words that repeatedly recur with other words. Hoey (e.g. 2007: 7–9), for example, argues that the strength of a relationship between words (i.e. as determined by frequency of collocation) leads speakers and writers become "primed" to use words in specific combinations to convey meaning. In other words, the argument is that through repeated exposure to authentic language use, speakers and writers retain a cognitive record of the context and co-text of use so that, cumulatively, they come to presume what is normally lexically and semantically associated with a word (Hoey 2011: 155; Morley and Partington 2009: 148). More broadly, this gradual adoption of discourse norms is part of a process of acculturation into a discourse community through which language users learn to effectively convey messages and understand their interlocutors (Morley and Partington 2009: 139–140; Partington 2004: 152; Stubbs 1996: 158, 2001: 59, 2003: 306).

The continued occurrence of a word with various other words results in "semantic preference" (see Baker et al. 2008: 278; Kemppanen 2004: 92; cf. Hoey 2007: 8). This means that a word tends to be repeatedly associated with a set of other related words because speakers replicate the contexts in which a word has been encountered (Hoey 2006: 53, 2007: 8). The result of these collocation patterns is that words have a "preference" for semantically associated words. Often, the strength of collocation is established using Mutual Information scores of statistical significance (see e.g. Baker 2006: 101). The strength of collocation helps researchers to establish how meaning is created when words are used and combined in specific patterned ways. In other words, collocation trends help to indicate discourse norms of a given community (Stubbs 2001: 7). When semantic preference takes an evaluative turn—that is, when a word tends to repeatedly collocate with other words that have predominantly negative or positive meanings—then a word is said to acquire "semantic prosody" (Kemppanen 2004: 93; Partington 2004: 151; cf. Baker et al. 2008: 278).

Semantic prosody is ultimately a contentious theory of evaluative collocation and connotation within corpus linguistics with numerous divergent accounts of existence and salience (for overviews, see e.g. Hunston 2007; Stewart 2010; Whitsitt 2005; Zhang 2009). Related and alternative concepts exist, such as "evaluative collocation" (Bednarek 2008), "semantic association" (Hoey, e.g. 2011), and "discourse prosody" (Stubbs, e.g. 2001; Tognini-Bonelli 1996). Here, the term "discourse prosody" will be adopted in order to emphasise the function of evaluative collocation in the creation of coherence and understanding within discourse communities (Baker 2006: 87, 2010: 133; Baker et al. 2006: 58; Stubbs 2001: 66; Tognini-Bonelli 1996: 193, 209).

Discourse prosody is a useful corpus linguistic concept to apply to studies of LI because ideologies are often evaluative (Preston 2004; Stubbs 2001: 215; Thompson and Hunston 2000: 8). While collocation and related concepts such as semantic preference show us how language users reproduce the phraseology of their community, discourse prosody goes a step further and suggests how language users reproduce the discourse of their community (Morley and Partington 2009: 140; Stubbs 2001: 215). By using language according to a community's discursive norms, an acculturated speaker tends to reproduce the values and judgments of his or her community. Discursive norms include such things as linking words together (i.e. collocation) in ways that are accepted by and used throughout the community; this accepted collocation, when evaluative, gives individual words their community-specific "discourse prosody". Certainly, language users can choose to "switch off" or "override" discourse prosodies, but it is argued that when this is done, it is usually with the intention of being ironic or humorous (see e.g. Louw 1993: 157; Morley and Partington 2009: 146; Stewart 2010: 3). The assumption that discourse prosody relies on discourse norms implies that discourse is ideological. If members of a discourse community are obliged to rely on common discursive norms in order to communicate effectively, since the discourse of that community is to some extent formulaic and value-laden (i.e. as a result of collocation trends that are at times evaluative), then most instances of language use will be unavoidably ideological (Manca 2008: 372; Morley and Partington 2009: 144–147; Stubbs 1996: 235). This, in turn, implies that individuals' use of language is manufactured and to some extent predetermined as an effect of their membership in a discourse community (Gramsci 1971). However, the discourse norms of any community are subject to the alternative and oppositional effects of competing ideologies from both within and outside the community (Williams 1973). This logic serves to highlight how ideologies, embedded in discourses and specific to discourse communities, may differ between groups. Furthermore, this theorisation of evaluative collocation functioning within discourse communities is one notable reason why the term "discourse prosody" is preferable to "semantic prosody".

Several corpus researchers have suggested that the discourse prosody of single words may differ between groups according to contexts of use (Hoey 2007: 9; Hunston 2007; Manca 2008: 383; Morely and Partington 2009: 155; Nelson 2006; Partington 2004: 154). If discourse prosodies vary across domains, then they may differ even more if translation equivalents are compared between language varieties because these so-called equivalents are derived not only from potentially different domains but also from different social groups that speak different languages (Baker 2010: 128; Berber Sardinha 2000; Dam-Jensen and Korning Zethsen 2008; Hoey 2011: 157; Kemppanen 2004; Korning Zethsen 2004; Lewandowska-Tomaszczyk 1996; Milizia and Spinzi 2008: 334; Morley and Partington 2009: 140; Munday 2011: 169; Partington 1998: 48–64, 77; Tognini-Bonelli 2001: 113–128; Xiao and McEnery 2006; Zhang 2009). This final point is particularly relevant to cross-linguistic studies of language ideologies.

Above and beyond discourse prosody, collocation trends more generally indicate the kinds of choices that speakers make and the denotational, connotational, and evaluative meanings that result from these choices (Cotterill 2001: 293). It is the task of the corpus analyst to interpret and explain lexical choices and the lexicogrammatical frame (i.e. collocational context) in which they occur (Qian 2010: 39). Importantly, even if linguistic choices and patterns are probabilistic, quantitative measures cannot provide explanations: choices and patterns must be explained by researchers (Biber et al. 2002: 3–4; Mautner 2009: 45). In sum, then, the Concord tool provides numerous functions that enable researchers to determine how words are being used, whether these uses are dominant or marginalised within the corpus, and whether words appear to be imbued with evaluative meaning by their repeated co-text (i.e. their discourse prosody according to repeated evaluative collocates). All of these collocational angles on the data could have potential implications for studies of LI.

Finally, we turn to the KeyWord tool. In popular language, a "keyword" tends to mean a word that is important in some way (Bondi 2010: 1; Stubbs 2010: 21; Williams 1976). The KeyWord tool is useful because it has defined specific criteria that determine which words are important and why. According to the KeyWord procedure, words are "key" when they are of statistically significant high frequency ("positive keywords") or low frequency ("negative keywords"). With this tool, significance is established by comparing one corpus (a "primary" or "specialised" corpus) with a "reference" or "comparator" corpus. Reference corpora tend to be very large, general, and compiled by research teams or institutions, whereas comparator corpora are designed and compiled according to the research purpose of individuals.

This KeyWord tool works by counting the words ("tokens") in each corpus, measuring their proportion of the overall lexical content of the corpus, and then using log-likelihood tests to determine whether the difference may have occurred by chance. Each word is accorded a "keyness" score according to its probability, and the words are then ranked according to their scores (i.e. the higher the keyness score, the lower the *p*-value). Words that are typical to both the primary and the comparator corpora are eliminated by the KeyWord calculations due to their similar frequencies. As a result, the KeyWord list includes only those words whose frequency or scarcity is significant. The calculation of statistical significance enables researchers to determine which words may have a specific ideological function in the discourse community from which the data are drawn. Keywords are therefore useful for uncovering "aboutness" (Mike Scott 2009), or salient thematic content, of a corpus, and can be invaluable in studies of ideology (Kemppanen 2004: 91).

However, keywords must be analysed in conjunction with other tools because, like frequency, statistical significance used in isolation can be misleading (Archer 2009: 4). Problems have also been noted in the KeyWord process in that comparator and reference corpora are used inconsistently (see e.g. Baker 2009a, 2010: 14; Johnson and Ensslin 2006: 10; Mike Scott 2009; Taylor 2008: 184). Also, some researchers (e.g. Gabrielatos and Marchi 2011; Kilgarriff 2009: 1) have taken issue with the subjectivity inherent in KeyWord. For example, the KeyWord tool produces far too many words for an individual, or even a team, to analyse in any kind of comprehensive way, and researchers are forced to subjectively decide which keywords to examine (Baker 2004: 351–352, 2010: 26; Berber Sardinha 1999: 4–6; Johnson and Ensslin 2006: 9–11; Kilgarriff 2009: 1–2; Rayson 2008: 526; Mike Scott 1997: 237). Also, the definitions of "keyness" and "keywords" are inconsistent, and the statistics used to measure "significance" are based on erroneous assumptions about what can be achieved (see e.g. Gabrielatos and Marchi 2011; Kilgarriff 2009). Here, keywords derived from the KeyWord process do not comprise the focal point of analysis in any chapter. Keywords are used to illustrate arguments rather than to draw conclusions. Thus, keywords are not studied exhaustively, because they are considered only "the tips of icebergs: pointers to complex lexical objects which represent the shared beliefs and values of a culture" (Stubbs 2010: 23; see also Sinclair 1996: 80). In general terms, then, keywords are useful in the study of LI because they indicate the topics that are possibly of significant (or even ideological) interest to members of a discourse community.

Despite their usefulness, the tools described above are unable by themselves to account for all aspects of LI. As we have seen, with the exception of concordance lines, most corpus analytic procedures principally rely on quantitative measures, which overlook the more subtle ways in which LI can function in discourse (Baker et al. 2008: 274; Bell 1998: 65; Blackledge and Pavlenko 2002: 122; Ricento 2006: 47). Even concordance lines, which show search terms in context, do not provide a theory or a method for determining how ideology may be functioning within the context of the sentence or even at the level of the discourse community. Moreover, the identification of probabilistic patterns is most useful in data sets that are normative in terms of both monolingualism (i.e. they consist of only one standard language so that patterns are not complicated by alternatives across languages or varieties) and syntax (e.g. standard grammar). When data sets become complicated with code-switching, code-mixing, spelling variation, and irregular syntax, then corpus tools prove to be less useful. In other words, corpus linguistics tools are useful for pinpointing some but not all characteristics of language ideologies. For the task of establishing how ideologies function as commonsense assumptions underlying discourse, discourse analysis plays an important role.

3.2.2 Critical Discourse Analysis

Critical discourse analysis (CDA) is unique among approaches to discourse in that it is intended to focus on studies of ideology and power (see e.g. Blommaert 2005: 25; Fairclough 1989, 2003; van Dijk 2006; Wodak 2001, 2007). In CDA, discourse analysis is not only seen as the analysis of text, even if the data are textual. Discourse (textual or otherwise) is understood as a sample of socially structured language use that is produced and consumed within specific socio-economic, geographic, and institutional contexts; thus, the analysis of discourse is to some extent the analysis of the society from which it emerges. In other words, language use is not considered to be isolated from the contexts in which it is produced; rather, societal power hierarchies and value systems are considered to be manifested in language.

Silverstein (1992: 315–316) (a linguistic anthropologist, not a critical discourse analyst) notes:

> there is no possible *absolutely* pre-ideological, i.e. *zero-order*, social semiotic – neither a purely 'sense'-driven denotational system for the referential-and-predicational expressions of any language, nor a totalizing system of purely 'symbolic' values for any culture.

If all language is to some extent ideological, then it is the task of the discourse analyst to determine the ways in which it is manifest or implicit in language. The objective of being "critical", however, does not exclude analysts themselves from scrutiny. An important tenet of critical discourse analysis (CDA) is the refusal to claim total objectivity (Fairclough 1989: 5). Since all language use is argued to be ideological and all individuals are members of one community or another, then analysts, themselves, must be as transparent as possible about their position with relation to the context and the data. This is similar to the principle of self-reflexivity in the field of linguistic anthropology and critical sociolinguistics (see e.g. Heller 2002).

Context and power are important considerations in the study of ideological discourse (Blommaert 2005: 12; Wodak 2001: 1). There are numerous relevant levels of context in CDA, including "co-text", "intertextuality" (the connections between a given text and those which it precedes and follows), "interdiscursivity" (the connections between discourses in use and other discourses circulating in society), and broader sociopolitical and historical contexts (Blommaert 2005: 46; Wodak 2008: 2). These levels of context, also used in other discourse analysis approaches, affect any discourse community and influence language users, who rely on assumptions about context in order to produce comprehensible discourse. For their language to be comprehensible, speakers and writers must, to a certain extent, draw on common understandings of language that include not only discourse norms but also discourse community norms, which include decisions as to what subject matter is relevant and how this subject matter should be described in such a way that it is logical to interlocutors.

Part of CDA is, then, determining why certain texts produced by certain individuals frame topics and individuals in specific ways, and whether these comprise part of a broader body of texts in which these topics and individuals are represented in similar ways. Contextual factors, such as intertextuality and interdiscursivity, are indicative of realms of power in society if these have an impact on the way individual speakers or writers use language. In other words, if in their own speech or writing individuals draw on the language of politicians, intellectuals, or the media, then this shows evidence of intertextuality or interdiscursivity and suggests the ways in which individuals are affected by power hierarchies in society (van Dijk 2003: 352; Wodak 2008: 3). In particular, the mass media is scrutinised since it is argued that the language of the media reflects the discourses of powerful members of society (Wodak et al. 2009: 214). Indeed, CDA has been used by many researchers to examine ideology in the news media (e.g. Jaworski et al. 2003; Kuo and Nakamura 2005), including language ideologies (Blackledge 2002; Milani 2007; Ricento 2005).

Although there is a fairly unified theory of discourse in CDA, there are numerous approaches to analysis within three dominant schools of thought: the discourse-historical, the sociocognitive, and the dialectical-relational (for an overview, see Wodak 2009: 311). The discourse-historical approach, used by Ruth Wodak and the Vienna School, applies argumentative, rhetorical, and pragmatic tools to examine social change and identity politics in large corpora of multiple genres. The sociocognitive approach of Teun van Dijk focuses on the impact of the media and the reproduction of racism through the study of context models that affect the pragmatics of discourse (Wodak and Meyer 2009: 25–26). The dialectical-relational approach used by Norman Fairclough relies on systemic functional grammar to analyse aspects of neo-liberal ideologies in British political developments. The approach used here draws on all of these schools, including, from the discourse-historical school, the argumentative and rhetorical tools for the analysis of national discourses (e.g. Wodak et al. 2009), the approaches to ideology and the media from the sociocognitive school (e.g. van Dijk 1991, 1998, 2006), and the use of systemic functional grammar from the dialectical-relational school (e.g. Fairclough 1989, 2003; for an overview, see Blommaert 2005: 22–23). All of these provide different means of accounting for language ideologies and nationalism in the Canadian media.

However, the discourse analytic tools used here are not limited to CDA. As Blommaert (2005: 6) notes, "CDA is part of a wider landscape of critical approaches to language and society", and thus by extension, "it would be a mistake to see CDA as the *only* possible critical perspective on language in society" (*ibid*: 21; emphasis in original). Thus, while largely subscribing to CDA, the approach to discourse analysis taken here also draws on other disciplinary methods that adopt a "critical" approach to the analysis of language (e.g. Blommaert 2005: 19; Fowler 2003 [1996]; Heller 2002), and also corpus linguistics and cross-linguistic studies. Part of the need for methodological fusion arises from the fact that discourse analysis has traditionally focused primarily on "monolingual discourse" not bilingual discourses (Blommaert 2007: 116), and this is particularly the case for studies of the media (Androutsopoulos 2007: 208). For the present purposes, the eclectic discourse analytic tools used here are outlined according to their use at the "micro" level (i.e. analysing LI at the local level of text) or at the "macro" level (i.e. analysing LI at the text, genre, and discourse level).

Micro-level tools are the tools that allow for ideology to be analysed in the lexicogrammar or at the clause level. These provide insight into how different angles of subjective experience are conveyed through lexicogrammatical choices. The micro tools used here draw predominantly on the transitivity system, which refers to the grammatical system that represents the "world of experience" through the categorisation of processes (i.e. verbs) and the ways in which they unfold—or are unfolded—through time and space (Conboy 2007: 56; Halliday and Matthiessen 2004: 170). This is a way of firmly rooting the grammar of a text into a theory of how language functions and which functions it serves in society (Fairclough 2003: 5). By situating the micro aspects of language—such as lexicogrammar—in society, we can establish the ideological implications of how and why messages are communicated in some ways and not others.

The transitivity system works by organising processes (e.g. processes of happening, doing, sensing, saying, being, or having) into "process types", each of which has its own structure for construing a "figure". According to Halliday and Matthiessen (2004: 175), a figure consists of (1) a process unfolding through time, (2) the participants involved in the process, and (3) the circumstances associated with the process. For example, "material" processes construe the actions and events of the external world (with actors, recipients, clients, scope, and attributes), whereas "mental" processes construe reflection, sensation, and awareness of the internal self (with sensers and phenomena that are sensed). "Relational" processes, on the other hand, serve to identify, classify, and characterise "carriers" and "tokens". There are also "behavioural" processes that represent outer manifestations of inner workings (e.g. consciousness), "verbal" processes that represent the exchange of communication through language or signs, and "existential" processes that simply denote existence or a happening (Halliday and Matthiessen 2004: 171). The importance of these process types is that once we are aware of the function(s) they serve, we can better understand the ways in which they are being used in a particular text.

In most instances, similar meanings can be conveyed in numerous different ways. For example, the official status of English and French in Canada can be conveyed in different ways (see Example 3.1).

3.3 Example 3.1

(a) Canada has two official languages.
(b) English and French are Canada's official languages.
(c) French and English are spoken in Canada.
(d) Canada is a bilingual country.
(e) Canadians speak English and French.

In each of these examples, the process type is different and with each different type the meaning is somewhat altered. In some cases (a, d), Canada is described in relation to languages; in other cases (b, c), the French and English languages are described in relation to Canada. In some cases (a), Canada is assigned possessions; in other cases (d), its possessions are merely attributes. In one case (d), "Canada" can be understood as a metonym for Canadians; in other cases (e), the linguistic abilities of some individuals are used to describe all citizens of the country. Thus, writers and speakers can convey different meanings within ostensibly synonymous expressions. The fact that a writer or speaker has chosen to convey a message through one process type rather than another may be suggestive of underlying ideology.

Other micro tools for discourse analysis are those used to study evaluative language. "Evaluation" refers to the language that expresses opinion, attitudes, feelings, or stance, and the term "evaluation" is used here to encompass a variety of near-synonymous terms, including "affect", "appraisal", "stance", "intensity", "affect", "evidentiality", and "hedging" (Thompson and Hunston 2000: 2; Conrad and Biber 2000: 57). According to Thompson and Hunston (2000: 6), evaluation serves three principal functions. First, evaluative language expresses the speaker or writer's opinion and, in so doing, reflects the value system of that person and sometimes their community. Second, evaluative language constructs and maintains relations between the speaker or writer and the hearer or reader. Finally, evaluative language can be used to organise discourse. Evaluation is important to studies of ideology because, as noted by Thompson and Hunston (2000: 8),

> ideologies do not exist in silence, but neither are they usually expressed overtly. They are built up and transmitted through texts, and it is in texts that their nature is revealed [...] Because ideologies are essentially sets of values – what counts as good or bad, what should or should not happen, what counts as true or untrue – evaluation is a key linguistic concept in their study.

The tools for analysing evaluative language, then, must take into account the various places in which evaluation can be located. At the micro level, evaluation can be studied in lexis (e.g. use of adjectives and adverbs) and grammar (e.g. use of intensifiers, explicatives, etc.) (Thompson and Hunston 2000: 14).

Evaluative lexis includes adjectives, adverbs, nouns, and verbs that indicate positivity or negativity, possibility or impossibility, or veracity or falsehood of a statement. Although there is not always consensus as to whether a word is clearly evaluative, comparison with other examples can shed light on the evaluative nature of a word (Channell 2000: 39). Evaluative grammar involves the use of intensifiers (such as quantifiers and repetition), comparators (such as negatives, futures, modals, questions, imperatives, or-clauses, superlatives, and comparatives), correlatives (such as progressives and attributives), and explicatives (i.e. clauses introduced by subordinators such as *while, though, since*, or *because*).

Evaluation also exists in syntactic structures and throughout longer phrases, which produce evaluation at the macro (text) level (Channell 2000; Thompson and Hunston 2000; van Dijk 1991: 46).

In sum, micro tools allow us to see the world of choices that is available to language users for providing a means of communication. Faced with these choices, speakers and writers make decisions—whether conscious or not—as to which process types suit the perspective being advanced in the message and which grammatical forms and lexicon will be used to talk about this subject. In some instances, speakers and writers simply choose the most common means of expressing a message, which is suggestive of the discourse norms of their community.

Macro tools rely on basic, interconnected understandings about what can be unearthed from the study of language use in society (from Blommaert and Verschueren 1998: 191). First, since no language user in any communicative context is able to fully express all that they wish to communicate in any entirely explicit way, all texts leave implicit assumptions that authors expect their readers to share with them. Thus, the careful analysis of these assumptions will reveal a common frame of reference or "ideology" in the discourse. There are two principal approaches to macro tools that will be outlined here: strategy analysis and genre analysis.

Strategies comprise a broad plane of analysis that Reisigl and Wodak (2009: 93–94) break down into five principal types: (1) referential or nominational; (2) predicative; (3) argumentative; (4) perspectival, and (5) intensifying/mitigating. The first category, referential or nominational strategies, refers to how people, things, and processes are named and categorised, and how these names and categories construct and represent social actors, in-groups, and out-groups. Referential or nominational strategies use categorisation devices, such as metaphors, metonymies, and synecdoches, to enable a part or a member to stand for (i.e. represent) the whole (Wodak 2009: 319–320). Predicative strategies are those where characteristics are attributed to participants through implicit or explicit predicates that serve to positively or negatively evaluate individuals, groups, or group members. Argumentative strategies involve attributions and claims and how these are justified. Often, justifications rely on culture-specific *topoi*, which are embedded assumptions that are used to conclude an argument. Perspectival strategies involve the expression of perspectives and positions, which rely to some extent on the use of intertextuality and interdiscursivity to allow writers or speakers to align with a certain perspective by using words, phrases, quotations, or even discourses that are central to that perspective (Wodak 2009: 320). More specifically, intertextuality involves the way in which the author of a text may draw upon a related set of other texts (Fairclough 1989: 152), and interdiscursivity refers to the way in which an author may draw upon other discourses for legitimisation, sustainment, or support (Wodak 2008: 3; Wodak 2009: 319). At times, an author will distance him or herself from a perspective through the use of "scare quotes", which are used to redirect responsibility for a contentious issue or remark away from the author and towards another source (Simpson 1993: 142). Finally, intensifying or mitigating strategies indicate the extent to which attributions and claims are given emphasis or modified, which may have ideological implications.

Genre analysis also has important implications for discourse analysis at the more macro level. Newspapers, for example, have specific genres that reflect the "information providing" function of newspapers in society. Newspapers exist to provide information to the public; however, subjective decisions affect what information is deemed to be "newsworthy" (Cotter 2010: 106–107). To a certain extent, newsworthiness is determined by evaluating events in terms of their contrast with the "norm". In other words, events are "newsworthy" if they are unexpected or unusual according to community values of "normality" (Cotter 2010: 9; Bednarek 2006: 191). Thus, the stories contained in a newspaper reflect ideological community values of what is normal and abnormal, what is important and unimportant, and sometimes what is positive versus what is negative. These community-specific values also determine where information is located within newspaper articles. For example, the structure of the "inverted pyramid" is the most common way of organising a news story (Aitchison 2007: 106). The pyramid structure means that the essential details of a story occur at the beginning of the article ("top of the pyramid"), whereas the less important details occur at the end of the article ("bottom of the pyramid").

Headlines, which occur before an article in a prominent position, are used to present the overall meaning and main topic of an article, including what is deemed to be the most important information in the event (Bell

1998: 83; van Dijk 1991: 51). The functions of headlines at the beginning of articles and their use of direct language have important effects on readers' interpretations of the body of the article (Brown and Yule 1983: 133). Similarly, the "lead" (i.e. the first paragraph or beginning of a story) of a newspaper article also has an important function since it is used to attract the reader. Indeed, Cotter (2010: 151) explains that it is in the lead that the information that is deemed "most interesting, relevant or new" is highlighted or "fronted". The decision of which information should be placed in the lead is subjective and based on news practice values as well as knowledge of the community for which the newspaper is designed: again, this decision indicates community-shared values and ideologies. Thus, when a newspaper in one community is compared with a newspaper in another, the differences between the two suggest "how newspapers with different audiences, identities, political commitments and hence editorial policies mediate the information they receive" (Richardson 2007: 106–107).

The discourse analysis of the articles began by establishing which categories of lexical items dominated each text with the aim of identifying lexical chains (e.g. hyponyms, synonyms, metonyms) that contributed to the cohesion of articles (Halliday and Hasan 1976). In addition, representations of languages were studied in articles, comments, and tweets and analyses focused on the extent to which languages were represented as descriptors of people, institutions, or locations, on the one hand, or stand-alone objects with or without agentive power, on the other. Above all, all analyses are comparative in terms of language (English/French), source country, and genre (news/social media).

In contrast, for online comments and tweets, the structure and analysis are not so straightforward. When there are patterns in the structure, these tend to emerge because of user-generated tendencies rather than because of institutional or genre requirements. The extent to which comments and tweets align or diverge often depends on the affordances of the given platform. For example, tweets are limited to 140 characters, and patterns often emerge because of the ability for Twitter users to "retweet" (repost a tweet verbatim), quote tweets, reach out to other Twitter users, and use established hashtags—or create new ones—to make tweets more findable (see Sect. 2.4). The reduction of word or character limits means that users must become more creative with their communication; often this means including innovative spelling (e.g. abbreviations, acronyms, rebuses) or multimodal (e.g. images, gifs), intertextual (e.g. quotation strategies), and hypertextual (e.g. URLs directing readers to other sites) means to communicate. However, the affordances of different platforms are constantly evolving, meaning that the structure and genre of online comments and tweeting are not established or fixed. Therefore, while some of the micro and macro tools are useful in studies of social media data, the differences in text type means that the tools sometimes must be adapted, as is discussed on a chapter-by-chapter basis throughout this book.

In sum, macro tools in discourse analysis enable researchers to examine how assumptions are embedded or organised within arguments and statements; these are relevant for the analysis of language ideologies and nationalism in Canadian newspapers.

The combination of corpus linguistics and discourse analysis, in the form of CADS, has been found to be useful by numerous researchers (see overview in Partington 2008). One of the primary advantages of the CADS approach is that it enables corpus linguists and discourse analysts to address criticisms that have plagued the component methods when used in isolation (see Baker et al. 2008: 275; Blommaert 2005: 31, 53; Blommaert and Bulcaen 2000: 447; Stubbs 1997: 102). Corpus linguistics and discourse analysis have faced criticisms ranging from theoretical incompleteness to methodological circularity; however, when used together in the CADS framework, researchers are able to address some of the weaknesses and exploit the strengths of each component part (see discussion in Baker et al. 2008: 284–285). Some advantages of the CADS approach include large amounts of contextualised data (Partington 2008: 97), reasonably high levels of objectivity (Baker et al. 2008: 277; Lee 2008: 92–93), and computerised coding, retrieval and analysis that mean findings are replicable (Lee 2008: 92–93). Another advantage of the CADS approach is that it is inherently flexible: researchers may adopt, adapt, and employ techniques and tools where and when they prefer (Baker et al. 2008: 275; Mautner 2009: 35; Morley 2009: 9; Rayson 2008: 520–521). The objective of CADS, Baker (2010: 123) notes, is not to replace but rather to enhance small-scale, qualitative analysis with corpus-based analysis of discourse. In sum, CADS not only enables researchers to combine qualitative and quantitative methods, but the combination in fact provides greater analytical capacity than either method on its own (Morley 2009: 10).

Still, there remains a lingering concern with the CADS approach: despite the fact that CADS is, at its heart, comparative (Partington 2008: 96, 2010: 90), nearly all comparisons have been between single-language corpora (for some exceptions, see Al-Hejin 2012; Freake et al. 2011; McEnery and Salama 2011; Qian 2010). Therefore, the remainder of this chapter explains how CADS can be adapted to cross-linguistic data.

3.3.1 Cross-Linguistic Corpus-Assisted Discourse Studies

The use of multilingual data adds important dimensions to CADS research, not least of which the capacity to compare discourses between groups that speak different languages. However, the study of multilingual data is not a defined area in the way that corpus linguistics and discourse analysis are. Here, the term "cross-linguistic studies" is used to refer to translation, contrastive linguistics, and other fields that can help to compare and contrast corpus and discourse (i.e. CADS) findings across languages.

Translation research shows that more or less identical perspectives can be expressed in different languages; however, the very need for translation emerges as a result of texts, perspectives, and even discourses being expressed only in one language (Dam-Jensen and Korning Zethsen 2008: 207). Lockerbie (2005: 39) explains:

> Since every culture has its own traditions and habits of thought, it also generates its own patterns in language, and its own rhetorical strategies which in turn lead to characteristic associations of words. These range from set idioms and expressions, many of them vernacular […], to looser collocations of words habitually grouped together either semantically or syntactically. Hence connotation and difference of meanings can occur in a grouping of words that in themselves are not distinctive.

Lockerbie's statement not only highlights the various ways in which patterns of language need to be explored in order for group differences to be fleshed out but also highlights some of the challenges that arise in cross-linguistic analysis. Lockerbie's argument becomes further complicated in multilingual contexts, when cultural differences are indexed and separated by languages. In an age where multilingual situations are increasingly common, the need for cross-linguistic analysis is incontrovertible. Dynamic methods are required for such cross-linguistic, cross-cultural analysis. However, there is no specific methodological procedure in "cross-linguistic studies". Rather, what is important is to highlight how the literature in translation and contrastive studies can contribute to CADS research. There are five issues worth noting.

First, ostensibly synonymous words across languages can serve different functions in the clause; thus, frequency can be misleading. Even languages with similar roots abound with "false friends" that can mislead researchers and translators alike (Korning Zethsen 2004). Even when translation "equivalents" share similar meanings, they may serve different functions in the clause, and this may affect frequency (Freake et al. 2011: 30). The second issue is that, since clause structures may differ between languages, discourse analytic techniques must be adapted (Johansson 2007: 3). Third, a reliance on pre-formulated categories may be inappropriate in comparisons between languages and cultures. Pre-formulated categories may lead to overgeneralisations and the "erasure" of some data to fit into categories. Good research practice means allowing categories to emerge from the data rather than imposing them there.

The fourth issue involves the comparison of the discourse prosody of translation equivalents. As discussed above, the comparison of translation "equivalents" can be a thorny area; this is further complicated when evaluative notions enter into discussion. To verify whether similar meanings and, moreover, evaluations are being conveyed, in-depth collocate and concordance analysis is required. Direct one-to-one equivalence cannot be assumed, and this means that the assessment of meaning and the comparison of frequency and statistical significance must nearly always be assessed on a case-by-case basis. Cross-linguistic studies of discourse prosodies are an under-researched area, but the literature that does exist suggests subtle evaluative differences in the uses of so-called translation equivalents (see Dam-Jensen and Korning Zethsen 2008; Korning

Zethsen 2004; Munday 2011; Partington 1998: 48–64; Stewart 2010: 18–19; Xiao and McEnery 2006; Zhang 2009).

Finally, the cross-linguistic comparison of keywords (e.g. using the KeyWord procedure outlined above) is complicated because (1) there are few parallel reference corpora available in different languages, (2) corpora of different languages cannot be directly compared against one another, and (3) keyness scores derived from different comparator corpora cannot be compared. Nevertheless, these obstacles can be overcome in cross-linguistic studies through the principled selection and design of comparator corpora in each language, each controlled for similar features such as genre, scope, size, and time period. With this approach, keywords can be produced that are reliable in terms of both their statistical significance and their ranked significance in comparison with keywords in the other language.

In sum, cross-linguistic CADS is a complex approach. It is especially complicated by the use of non-normative data, for example that of new and social media, which tends to be non-standard, multilingual, and even "superdiverse" (Vertovec 2007). However, given that corpus linguistics, discourse analysis, and cross-linguistic studies tend to draw on similar theoretical foundations about, for example, the importance of empirical data and the function of language in society, the three component parts are complementary. Together, these form a useful approach that enhances the predominantly monolingual research that has been done in recent years (e.g. Blommaert 2007; Johansson 2007: 6), and they shed light on the numerous facets through which meaning is conveyed. Now, with each component of the approach explicated, we can turn to the way in which the method can be applied to data.

3.4 Cross-Linguistic Corpus-Assisted Discourse Studies Procedure

The procedure used for the analysis of the various data sets was not unidirectional or uniform across all cases. Indeed, this would have been impossible, given the linguistic and genre differences across the data sets (i.e. print newspapers, online news, comments, and Twitter). The analytic procedure tended to involve a cycle of related and increasingly precise steps of analysis. Although initial approaches to all data sets tended to be quantitative, qualitative procedures followed and then these results were supplemented by further quantitative and qualitative analyses. More specifically, the first steps of analysis involved corpus procedures to determine the most frequent words and phrases, and sometimes the highest-ranked keywords. Frequent words and keywords were then often grouped together in thematic categories to establish trends in the data (although this differed according to the data set). The collocates, clusters, and concordance lines of relevant frequent and statistically significant words were then examined in order to flesh out the details of how these words were used in context. When frequent words or keywords were expanded into full concordance lines, these lines were analysed using micro discourse analytic tools as appropriate. When a saturation point was reached with the findings from keywords and frequent words, further qualitative procedures were often used. In some cases, this involved downsampling individual texts according to specific criteria for in-depth discourse analysis (see Chap. 4).

This alternation between the examination of large-scale (i.e. entire corpora) and small-scale (e.g. downsampled) data sets was used to ensure the reliability of the findings (Baker 2010: 139–141). In sum, then, analyses generally started with corpus linguistics procedures that were used to uncover and analyse frequency and statistical significance. Analyses then proceeded with a combined corpus linguistics and micro discourse analysis approach to concordance lines, collocates, and clusters. Next, micro and macro discourse analysis tools were used to study specific texts, and these qualitative findings were used to assess the reliability of the broader-scale findings uncovered from the corpus analysis. If and when needed, more corpus linguistics procedures were used and then followed by more discourse analytic procedures.

In summary, the approach used for the analysis of LI in the data sets under examination in this book involved, as a first step, the identification of words of high, low, and statistically significant frequency. The frequency of references to languages was used to identify sites where metalanguage was more or less salient and comparisons of metalanguage across corpora—and especially corpora of different languages—was used to help explore representations of languages within the data sets.

Furthermore, the identification of and comparisons between high- and low-frequency words helped to establish where language ideologies were more explicit or implicit. While frequency findings in and of themselves could not reveal the "explicitness" or "implicitness" of language ideologies, they tended to pinpoint potentially fruitful sites for more in-depth investigations. Collocation data also provided greater insight into the ways in which languages were represented within sites identified through frequency and statistical significance, and fixed and semi-fixed phrases served to reveal patterns in metalanguage (i.e. the ways in which languages were being represented). Although keywords were used to a lesser extent in some chapters, when the KeyWord procedure was used, it shed light on some of the ways in which texts containing references to languages differed from texts discussing other issues. These differences helped to establish some of the general ways in which language ideologies became embedded in Canadian media.

However, corpus linguistics was not the only approach used in the analysis; discourse analysis proved to be essential for understanding the more nuanced ways in which language ideologies became embedded in the data. Discourse analysis allowed the findings to be examined according to various levels of context and for findings to be interpreted according to relevant discourse theory. More specifically, strategy analysis showed how language ideologies were operationalised in arguments in specific texts; genre analysis showed how language issues were foregrounded or backgrounded according to text structure; and the micro tools showed how this took place in incremental ways in the discourse.

Nevertheless, discourse analysis, too, had its limitations in the multilingual data sets under examination in these chapters. Therefore, in some cases data sets were compared and contrasted in more ad hoc ways in order to assess the similarities and differences between the explicit and implicit language ideologies in the English and French data examined here. These are methods that had to be adapted to the data at hand and, rather than serving as a model for future research, it is hoped that these methods and procedures can be informative for research on comparisons of language ideologies across other multilingual datasets in the future.

References

Aitchison, J. (2007). *The word weavers: Newshounds and wordsmiths*. Cambridge: Cambridge University Press.

Al-Hejin, B. (2012). Linking critical discourse analysis with translation studies: An example from BBC News. *Language and Politics, 11*(3), 311–335.

Androutsopoulos, J. (2007). Bilingualism in the mass media and on the internet. In M. Heller (Ed.), *Bilingualism: A social approach* (pp. 207–230). New York: Palgrave.

Archer, D. (2009). Does frequency really matter? In D. Archer (Ed.), *What's in a word list?* (pp. 1–16). Farnham/Burlington: Ashgate.

Baker, P. (2004). Querying keywords: Questions of difference, frequency, and sense in keywords analysis. *Journal of English Linguistics, 32*(4), 346–359.

Baker, P. (2006). *Using corpora in discourse analysis*. London/New York: Continuum.

Baker, P. (2009a). "The question is, how cruel is it?" Keywords, fox hunting and the House of Commons. In D. Archer (Ed.), *What's in a word list?* (pp. 125–136). Farnham/Burlington: Ashgate.

Baker, P. (2009b). Introduction. In P. Baker (Ed.), *Contemporary corpus linguistics* (pp. 1–8). London: Continuum.

Baker, P. (2009c). Issues arising when teaching corpus-assisted (critical) discourse analysis. In L. Lombardo (Ed.), *Using corpora to learn about language and discourse* (pp. 63–98). Bern: Peter Lang.

Baker, P. (2010). *Sociolinguistics and corpus linguistics*. Edinburgh: Edinburgh University Press.

Baker, P., Gabrielatos, C., Khosravinik, M., Krzyzanowski, M., McEnery, T., & Wodak, R. (2008). A useful methodological synergy? Combining critical discourse analysis and corpus linguistics to examine discourses of refugees and asylum seekers in the UK press. *Discourse & Society, 19*(3), 273–306.

Bednarek, M. (2006). *Evaluation in media discourse. Analysis of a newspaper corpus*. London: Continuum.

Bednarek, M. (2008). "An increasingly familiar tragedy": Evaluative collocation and conflation. *Functions of Language, 15*(1), 7–34.

Bell, A. (1998). The discourse structure of news stories. In A. Bell & P. Garrett (Eds.), *Approaches to media discourse* (pp. 64–104). Oxford: Blackwell.

Berber Sardinha, T. (1999). *Using key words in text analysis: Practical aspects* (DIRECT Working Papers 42). São Paulo and Liverpool. Retrieved from http://www2.lael.pucsp.br/direct/DirectPapers42.pdf

Berber Sardinha, T. (2000). Semantic prosodies in English and Portuguese: A contrastive study. *Cuadernos de Filologia Inglesa, 9*(1), 93–109.

Biber, D., Conrad, S., & Leech, G. (2002). *Longman student grammar of spoken and written English*. Essex: Longman.

Blackledge, A. (2002). "What sort of people can look at a chicken and think dofednod?": Language, ideology and nationalism in public discourse. *Multilingua, 21*(2/3), 197–226.

Blackledge, A., & Pavlenko, A. (2002). Introduction. *Multilingua, 21*, 121–140.

Blommaert, J. (Ed.). (1999a). *Language ideological debates*. Berlin: Mouton de Gruyter.

Blommaert, J. (2005). *Discourse: A critical introduction*. Cambridge: Cambridge University Press.

Blommaert, J. (2007). Sociolinguistics and discourse analysis: Orders of indexicality and polycentricity. *Journal of Multicultural Discourses, 2*(2), 115–130.

Blommaert, J., & Bulcaen, C. (2000). Critical discourse analysis. *Annual Review of Anthropology, 29*, 447–466.

Blommaert, J., & Verschueren, J. (1998). The role of language in European nationalist ideologies. In B. B. Schieffelin, K. A. Woolard, & P. V. Kroskrity (Eds.), *Language ideologies. Practice and theory* (pp. 189–210). Oxford: Oxford University Press.

Bondi, M. (2010). Perspectives on keywords and keyness: An introduction. In M. Bondi & M. Scott (Eds.), *Keyness in texts* (pp. 1–20). Amsterdam: John Benjamins.

Boudreau, A. (2008). Le français parlé en Acadie: idéologies, représentations et pratiques. In *La langue française dans sa diversité* (pp. 59–74). Government of Quebec. Available http://www.spl.gouv.qc.ca/fileadmin/medias/pdf/actes_colloque_langue_francaise_2008.pdf

Bourdieu, P. (1991). *Language and symbolic power* (Thompson, J. Ed., trans: Raymond, G., & Adamson, M.). Cambridge, MA: Harvard University Press.

Briggs, C. L. (1998). 'You're a liar—you're just like a woman!': Constructing dominant ideologies of language in Warao Men's gossip. In B. B. Schieffelin, K. A. Woolard, & P. V. Kroskrity (Eds.), *Language ideologies: Practice and theory* (pp. 229–255). New York: Oxford University Press.

Brown, G., & Yule, G. (1983). *Discourse analysis*. Cambridge: Cambridge University Press.

Channell, J. (2000). Corpus-based analysis of evaluative lexis. In S. Hunston & G. Thompson (Eds.), *Evaluation in text. Authorial stance and the construction of discourse* (pp. 38–55). Oxford: Oxford University Press.

Conboy, M. (2007). *The language of the news*. Abingdon: Routledge.

Conrad, S., & Biber, D. (2000). Adverbial marking of stance in speech and writing. In S. Hunston & G. Thompson (Eds.), *Evaluation in text. Authorial stance and the construction of discourse* (pp. 56–73). Oxford: Oxford University Press.

Cotter, C. (2001). Discourse and media. In D. Schiffrin, D. Tannen, & H. E. Hamilton (Eds.), *The handbook of discourse analysis* (pp. 416–436). Oxford: Blackwell Publishers.

Cotter, C. (2010). *News talk: Investigating the language of journalism*. Cambridge: Cambridge University Press.

Cotterill, J. (2001). Domestic discord, rocky relationships: Semantic prosodies in representations of marital violence in the O. J. Simpson trial. *Discourse & Society, 12*(3), 291–312.

Dam-Jensen, H., & Korning Zethsen, K. (2008). Translator awareness of semantic prosodies. *Target, 20*(2), 201–221.

Davies, M. (2009). Word frequency in context: Alternative architectures for examining related words, register variation and historical change. In D. Archer (Ed.), *What's in a word list?* (pp. 53–68). Farnham/Burlington: Ashgate.

De Costa, P. I. (2010). Language ideologies and standard English policy in Singapore: Responses of a 'designer immigrant, student'. *Language Policy, 9*(3), 217–239.

Dubois, L., LeBlanc, M., & Beaudin, M. (2006). La langue comme ressource productive et les rapports de pouvoir entre communautés linguistiques. *Langage and société, 118*(4), 17–41.

Duchêne, A. (2009). Marketing, management and performance: multilingualism as commodity in a tourism call centre. *Language Policy, 8*(1), 27–50.

Eades, D. (2012). The social consequences of language ideologies in courtroom crossexamination. *Language in Society, 41*(4), 471–497.

Fairclough, N. (1989). *Language and power*. Essex: Longman.

Fairclough, N. (2003). *Analysing discourse: Textual analysis for social research*. London/New York: Routledge.

Fitzsimmons-Doolan, S. (2009). Is public discourse about language policy really public discourse about immigration? A corpus-based study. *Language Policy, 8*, 377–402.

Fitzsimmons-Doolan, S. (2014). Using lexical variables to identify language ideologies in a policy corpus. *Corpora, 9*(1), 57–82.

Fowler, R. (1991). *Language in the news: Discourse and ideology in the press*. London: Routledge.

Fowler, R. (2003[1996]). On critical linguistics. In C. R. Caldas-Coulthard & M. Coulthard (Eds.), *Readings in critical discourse analysis* (pp. 3–14). London: Routledge.

Freake, R., Gentil, G., & Sheyholislami, J. (2011). A bilingual corpus-assisted discourse study of the construction of nationhood and belonging in Quebec. *Discourse & Society, 22*(2), 21–47.

Gabrielatos, C., & Marchi, A. (2011). Keyness: Matching metrics to definitions. In Theoretical-methodological challenges in corpus approaches to discourse studies—And some ways of addressing them. University of Portsmouth, Portsmouth. Available http://eprints.lancs.ac.uk/51449/

Gal, S. (2006). Migration, minorities and multilingualism: Language ideologies in Europe. In C. Mar-Molinero & P. Stevenson (Eds.), *Language ideologies, policies, and practices: Language and the future of Europe* (p. 1327). Basingstoke: Palgrave Macmillan.

Giddens, A. (1984). *The constitution of society*. Berkeley: University of California Press.

Gramsci, A. (1971). *Selections from the prison notebooks.* (Ed. & trans: Hoare, Q., & Nowell, G.). New York: International Publishers.

Greaves, C. (2009). *ConcGram 1.0. A phraseological search engine.* Available http://www.edict.com.hk/pub/concgram/

Gries, S. T. (2008). Dispersions and adjusted frequencies in corpora. *International Journal of Corpus Linguistics, 13*(4), 403–437.

Griswold, O. V. (2011). The English you need to know: Language ideology in a citizenship classroom. *Linguistics and Education, 22*(4), 406–418.

Halliday, M., & Hasan, R. (1976). *Cohesion in English.* London: Longman.

Halliday, M. A. K., & Matthiessen, C. (2004). *An introduction to functional grammar.* London: Arnold.

Heller, M. (2002). *Éléments d'une sociolinguistique critique.* Paris: Didier.

Hoey, M. (2006). Language as choice: What is chosen? In G. Thompson & S. Hunston (Eds.), *System and corpus: Exploring connections* (pp. 37–54). London: Equinox.

Hoey, M. (2007). Lexical priming and literary creativity. In M. Hoey, M. Mahlberg, M. Stubbs, & W. Teubert (Eds.), *Text, discourse and corpora: Theory and analysis* (pp. 7–30). London: Continuum.

Hoey, M. (2011). Lexical priming and translation. In A. Kruger, K. Wallmach, & J. Munday (Eds.), *Corpus-based translation studies: Research and applications* (pp. 153–168). London: Continuum.

Hoffmann-Dilloway, E. (2011). Writing the smile: Language ideologies in, and through, sign language scripts. *Language and Communication, 31*(4), 345–355.

Hunston, S. (2002). *Corpora in applied linguistics.* Cambridge: Cambridge University Press.

Hunston, S. (2007). Semantic prosody revisited. *International Journal of Corpus Linguistics, 12*(2), 249–268.

Hunston, S., & Thompson, G. (2006). System and corpus: Two traditions with a common ground. In G. Thompson & S. Hunston (Eds.), *System and corpus: Exploring connections* (pp. 1–14). London: Equinox.

Hymes, D. (1974). *Foundations in sociolinguistics: An ethnographic approach.* Philadelphia: University of Pennsylvania Press.

Jaworski, A., Thurlow, C., Lawson, S., & Ylanne-McEwen, V. (2003). The uses and representations of local languages in tourist destinations: A view from British TV holiday programmes. *Language Awareness, 12*(1), 5–29.

Johansson, S. (2007). *Seeing through multilingual corpora: On the use of corpora in contrastive studies.* Amsterdam: John Benjamins.

Johnson, S., & Ensslin, A. (2006). Language in the news: Some reflections on keyword analysis using WordSmith Tools and the BNC. *Leeds Working Papers in Linguistics and Phonetics, 11*, 96–109.

Kemppanen, H. (2004). Keywords and ideology in translated history texts: A corpus-based analysis. *Across Languages and Cultures, 5*(1), 89–106.

Kilgarriff, A. (2009). Simple maths for keywords. *Proceedings of the corpus linguistics conference 2009.* University of Liverpool, UK. Retrieved from http://ucrel.lancs.ac.uk/publications/CL2009/

Kirk, J. M. (2009). Word frequency use or misuse? In D. Archer (Ed.), *What's in a word list?* (pp. 17–34). Farnham/Burlington: Ashgate.

Korning Zethsen, K. (2004). Latin-based terms. True or false friends? *Target, 16*(1), 125–142.

Kuo, S., & Nakamura, M. (2005). Translation or transformation? A case study of language and ideology in the Taiwanese press. *Discourse & Society, 16*(3), 393–417.

Laihonen, P. (2008). Language ideologies in interviews: A conversation analysis approach. *Journal of Sociolinguistics, 12*(5), 668–693.

Lee, D. Y. W. (2008). Corpora and discourse analysis: New ways of doing old things. In V. K. Bhatia, J. Flowerdew, & R. H. Jones (Eds.), *Advances in discourse studies* (pp. 86–99). London/New York: Routledge.

Lewandowska-Tomaszczyk, B. (1996). Cross-linguistic and language-specific aspects of semantic prosody. *Language Sciences, 18*(1–2), 153–178.

Lockerbie, I. (2005). The debate on l'amenagement du français in Québec. In I. Lockerbie, I. Molnaro, K. Larose, & L. Oakes (Eds.), *French as the common language in Québec: History, debates and positions* (pp. 15–65). Québec: Éditions nota bene.

Louw, B. (1993). Irony in the text or insincerity in the writer? The diagnostic potential of semantic prosodies. In M. Baker, G. Francis, & E. Tognini-Bonelli (Eds.), *Text and technology: In honour of John Sinclair.* Amsterdam: John Benjamins.

Manca, E. (2008). From phraseology to culture: Qualifying adjectives in the language of tourism. In U. Römer & R. Schulze (Eds.), *Patterns, meaningful units and specialized discourses* (pp. 368–385). Amsterdam: John Benjamins.

Mautner, G. (2009). Corpora and critical discourse analysis. In P. Baker (Ed.), *Contemporary corpus linguistics* (pp. 32–46). London: Continuum.

McEnery, T., & Salama, A. (2011). *De/victimizing Christian copts in/outside contemporary Egypt: A critical corpus-based study*. Paper presented at the International Corpus Linguistics Conference, Birmingham.

Milani, T. (2007). A language ideology in print: The case of Sweden. In S. Johnson & A. Ensslin (Eds.), *Language in the media: Representations, identities, ideologies* (pp. 111–129). London: Continuum.

Milani, T. M., & Johnson, S. (2008). CDA and language ideology: Towards a reflexive approach to discourse data. In I. H. Warnke & J. Spitzmuller (Eds.), *Methoden der Diskurslinguistik Sprachwissenschaftliche Zugaenge zur transtextuellen Ebene* (pp. 361–384). Berlin: Mouton de Gruyter.

Milizia, D., & Spinzi, C. (2008). The 'terroridiom' principle between spoken and written discourse. In U. Römer & R. Schulze (Eds.), *Patterns, meaningful units and specialized discourses* (pp. 322–350). Amsterdam: John Benjamins.

Morley, J. (2009). Introduction: A description of *CorDis*. In J. Morley & P. Bayley (Eds.), *Corpus-assisted discourse studies on the Iraq conflict: Wording the war* (pp. 1–12). New York: Routledge.

Morley, J., & Partington, A. (2009). A few *frequently asked questions* about semantic—Or evaluative—Prosody. *International Journal of Corpus Linguistics, 14*(2), 139–158.

Moschonas, S. & Spitzmuller, J. (2010). Prescriptivism in and about the media: A comparative analysis of corrective practices in Greece and Germany. In Language Ideologies and Media Discourse: Texts, Practices, Politics, S. Johnson & T.M. Milani (eds), 17–40. London: Continuum.

Munday, J. (2011). Looming large: A cross-linguistic analysis of semantic prosodies in comparable reference corpora. In A. Kruger & K. Wallmach (Eds.), *Corpus-based translation studies: Research and applications* (pp. 169–186). Manchester: St. Jerome.

Nelson, M. (2006). Semantic associations in business English: A corpus-based analysis. *English for Specific Purposes, 25*, 217–234.

Partington, A. (1998). *Patterns and meanings—Using corpora for English language research and teaching*. Amsterdam/Philadelphia: John Benjamins.

Partington, A. (2004). Corpora and discourse, a most congruous beast. In A. Partington, J. Morley, & L. Haarman (Eds.), *Corpora and discourse* (pp. 11–20). Bern: Peter Lang.

Partington, A. (2008). Teasing at the white house: A corpus-assisted study of face work in performing and responding to teases. *Text & Talk, 28*(6), 771–792.

Partington, A. (2009). Evaluating evaluation and some concluding thoughts on CADS. In J. Morley & P. Bayley (Eds.), *Corpus-assisted discourse studies on the Iraq conflict: Wording the war* (pp. 261–304). New York: Routledge.

Partington, A. (2010). Modern diachronic corpus-assisted discourse studies (MD-CADS) on UK newspapers: An overview of the project. *Corpora, 5*(2), 83–108.

Phillips, S. U. (1998). Language ideologies in institutions of power: A commentary. In B. B. Schieffelin, K. A. Woolard, & P. V. Kroskrity (Eds.), *Language ideologies. Practice and theory* (pp. 211–228). Oxford: Oxford University Press.

Preston, D. R. (2004). Folk metalanguage. In A. Jaworski, N. Coupland, & D. Galasiński (Eds.), *Metalanguage: Social and ideological perspectives* (pp. 75–104). Berlin: Mouton de Gruyter.

Qian, Y. (2010). *Discursive construction around terrorism in the People's Daily (China) and The Sun (UK) before and after 9.11*. Oxford: Peter Lang.

Rahman, T. (2009). Language ideology, identity and the commodification of language in the call centres of Pakistan. *Language in Society, 38*(2), 233–258.

Rayson, P. (2008). From key words to key semantic domains. *International Journal of Corpus Linguistics, 13*(4), 519–549.

Reisigl, M., & Wodak, R. (2009). The discourse-historical approach. In M. Meyer & R. Wodak (Eds.), *Methods of critical discourse analysis* (pp. 87–121). London/Thousand Oaks: SAGE.

Ricento, T. (2005). Problems with the 'language-as-resource' discourse in the promotion of heritage languages in the U.S.A. *Journal of Sociolinguistics, 9*(3), 348–368.

Ricento, T. (2006). Americanization, language ideologies, and the construction of European identities. In C. Mar-Molinero & P. Stevenson (Eds.), *Language ideologies, policies, and practices: Language and the future of Europe* (pp. 44–57). Basingstoke: Palgrave Macmillan.

Richardson, J. E. (2007). *Analysing newspapers: An approach from critical discourse analysis*. Basingstoke: Palgrave.

Schieffelin, B. B., & Doucet, R. C. (1998). The "real" Haitian creole: Ideology, metalinguistics, and orthographic choice. In B. B. Schieffelin, K. A. Woolard, & P. V. Kroskrity (Eds.), *Language ideologies. Practice and theory* (pp. 285–316). Oxford: Oxford University Press.

Scott, M. (1997). PC analysis of key words—And key key words. *System, 25*(1), 233–245.

Scott, M. (2009). In search of a bad reference corpus. In D. Archer (Ed.), What's in a word-list? Investigating word frequency and keyword extraction (pp. 79–92). Oxford: Ashgate.

Scott, M. (2014). *WordSmith Tools, Version 6*. Liverpool: Lexical Analysis Software.

Silverstein, M. (1979). Language structure and linguistic ideology. In P. Clyne, W. Hanks, & C. Hofbauer (Eds.), *The elements: A parasession on linguistic units and levels* (pp. 193–247). Chicago: Chicago Linguistic Society.

Silverstein, M. (1992). The uses and utility of ideology: Some reflections. *Pragmatics, 2*(3), 311–323.

Simpson, P. (1993). *Language, ideology and point of view*. London: Routledge.

Sinclair, J. (1991). *Corpus, concordance, collocation*. Oxford: Oxford University Press.

Sinclair, J. (1996). The search for units of meaning. *Textus, 9*(1), 75–106.

Stewart, D. (2010). *Semantic prosody: A critical evaluation*. London: Routledge.

Stewart, C. M. (2012). Mapping language ideologies in multi-ethnic urban Europe: The case of Parisian French. *Journal of Multilingual and Multicultural Development, 33*(2), 187–202.

Stubbs, M. (1996). *Text and corpus analysis: Computer-assisted studies of language and culture*. Oxford/Cambridge: Blackwell Publishers.

Stubbs, M. (1997). Whorf's children: Critical comments on critical discourse analysis (CDA). In A. Ryan & A. Wray (Eds.), *Evolving models of language: Papers from the annual meeting of the British Association for Applied Linguistics held at the University of Wales, Swansea, September 1996* (pp. 100–116). Clevedon: Multilingual Matters.

Stubbs, M. (2001). *Words and phrases: Corpus studies of lexical semantics*. Oxford: Blackwell.

Stubbs, M. (2003). Computer-assisted text and corpus analysis: Lexical cohesion and communicative competence. In D. Schriffen, D. Tannen, & H. E. Hamilton (Eds.), *The handbook of discourse analysis* (pp. 305–320). Malden: Blackwell Publishing.

Stubbs, M. (2006). Corpus analysis: The state of the art and three types of unanswered questions. In G. Thompson & S. Hunston (Eds.), *System and corpus: Exploring connections* (pp. 15–36). London: Equinox.

Stubbs, M. (2007). An example of frequent English phraseology: Distributions, structures and functions. In R. Facchinetti (Ed.), *Corpus linguistics: 25 years on* (pp. 89–105). New York: Rodopi BV.

Stubbs, M. (2010). Three concepts of keywords. In M. Bondi & M. Scott (Eds.), *Keyness in texts* (pp. 21–42). Amsterdam: John Benjamins.

Subtirelu, N. C. (2013). 'English… it's part of our blood': Ideologies of language and nation in United States Congressional discourse. *Journal of Sociolinguistics, 17*(1), 37–65.
Taylor, C. (2008). What is corpus linguistics? What the data says. *ICAME, 32*, 179–200.
Teubert, W. (2007). Natural and human rights, work and property in the discourse of Catholic social doctrine. In M. Hoey, M. Mahlberg, M. Stubbs, & W. Teubert (Eds.), *Text, discourse and corpora: Theory and analysis* (pp. 89–126). London: Continuum.
Thompson, G., & Hunston, S. (2000). Evaluation: An introduction. In S. Hunston & G. Thompson (Eds.), *Evaluation in text. Authorial stance and the construction of discourse* (pp. 1–27). Oxford: Oxford University Press.
Tognini-Bonelli, E. (1996). *Corpus theory and practice*. Birmingham: TWC Publishers.
Tognini-Bonelli, E. (2001). *Corpus linguistics at work*. Amsterdam: John Benjamins.
Van Dijk, T. A. (1991). *Racism and the press*. London: Routledge.
Van Dijk, T. A. (1998). Opinions and ideologies in the press. In A. Bell & P. Garrett (Eds.), *Approaches to media discourse* (pp. 21–63). Oxford: Blackwell.
Van Dijk, T. A. (2003). Critical discourse analysis. In D. Schiffrin, D. Tannen, & H. E. Hamilton (Eds.), *The handbook of discourse analysis* (pp. 352–371). Malden: Blackwell Publishing.
Van Dijk, T. A. (2006). Ideology and discourse analysis. *Journal of Political Ideologies, 11*(2), 115–140.
Van Hout, T., & Macgilchrist, F. (2010). Framing the news: An ethnographic view of business newswriting. *Text and Talk, 30*(2), 168–191.
Vertovec, S. (2007). Super-diversity and its implications. *Ethnic and racial studies, 30*(6), 1024–1054.
Wassink, A. B., & Dyer, J. (2004). Language ideology and the transmission of phonological change changing indexicality in two situations of language contact. *Journal of English Linguistics, 32*(3), 3–30.
Whitsitt, S. (2005). A critique of the concept of semantic prosody. *International Journal of Corpus Linguistics, 10*(3), 283–305.
Williams, R. (1973). Base and superstructure in Marxist cultural theory. *New Left Review, 82*, 1–14. Retrieved from http://www.newleftreview.org/?getpdf=NLR08101&pdflang=en.
Williams, R. (1976). *Keywords: A vocabulary of culture and society*. New York: Oxford University Press.

Williams, R. (1977). *Marxism and literature*. Oxford: Oxford University Press.

Wodak, R. (2001). What CDA is about—A summary of its history, important concepts and its developments. In M. Meyer & R. Wodak (Eds.), *Methods of critical discourse analysis* (pp. 1–13). London/Thousand Oaks: Sage.

Wodak, R. (2007). Language and ideology—Language in ideology. *Journal of Language and Politics, 6*(1), 1–5.

Wodak, R. (2008). Introduction: Discourse studies—Important concepts and terms. In R. Wodak & M. Kryzanowsky (Eds.), *Qualitative discourse analysis in the social sciences* (pp. 1–29). Basingstoke: Palgrave MacMillan.

Wodak, R., & Meyer, M. (2009). Critical discourse analysis: history, agenda, theory and methodology. In R. Wodak & M. Meyer (Eds.), *Methods of critical discourse analysis* , 2nd Ed. (pp. 1–33). London: sage.

Woolard, K. A. (1998). Introduction: Language ideology as a field of inquiry. In B. B. Schieffelin, K. A. Woolard, & P. V. Kroskrity (Eds.), *Language ideologies. Practice and theory* (pp. 3–50). Oxford: Oxford University Press.

Xiao, R., & McEnery, T. (2006). Collocation, semantic prosody, and near synonymy: A cross-linguistic perspective. *Applied Linguistics, 27*(1), 103–129.

Zhang, W. (2009). Semantic prosody and ESL/EFL vocabulary pedagogy. *TESL Canada Journal/Revue TESL du Canada, 26*(2), 1–12.

4

Language Ideologies in Canadian Print Newspapers

As a first step of investigating language ideologies in Canadian media, newspapers are an obvious choice of data. As outlined in Sect. 2.2, newspapers have never had the status that they have in, for example, the UK, but they have nonetheless played a defining part in Canada's self-definition in contrast to its colonial parentage and Southern neighbour. Newspapers have also been shown to be an important site for the study of language ideologies in other countries. However, they have rarely been tackled in Canada for this purpose (for some exceptions, see e.g. the work of Boudreau 2011; Boudreau and Urbain 2014), and there are no examples comparing English and French newspapers. This chapter aims to address this gap and to identify some of the principal language ideologies that emerge from a comparison of large corpora of English and French Canadian newspaper data. It proceeds as follows: Section 4.1 provides an overview of the data, Sect. 4.2 discusses language ideologies in English Canadian newspapers, and Sect. 4.3 discusses language ideologies in French Canadian newspapers. The chapter concludes in Sect. 4.4.

R. Vessey, *Language and Canadian Media*,
DOI 10.1057/978-1-137-53001-1_4

4.1 Data

In order to account for the geographic diversity of Canada, two newspapers were selected from each region delineated by Newspapers Canada (see Sect. 2.2). Within each region, newspapers were selected from different provinces where possible, or from different cities where a region consisted only of a single province. In this way, even if in Ontario Toronto is home to the newspapers with the highest circulation figures, only one Toronto newspaper is selected for the corpus; a newspaper with the next highest circulation figures from another Ontarian city is selected as the second newspaper for the corpus. This was found to be a useful way to balance circulation figures against regional representation. In addition to the five regions, a category of "national newspapers" was included, which consisted of two nationally distributed English newspapers that have a pan-Canadian scope and two widely read French newspapers that have been argued to be national in nature (see discussion in Sect. 2.2). With this reasoning, the English corpus is composed of newspapers from the regional and national newspapers with the highest circulation figures (see Table 4.1), and the French corpus is composed of newspapers with the highest circulation figures drawn from the same geographic areas where available (see Table 4.2).

Notably, the French corpus draws on considerably fewer data sources than the English corpus. While it is unfortunate for the sake of literal comparison that the two corpora are not of the same size, the English and French corpora are equally valid in terms of their representation of newspaper readership across the country according to the geographic coverage, and it is therefore reasonable to compare them.

Table 4.1 English corpus with data sources by region

English corpus	Data source (newspapers)	
Atlantic Canada	*Moncton Times & Transcript*	*The Halifax Herald*
Quebec	*The Gazette*	*The Record*
Ontario	*The Toronto Star*	*The Ottawa Citizen*
Prairies	*Winnipeg Free Press*	*Calgary Herald*
BC & Yukon	*Vancouver Sun*	*Whitehorse Star*
National newspapers	*The Globe and Mail*	*The National Post*

Table 4.2 French corpus with data sources by region

French corpus	Data source (newspapers)	
Atlantic Canada	*L'Acadie Nouvelle*	(No data)
Quebec	*Le Soleil*	(No data)
Ontario	*Le Droit*	(No data)
Prairies	(No data)	(No data)
BC & Yukon	(No data)	(No data)
National newspapers	*La Presse*	*Le Devoir*

All articles, editorials, and columns published by these newspapers between 15 June and 8 July 2009 were collected using the news databases *Canadian Newsstand, Eureka.cc*, and *Actualité Francophone Plus.* Photo captions, editorials, and community announcements were also considered news items, since they serve as part of the newspaper content to enhance, clarify, and add to the news story (Blommaert and Verschueren 1998: 190–191; Cotter 2010: 58; Kariel and Rosenvall 1983: 432). The complete data sets consist of 8759 articles (3,589,786 words) from 5 French newspapers and 18,271 articles (7,524,331 words) from 12 English newspapers (see Table 4.3).

From this sample, individual whole texts were downsampled for close discourse analysis. The findings from these specific texts were used for corroboration against the more macro findings uncovered using corpus linguistics. The criterion for the selection of these texts was their proportion of specific language-related terms: LANGUAGE/*LANGUE*, ENGLISH/*ANGLAIS/E*, and FRENCH/*FRANÇAIS/E.* These terms were used to select two categories of downsampled texts. First, articles that contained high proportions of these terms were selected because it was presumed that therein would be overt and explicit discussions of language issues. In addition, articles that contained low proportions of these terms were selected because in these cases it was assumed that language issues were mentioned only in passing. While it would have been useful to examine articles where language issues were entirely inexplicit (i.e. presupposed and/or naturalised), it is very difficult to objectively find inexplicit references. In other words, finding a newspaper article without references to language issues and then to assume that language issues should be present would mean imposing researcher bias on the data. Instead, by selecting articles that only mention language issues in passing, the role, function, or nature of language is implied by its marginal

Table 4.3 English and French corpora

Corpus		Total number of texts	Total tokens (running words)	Types (distinct words)	Type/token ratio	% of corpus
Atlantic Canada	*L'Acadie Nouvelle*	1421	504,979	32,628	6.66	14.07
Quebec	*Le Soleil*	2212	778,320	45,684	6.03	21.68
Ontario	*Le Droit*	1567	600,311	33,842	5.78	16.72
Prairies	(No data)					
BC & Yukon	(No data)					
National newspapers	*La Presse*	2310	1,067,634	55,470	5.33	29.74
	Le Devoir	1249	638,542	45,196	7.22	17.79
Total French corpus		**8759**	**3,589,786**	**100,286**	**2.87**	**100 %**
Atlantic Canada	*Moncton Times & Transcript*	2095	956,575	34,704	3.77	12.73
	The Halifax Herald	2453	1,048,651	40,265	4.05	13.96
Quebec	*The Gazette*	1462	437,310	27,805	6.55	5.8
	The Record	188	64,853	9176	14.48	0.86
Ontario	*The Toronto Star*	1568	525,760	30,812	6.04	7.00
	The Ottawa Citizen	1825	563,159	29,126	5.31	7.49
Prairies	*Winnipeg Free Press*	1085	623,717	33,547	5.62	8.30
	Calgary Herald	1476	371,847	24,450	6.76	4.95
BC & Yukon	*Vancouver Sun*	1205	403,944	24,271	6.2	5.38
	Whitehorse Star	501	230,204	17,509	7.88	3.06
National newspapers	*The Globe and Mail*	3004	1,731,889	56,018	3.23	23.05
	The National Post	1409	493,496	28,061	5.82	6.57
Total English corpus		**18,271**	**7,524,331**	**107,295**	**1.48**	**100 %**

function in the text. In sum, the goal was to analyse (1) entire articles where language plays a dominant role and (2) entire articles where language plays a marginal role.

In order to select a feasible number of texts for analysis, 15 texts were first selected, each with the highest proportion of each term per 1000 words, for a total of six groups of 15 articles each (i.e. one list of 15 articles with the highest proportion of references to LANGUAGE, one list of 15 articles with the highest proportion of references to ENGLISH, etc.). Next, the lists were cross-referenced in order to determine which individual articles contained the most references to multiple terms. Five articles emerged from this process in French, and six articles emerged from the English corpus. These 11 articles were then quickly reviewed for length and relevance: length was an important consideration in order to avoid articles that would be either prohibitively long or uncharacteristically short for analysis (some opinion articles or letters to the editor tended to be very short, and hence the inclusion of even just one reference to language could mean that its proportion of language-related terms appeared to be very high). Relevance was another important consideration since some references to FRANÇAIS, for example, refer to French nationality rather than language. From the 11 articles, then, 8 (four in French and four in English) were selected for analysis (see Box 4.1).

Box 4.1 Downsampled Articles with Highest Proportion of Language-Related Terms

Anonymous (2009c). Vigilance essential for French. *Toronto Star,* 1 July 2009, p. A17.

Bélair-Cirino (2009). Le français à Montréal: 90 % des francophones sont inquiets. *Le Devoir,* 22 June 2009, p. A1.

Ferenczy (2009). Broader opportunities. *Ottawa Citizen,* 3 July 2009, p. A9.

Havrankova (2009). Apprendre le français, un privilège. *Le Devoir,* 22 June 2009, p.A6.

Howlett (2009). French schools will be available to more students. *The Globe and Mail,* 17 June 2009, p. A12.

Meurice (2009). Pauvres touristes. *La Presse,* 7 July 2009, p. A13.

Ravindran (2009). How to speed immigrants' entry into the workforce. *Vancouver Sun,* 30 June 2009, p. A10.

Rioux (2009). Full bilingue. *Le Devoir,* 3 July 2009, p. A3.

The procedure for selecting articles with the lowest proportion of terms was similar to the procedure for selecting the articles with the highest proportion of terms. First, 15 articles were selected from each corpus according to their low proportion of each term (per 1000 words). This produced six lists of 15 articles each (i.e. one list of 15 articles with the fewest references to LANGUE, one list with the fewest references to ANGLAIS, etc.). These lists were then cross-referenced to determine which articles had the lowest proportion of at least two different terms. From this list, all 12 relevant (i.e. language-related) examples were examined (see Box 4.2).

Box 4.2 Downsampled articles with lowest proportion of language-related terms

Anonymous (2009a). Divine liturgy to be held tomorrow. *Moncton Times & Transcript,* 4 July 2009, p. E6.

Aubry (2009). Le plus grand vin canadien? *Le Devoir,* 19 June 2009, p. B6.

Blatchford and Leeder (2009). Did we push her too much? *The Globe and Mail,* 20 June 2009, p. A1.

Cornellier (2009). Pierre Falardeau et son Elvis. *Le Devoir,* 27 June 2009, p. E5.

Lawrence (2009). De l'évanescence à l'efferevescence. *Le Devoir,* 20 June 2009, p.D1.

Le Bouthillier (2009). Le Grand Caraquet—suite. *L'Acadie Nouvelle,* 25 June 2009, p. 13.

Lussier (2009a). De père en flic. *La Presse,* 4 July 2009, p. Cinema 2.

Mazerolle (2009). The quintessential Canadian. *Moncton Times & Transcript,* 25 June 2009, p. A1.

Nolen (2009). India's gay community fights for 'dignity'. *The Globe and Mail,* 19 June 2009, p. A16.

Valpy (2009). The emperor and the tennis pro. *The Globe and Mail,* 27 June 2009, p. A1.

Vigor (2009). Cet art qu'est la composition florale. *Le Devoir,* 20 June 2009, p. D6.

York (2009). Sterilized, stigmatized. *The Globe and Mail,* 15 July 2009, p. A7.

These downsampled articles were investigated with the aim of finding evidence of language ideologies and corroborating findings from the corpus analysis.

4.2 Language Ideologies in English Canadian Newspapers

4.2.1 Monolingual Ideologies

First and foremost, the findings from the English Canadian newspapers suggest that language issues are not normally a topic of discussion. The implicit role of language suggests the importance of monolingual ideologies that naturalise the understanding of Canada as a monolingual English-speaking society.

The term "monolingual ideologies" refers to the taken-for-granted norm of monolingualism, in this case, English monolingualism. These ideologies normalise linguistic homogeneity, which is sometimes understood to be the guarantee of state legitimacy (see Blackledge 2000; Boudreau and Urbain 2014; Boyer 2001). In the case of English monolingual ideologies, which tend to be taken for granted, their unmarked, implicit nature makes them rather difficult to pinpoint. However, their role seems to be consistent throughout recent Canadian language history. In 1955, Matthew Henry Scargill, who pioneered research on Canadian English, noted English Canadians' lack of interest in their own language:

> Our French Canadian colleagues have a culture and a language of their own and study them. Our many Slavic communities are advanced in the study of their own language in Canada. It is the English-speaking Canadians who lag behind, who do not consider their language worthy of study, who do not seem to know or care if they have a culture and a language to give expression to it (cited in Rea 2006: 83).

Ten years later, Walter S. Avis, who edited several dictionaries of Canadian English, noted the continuing trend: "[l]anguage in Canada [...] is taken for granted" (cited in Rea 2006: 84). More recently, other researchers have noted the relevance of unmarked monolingualism in English-speaking Canada. Heller (e.g. 2003a: 14), for example, has contended that the study of language and power in English-speaking Canada is difficult because "one of the hallmarks of dominant discourses is their ability to erase salient features". In this sense, English-speaking Canada is like many other contexts where, despite a wealth of multilingualism, there are "monolingualising tendencies" that mean that English tends to dominate (Heller 1995: 374; see also Blackledge 2002: 69–71; Bucholtz 2003: 405; Jaspers and Verschueren 2011: 1157).

Monolingual ideologies emerge in the English Canadian newspaper corpus because the English language often goes unmentioned. The taken-for-grantedness of language issues is most evident from comparisons with the French data: while 7.86 % of all English newspaper articles contain at least one reference to language, twice the proportion of French newspaper articles contain at least one reference to language[1] (15.9 %). Also, references to the French language are far more frequent than references to the English language in the English corpus. In fact, FRENCH occurs nearly twice as often as ENGLISH (198 wpm[2] vs. 105 wpm, respectively). This is arguably because the French language is less taken for granted and discussed more frequently; in contrast, the English language is naturalised and taken for granted and therefore less frequently discussed in English Canadian newspapers.

It is not only the English language that is taken for granted. English speakers, too, are presupposed to be the norm, and therefore there are fewer discussions of "anglophone" and "anglophones" (4 wpm and 6 wpm, respectively) than there are discussions of "francophone" and "francophones" (18 wpm and 14 wpm, respectively). Indeed, anglophones tend not to be discussed unless in contexts where speakers of other languages ("-phones") are also under discussion. In fact, nearly half (42.5 %) of occurrences of ANGLOPHONES collocate with FRANCOPHONES (nine occurrences), FRENCH (six occurrences), and ALLOPHONES (five occurrences). This contrasts with discussions

---

[1] In English, these "references to language" included the following: ANGLO, ANGLOS, ANGLICIZE, ANGLOPHONE, ANGLOPHONES, BILINGUAL, BILINGUALS, BILINGUALISM, ENGLISH, FRANCO, FRANCOPHONE, FRANCOPHONES, FRANCOPHONIE, FRENCH, LANGUAGE, LANGUAGES, LINGUISTIC, LINGUISTICS, MONOLINGUAL, MULTILINGUAL, and UNILINGUAL. In French, these "references to language" included the following: ANGLAIS, ANGLAISE, ANGLAISES, ANGLICISME, ANGLICISE, ANGLO, ANGLOS, ANGLOPHONE, ANGLOPHONES, BILINGUE, BILINGUES, BILINGUISME, FRANÇAIS, FRANÇAISE, FRANÇAISES, FRANCO, FRANCOS, FRANCOPHONE, FRANCOPHONES, FRANCOPHONIE, LANGAGE, LANGAGES, LANGAGIER, LANGAGIÈRE, LANGAGIÈRES, LINGUISTIQUE, LINGUISTIQUES, LANGUE, and LANGUES.

[2] wpm = "words per million". Frequencies are normalised per million words, which facilitate comparisons of frequency across corpora of different sizes.

of francophones: only 15 % of occurrences of FRANCOPHONES collocate with ANGLOPHONES (nine occurrences), FRENCH (nine occurrences), and ENGLISH (no occurrences). In other words, discussions of francophones can occur on their own; in contrast, discussions of anglophones tend to take place in discursive contexts where other language groups are also under discussion.

Concordance lines demonstrate the various ways in which the term ANGLOPHONE/S is used in contrast with the French language. Most instances explicitly juxtapose the term ANGLOPHONES with FRANCOPHONES (six occurrences), or juxtapose fluency in French with being anglophone (six occurrences). One line suggests that Quebec is French-speaking by juxtaposing "anglophones" with "Quebec" ("anglophones who have weathered Quebec's political storms") (see Fig. 4.1).

In contrast, the fact that the term FRANCOPHONES most often occurs on its own suggests that those who are not labelled as "francophones" tend to be anglophones. Thus, "Englishness" seems to be normalised and taken for granted in English Canadian newspapers (cf. on the normalisation of heterosexuality vs. homosexuality in corpus data, Baker 2010: 126).

Another indicator of monolingual ideologies is that the English language is presented as the language of integration for Canada. The unmarked role of English monolingualism is at the crux of many debates about language and immigration. Although Canada has two official languages and numerous indigenous languages, English is often presupposed to be the language of integration for newcomers to the country. This presupposition belies the perceived importance of English in Canada. Vipond (2008: 332) notes that even in the 1930s, English was perceived to be essential to assimilate immigrants. More recently, Pacini-Ketchabaw

```
 have a facility for languages. Well, anglophones are just as smart as francophones."
atural fear when speaking French that anglophones feel more than francophones (who sp
er cent of non-francophones feel that anglophones speak French at a satisfactory leve
007). </p><p style="margin-top:0px;"  Anglophones speak satisfactory French: 36 per c
onsidered a francophone is a Canadian anglophone who also speaks French. Not content
n English. After all, the majority of anglophones who have weathered Quebec's politic
kely to be able to speak English than anglophones are to speak French, with 43.4 per
ts of eyes to see if francophones and anglophones can appreciate the humour. In this
into heavily-francophone regions than anglophones might do. But as long as Montreal I
rtunities to use the French language. Anglophones will develop their skills in conte
```

Fig. 4.1 English concordance lines ANGLOPHONE/S, FRANCOPHONE/S

and de Almeida (2006) have found that Canadian immigration documents and settlement services present English monolingualism as the ideal norm to newcomers to Canada and learning English is depicted as crucial for integration.

In the English Canadian newspapers, an editorial in the *Calgary Herald* (Corbella 2009) clearly argues that English is a delineating marker between Canadians (implied: English-speaking) and others. The editorial, entitled "No surprise burka-clad women didn't write in", focuses on whether the burka should be banned in Canada. In the debate over burka banning, the columnist writes that she received a great deal of mail but none from women who wear burkas. This, she argues, is because they have not learned English as a result of their isolation and lack of freedom. The columnist emphasises that those who wear burkas should speak English in order to not be isolated (see Example 4.1).

Example 4.1 (Corbella 2009)

Several days ago, a Calgary Muslim man asked me if I wanted to run a column by a niqab-wearing woman. "Of course," was my answer. A day later, he wrote this: "There aren't a lot of Niqabis in Calgary who feel they're fluent enough in English, and by definition they're a shy bunch!" He didn't refer to them as women wearing niqabs but as "Niqabis." They are defined by their garb which only leaves a slit for their eyes. Is it any wonder they are so isolated they haven't learned English and that "they're a shy bunch?"

The assumption of Corbella's (2009) editorial is that irrespective of the gender/culture dimension, English is necessary for integration into and participation in Canadian society. In another example of a letter to the editor, Wai (2009) notes that in her experience some people "have no English despite having been in Canada for years". Their lack of fluency is noted in part because of the length of time spent in a country that is implied to be English-speaking. These examples parallel the assumptions made in a downsampled text discussing immigrant employment (Ravindran 2009).

In a letter to the editor, Ravindran (2009) stresses the need for immigrants to have access to English education in order for them to be able to earn beyond "hand to mouth" wages. The implication is that English skills are required for any job that pays above minimum wage because English is the language that is spoken most widely in Canadian society (see Example 4.2).

Example 4.2 (Ravindran 2009)

Non-English-speaking immigrants arriving with families face a significant dilemma: seek low-paying work that will provide only hand-to-mouth wages or attend English classes and generate little-to-no income.

Indeed, Ravindran (2009) argues that fluency in English is crucial for integration into Canadian society (see Example 4.3).

Example 4.3 (Ravindran 2009)

Government programs such as English Language Services for Adults do facilitate economic and cultural integration into Canadian society, but I believe more pragmatic solutions need to be implemented.

The English language figures in discussions of integration with regard to immigration. ENGLISH collocates with IMMIGRANTS lemmas eight times, and no other languages are collocates of IMMIGRATION (313 occurrences), IMMIGRANTS (273 occurrences), IMMIGRANT (122 occurrences), IMMIGRATED (19 occurrences), IMMIGRATE (4 occurrences), or IMMIGRATING (3 occurrences). In these ways, then, English is implied to be necessary for the integration of immigrants, since English monolingualism is the norm in English Canada.

The final indicator of monolingual ideologies emerges from evaluations of fluency in English. Numerous concordance lines emphasise the necessity and the benefits of speaking English and negatively evaluate poorly spoken English or a lack of fluency in English. Some concordance lines (three occurrences) simply note an ability to speak English ("can speak", "able to speak"); others (eight occurrences) note a lack of fluency ("didn't speak", "refused", "speak little", "not speak", "speak neither", "didn't speak very good"; "halting"; "to improve"; "make sure his English was understood"; "isn't very strong"; "no English"). There are also seven references to "broken English" (see Fig. 4.2).

These concordance lines indicate that although language issues tend not to be topical in English Canadian news, when languages are discussed it is often with reference to fluency or a lack of fluency. Since there are far more references to French than there are to English, it is particularly notable that there are references to "broken English" but not to "broken French". Indeed, the fact that a lack of fluency in English (but not in French) is salient suggests that fluency in English is perceived as more important than fluency in French. Indeed, the downsampled text

```
MODALIZED
ou for two years and can speak English or French. Q. I will
eror and the Empress can speak English, but at no point duri
ore likely to be able to speak English than anglophones are

LACK OF FLUENCY
 three."My mother didn't speak English," Frank said.At first
 but they might not speak both English and French, so some m
 Polish man, who did not speak English and had spent hours a
ly explained she did not speak English. After that, we excha
d Mamma also to speak to us in English which she refused. Sh
on, and a few who speak little English. At least one worker
s who speak neither French nor English. The raison d'etre of
ear."He didn't speak very good English, but the big fish tur
 says the director, in halting English."At the beginning of
ian. He intends to improve his English so he can volunteer a
ipal portfolio, to improve his English. Charest recalled the
owski, wanted to make sure his English was understood last w
owski, wanted to make sure his English was understood last w
s while in Moncton.He says his English isn't very strong, bu
aid in his gradually improving English. "Now, we're couple y
 before him, is not at ease in English, although he made a c
 a huge number of them have no English at all. I volunteered
; his mother Nathalie spoke no English but somehow managed t
e. Most of the clients have no English despite having been i
ound. Dziekanski, who spoke no English, eventually began thr

BROKEN ENGLISH
usually passed along in broken English and riddled with grammat
etsova said in slightly broken English. "They don't have to put
usually passed along in broken English and riddled with grammat
about Canada, but spoke broken English. Then again, we could ba
es. I was questioned in broken English for about 20 minutes - s
 Jar Binks, the clumsy, broken-English speaking alien from "Sta
 Jar Binks, the clumsy, broken-English speaking alien from Star
```

Fig. 4.2 English concordance lines: fluency in English

discussed previously (Ravindran 2009) also stresses the need for fluency in English in order for immigrants to obtain well-paying jobs.

Some discussions of fluency also discuss accents, which are sometimes compared against a Canadian standard (i.e. unmarked) accent. There are three references to "heavily accented English" in three separate newspapers (*The Halifax Herald*, *Moncton Times & Transcript*, and *National Post*), and two of the three are used in discussions of Canadians. The fact that accents are noted suggests that English is normally spoken in a certain way in order to blend in, and perhaps in order to appear authentically Canadian (Karim 1993). Indeed, one example (Delaney 2009) refers to "heavily accented English" within the context of a report on citizenship for new Canadians. One individual who had recently taken the oath of citizenship is quoted as saying "I believe in this country there are lots of open-minded people, and that's very important for me". However, she is noted as speaking with "heavily accented English"; her language skills perhaps reify her status as a new—and thus not unmarked—Canadian.

To conclude, monolingual ideologies seem to permeate the English newspapers through the unmarked and naturalised status of the English language, the role of English as a language of integration, and evaluations of fluency.

4.2.2 Instrumental Language Ideologies

The findings from the English Canadian newspapers also indicate that when languages are discussed, most often it is with relation to their functional role in society. The perceived functional importance of language aligns with what Kulyk (2010: 84) calls the "ideology of understanding (or communication)", which he argues "sees language primarily as a conduit for conveying information and thus prescribes the use of a language that is best understood for all participants in a given communication act". Here, the assumptions and beliefs that languages serve predominantly functional or instrumental purposes are referred to as "instrumental language ideologies", and these permeate the English Canadian newspaper corpus.

Instrumental language ideologies do not just concern the English language; they concern other languages, too. In other words, one predominant motivation for discussing language is to refer to its use(s) in society. Moreover, the more languages that a person can use, the better. Thus, discussions of multilingualism tend to foreground the importance of language as a communicative resource. Nevertheless, when multilingualism is discussed, the English language plays a key role. In other words, in almost all cases multilingual individuals are noted to speak English alongside other languages (see Fig. 4.3).

One downsampled article shows how multilingualism is understood to be an asset for individuals; in Example 4.4, a Canadian military officer's linguistic abilities are discursively paired with "marvellous intellect and work ethic".

> **Example 4.4 (Blatchford and Leeder 2009)**
>
> "She got far more high-level attention than a normal RMC [Royal Military College] grad would get," said a now-retired senior officer who once lobbied for her. But then, he said, she deserved it—she was trilingual (English, French and Portuguese), and she had that marvellous intellect and work ethic.

This representation indicates the way that language skills can serve as an asset and a symbol of intelligence, but importantly the English language figures among these praised assets.

```
SPEAKING MULTIPLE LANGUAGES
sers to speak either Arabic or English into their phone, hea
ou for two years and who speak English or French. These peop
tually speak Latin, as well as English, French and a smatter
e than francophones (who speak English), but francophones ar
pan>Re: [Immigrants] who speak English find better jobs, Wes
aiwanese children how to speak English, before returning to
who speak languages other than English will be connected to

years and who speak English or French. These people could be
rson born in Russia who speaks French (and English) must als
ght not speak both English and French, so some measure of la
their mother tongue, know both French and English, and speak
es feel that anglophones speak French at a satisfactory leve
ian anglophone who also speaks French. Not content with that
s English and the other speaks French."We need to tell (fami
rson born in Russia who speaks French and English. About the
```

Fig. 4.3 English concordance lines of multilingualism

In other multilingual contexts, English is sometimes favourably represented in contrast with other languages. One downsampled article highlights the power and hegemony of the English language in comparison with French (see Example 4.5).

Example 4.5 (Anonymous 2009c)

while the power of attraction of English ensures that it is the common language of multicultural Toronto, French would hardly be as dominant as it is in Montreal without some legislative assistance.

Another newspaper explains how the French language serves little purpose on the West coast of Canada. Bilingualism, the journalist writes, would be better served by furthering Mandarin or Spanish, which are implied to be more useful or at least *used* languages than French (see Example 4.6).

Example 4.6 (Fralic 2009)

We are also woefully baffled by the French language spat, finding it hard to relate to or even take seriously the perennial debate that is all things francophone. You want bilingual? Try Mandarin. Or, lately, Spanish.

These examples have indicated the extent to which the preservation of languages without immediate and widespread use in society seems incomprehensible. There is also an indication of a "benign neglect" approach to language, that is, a belief that individuals' language choices are self-regulating and should therefore be unrestricted and ungoverned (Kymlicka and Patten 2003: 10). In such a context, the most widely used languages (e.g. English, Mandarin, Spanish) would also be the most useful—there would be no need for linguistic protectionism.

Instrumental language ideologies also seem to underpin the emphasis on language education in the English Canadian newspapers. When all of the English Canadian newspapers that contain at least one reference to language (see Note 1) are compared against the rest of the newspapers using the KeyWord procedure (see Sect. 3.2), then a substantial number of keywords pertain to language education (see Table 4.4).

Table 4.4 English keywords pertaining to education

Positive key word	Frequency	Number of texts in which word occurs	% of words in corpus	Reference corpus frequency	% of words in reference corpus	Keyness score
School	866	287	0.09	6658	0.04	306.75
Students	397	127	0.04	2849	0.02	166.23
Education	312	128	0.03	2034	0.01	160.67
Immersion	57	20		65		158.06
Literacy	85	30		213		145.49
Schools	225	97	0.02	1479	0.01	113.93
Classes	120	58	0.01	598		97.90
Teachers	129	56	0.01	787		75.49
Courses	79	36		389		65.58
Student	148	88	0.01	1172		48.47
Teaching	78	56		472		46.33
Kindergarten	55	19		279		43.70
Campus	56	21		290		43.13
Learning	125	87	0.01	993		40.59
Graduates	61	28		373		35.54
Taught	58	50		368		31.50
Teach	56	42		354		30.64
Academic	60	49		394		30.44

Since keywords are words that are unusually frequent in comparison with another data set, these words suggest that discussions of education are particularly prominent in English Canadian newspaper texts that (even when in passing) discuss language issues.

This is not the only indication that language education is topical in English Canadian newspapers. When the words LANGUAGE, FRENCH, and ENGLISH are examined, they have a semantic preference for (i.e. they collocate frequently with) education-related words (collocates marked with an asterisk (*) are statistically significant using Mutual Information scores of 3.0 or above). The word LANGUAGE (671 occurrences) collocates with SCHOOL* (10), LEARNING (11), SKILLS* (11) LEARN (9), TEACHING (6), STUDENTS (6), TRAINING (6), CLASSES* (6), and EDUCATION (5). The word ENGLISH (794 occurrences) collocates with SCHOOL* (25), SCHOOLS* (19), CLASSES* (11), UNIVERSITY* (8), INSTRUCTOR (6), STUDENTS* (6), TEACHER* (5), and TEACHING (5). Finally, FRENCH (1489 occurrences) collocates with IMMERSION* (48), SCHOOL* (39), SCHOOLS* (20), EDUCATION (14), STUDENTS (13), LEARNED* (9), CLASSES* (7), KINDERGARTEN* (7), and STUDENT (7). In other words, education tends to be discussed frequently within the context of language issues, suggesting the topical nature of language education.

Finally, individual texts, too, can attest not only the importance of language education in English Canadian newspapers but also the contentious nature of language education in Canada. Two of the four downsampled English texts focus specifically on issues of language education, and more specifically, the proposed expansion of French Ontario school admissions. With the changes, students from outside Canada who acquired French in their country of origin would be able to attend Ontario's French schools. However, this expansion would not extend to English-speaking Canadians. Howlett (2009) notes that this announcement occurs at a time when cuts are being made to French immersion programmes and contrasts this expansion of admission eligibility (which is due to the low enrolment of French Ontarians, i.e. those constitutionally entitled to such education) with cuts made to the highly popular French immersion programmes for English-speaking Canadians. The cuts are evaluated negatively; for example, the government is described as "under siege over cuts to French immersion programmes", and Howlett reports that communities are calling for boycotts of the alternatives (i.e. travelling to more remote schools where French immersion is still offered). The other downsampled text is a letter to the editor from Monika Ferenczy, former President of Canadian Parents for French (Ontario). Ferenczy (2009) argues in favour of expanding admission guidelines for French-language schools in Ontario because "all students should have opportunities to become proficient and literate in both official languages". Ferenczy explains that Canadian Parents for French "encourages initiatives to improve access to education in French".

The debate over these changes to admissions is underpinned by the understanding of the value of languages in Canadian society and the role of education in distributing this resource equally to Canadian students. In other words, Howlett's text implies that although the English-speaking majority continues to demonstrate interest in French, the infrastructure to support it is dwindling. At the same time, non-English Canadians are being provided unequal access to this valuable social commodity. Ferenczy's argument that all students should have opportunities "to become proficient and literate" in the official languages foregrounds the importance of bilingual fluency while backgrounding the intrinsic role of languages in social life (i.e. the symbolic role of language for French Canadians; the symbolic role of bilingualism for Canadians). In other words, in these examples, equality of access to fluency in official languages is privileged over French-speaking Canadians' desire for intergenerational linguistic and cultural transmission—which is, in fact, at the heart of their constitutional rights. Language education is represented as the means by which to access valuable social resources, and the argument is that it should be democratically available to all. These findings corroborate the argument made by Heller (1990: 79):

> To the extent that Franco-Ontarian schools represent a particularly attractive path to the valued resource that bilingualism has become, they have also become a battleground between francophones and anglophones over who will have access to those schools. Many francophones claim that anglophone access effectively destroys any possibility francophones may have to really preserve their language and their identity. Many anglophones, essentially not understanding the fragile position of minorities in Canadian society, argue for open, democratic access to any and all forms of education (after all, there are no obstacles to francophone access to English-language schools).

As Heller argues, the value of bilingualism is recognised by English-speaking Ontarians (and arguably English-speaking Canadians more generally), and this suggests that the instrumental value of languages is being foregrounded. Moreover, this finding supports Garvin's (1993: 51) arguments about the privileging of fluency and the instrumental value of languages in English-speaking countries.

One final reason why English in particular appears to be perceived as a valuable language of communication in Canadian newspapers is because of its value internationally. English has real, valuable currency in society because fluency and skills in English have been "commodified" (Heller 2003b) as marketable resources. Because it is a common language for many diverse groups of people, English tends to be seen as serving functional, utilitarian, and "instrumental" purposes. Most of the downsampled articles with the lowest proportion of language-related terms (see Sect. 4.1) are useful for studying this angle on English. These examples tend to discuss languages in passing in such a way that they are presented as assets to individuals rather than as social goods with inherent value. The English language in particular is framed as an invaluable asset that enables individuals to access opportunities that otherwise would be unavailable to them. For example, one article represents fluency in English as a positive trait of the educated elite in Indian society. According to this description, being educated and fluent in English allows gay men and lesbians more freedom, both on the Internet and in elite establishments (see Example 4.7).

Example 4.7 (Nolen 2009, emphasis added)

Gay and transgendered Indians, especially those who belong to the visible *hijira* (transgendered) and *kothi* communities, and femme and proud boys like Rajiv, are particular targets for police brutality carried out in the name of 377 [the section of the Indian Penal Code that criminalizes homosexual acts between consenting adults]. *An elite of educated, English-speaking gay men and lesbians moves relatively freely*, meeting on the Internet or at dedicated queer nights at upscale bars; their money insulates them from the threat of police harassment.

Fluency in English is a coveted skill, it would seem, since another downsampled article discusses the English language education of a Japanese royal prince. In this case, the English language is paired with "international etiquette" and "democratic principles", suggesting the important value of the English language in geopolitics (see Example 4.8).

Example 4.8 (Valpy 2009, emphasis added)

Elizabeth Gray Vining was engaged to teach him *English, international etiquette, democratic principles and – Ms. Vining being a Quaker – pacifism.* The director of the Prince's education, Shinzo Koizumi, a former university president, taught his young charge the maxim that "Heaven never created a man above or below another man" and instructed him to emulate Britain's King George V as a constitutional monarch who placed himself at the service of his people.

Finally, another downsampled article (York 2009) discusses how a lack of fluency in English can have hugely detrimental effects. The article discusses the non-consensual sterilisation of HIV-positive African women, and gives the example of a woman who was asked to "sign some papers" as she entered the hospital for a C-section but was unaware that these confirmed her acceptance of sterilisation. The story contends that her lack of fluency in English meant she was unable to participate in actions that concerned her directly. Indeed, the explanation for her non-consensual sterilisation is that the woman "barely spoke English": she was unable to read the doctor's handwriting apart from a few words.

These examples all serve to show how the English language is represented as an asset with real, operable instrumental value not only in Canada but also internationally. According to this line of reasoning, rather than questioning or critiquing the role of English in places such as Africa, Japan, and India, the importance of English is strongly asserted: fluency in English can help in a variety of situations, including health, safety, career progress, and international relations.

4.3 Language Ideologies in French Canadian Newspapers

4.3.1 Monolingual Ideologies and Instrumental Language Ideologies

The findings from the French Canadian newspapers are somewhat similar to the findings from the English Canadian newspapers in two ways: first, the French Canadian newspapers contain monolingual ideologies—but these tend to be explicit rather than implicit; and second, the French Canadian newspapers contain instrumental language ideologies—but these concern the English language much more than they concern French.

In the French newspaper corpus, 15.9 % of all articles contained at least one reference to language, which is more than double the proportion of English newspaper articles[3] (7.86 %). Notably, while the English newspapers exhibited monolingual ideologies through the implicit role of English in comparison to other languages, in the French newspapers, monolingual ideologies are explicit and surface especially with relation to discussions of French. French is the language most frequently discussed, and references to French occur more than three times more often than references to English (*FRANÇAIS* 320 wpm, *FRANÇAISE* 107 wpm, *ANGLAIS* 104 wpm, *ANGLAISE* 14 wpm). Although the French Canadian newspapers do not represent Canada as a monolingual French-speaking country the way that the English Canadian newspapers represent it as a monolingual English-speaking country, most (3) of the newspapers in the data set are drawn from Quebec and they tend to represent this province as monolingual.

In the French newspapers, references to *QUÉBEC* and *QUÉBÉCOIS* are more frequent than references to *CANADA* and *CANADIEN* (1621 and 692 occurrences vs. 1025 and 471 occurrences, respectively), and *QUÉBEC* frequently collocates with *FRANÇAIS/E* (43 occurrences). Some concordance lines attest to the French character of Quebec (*le caractère français du Québec*, two occurrences), or simply refer to "French Quebec" (*Québec français,* three occurrences). Other concordance lines (two occurrences) highlight the goal of making Quebec more French. Still other concordance lines (six occurrences) highlight activities taking place in French, the official status of the French language in Quebec, or use Quebec as metonymy for the French-speaking people of Quebec (*Le reste du Québec parle français;* "The rest of Quebec speaks French"). The dominant trend (14 occurrences), however, is simply to locate the French

[3] In French, these "references to language" included the following: ANGLAIS, ANGLAISE, ANGLAISES, ANGLICISME, ANGLICISE, ANGLO, ANGLOS, ANGLOPHONE, ANGLOPHONES, BILINGUE, BILINGUES, BILINGUISME, FRANÇAIS, FRANÇAISE, FRANÇAISES, FRANCO, FRANCOS, FRANCOPHONE, FRANCOPHONES, FRANCOPHONIE, LANGAGE, LANGAGES, LANGAGIER, LANGAGIÈRE, LANGAGIÈRES, LINGUISTIQUE, LINGUISTIQUES, LANGUE, and LANGUES. In English, these "references to language" included the following: ANGLO, ANGLOS, ANGLICIZE, ANGLOPHONE, ANGLOPHONES, BILINGUAL, BILINGUALS, BILINGUALISM, ENGLISH, FRANCO, FRANCOPHONE, FRANCOPHONES, FRANCOPHONIE, FRENCH, LANGUAGE, LANGUAGES, LINGUISTIC, LINGUISTICS, MONOLINGUAL, MULTILINGUAL, and UNILINGUAL.

language and its use in geographic relation to Quebec (e.g. "the French language in Quebec"/*la langue française au Québec*).

One of the four articles downsampled from the French corpus provides a useful site for explicating monolingual language ideologies in greater detail. "Full bilingue" (Rioux 2009) discusses the Quebec Premier's visit to Brussels for an international conference on the environment. While there, Jean Charest gave a speech half in French and half in English, and Rioux argues that the Premier of Quebec should always speak French unless an audience's lack of fluency in French makes it necessary for him to speak another language.

Rioux refers to Law 101 (the Charter of the French Language), which begins with the declaration that French is the official language of Quebec, and he also notes that Quebec has only one official language—French (*une province dont l'unique langue officielle est le français;* "a province wherein the only official language is French"). Rioux clarifies that the Premier should not be reproached every time he speaks English when it is necessary; on the contrary, the Premier should speak English any time his audience does not understand French (*chaque fois que cela est necessaire;* "every time it is necessary"*; chaque fois que son auditoire ne comprend pas le français;* "every time his audience does not understand French"). However, since the Premier was in Brussels—a city with a higher percentage of francophones than Montreal—when he gave his bilingual speech, and because there was simultaneous translation available, Charest had no need to speak English. Moreover, Rioux argues that the English and French languages should be kept separate and used separately rather than be interwoven with one another in speeches. This interweaving of languages Rioux labels "speaking bilingual" (*le bilingue*): an "exotic language that is spoken nowhere apart from in small corners of Ottawa" (*langue exotique qui n'est parlée que dans certains quartiers d'Ottawa: le bilingue*). Furthermore, Rioux implies that if Charest is to speak English, let it be only English (*anglais, et anglais seulement*), rather than a mix with French.

Thus, monolingual ideologies seem to underpin Rioux's arguments that, first, wherever possible, French should be the (only) language spoken and, second, even when it is not possible to speak only French, the language should nonetheless be kept separate and distinct from other languages, such as English. Rioux's arguments suggest that one of the reasons why the French language and its role in society continue to be discussed explicitly is due to the challenges it faces in an English-dominated globalised world. These challenges mean that it is important to explicitly articulate why French—and only French—should be spoken.

The French newspapers also express some instrumental language ideologies along the lines of those discussed in Sect. 4.2.2. Similar to the English newspapers, the instrumental language ideologies notably tend to be focused on the English language, and not French. For example, fluency in English is sometimes evaluated. There is one positive evaluation of English skills (*parlant un bon anglais*), but there are three references to "poor English" (*parlait mal anglais*), one reference to "barely speaking English" (*parlait à peine anglais*), and one reference to unintelligible English (*son anglais était pratiquement inintelligible*). In contrast, the French corpus contains only positive—not negative—evaluations of French (seven occurrences). Neither *À PEINE* nor *ININTELLIGIBLE* (the negative evaluation terms used to describe a lack of fluency in English) collocate with *FRANÇAIS,* and *MAL* only collocates with *FRANÇAIS* twice—neither instance using *MAL* to evaluate French skills.

Although findings are small in number, they suggest that English skills may be important to French speakers as well as English speakers. This would confirm recent arguments made by researchers (e.g. Cardinal 2008: 69; Oakes 2010), who have noted that many francophones want to improve their fluency in English. They would also support Garvin's (1993) conceptual framework of language standardisation (see Sect. 1.1), which posited that when a language has predominantly instrumental value, individual fluency in a standard language is highly prized. In contrast, if a language has a predominantly integrative value, then expectations for individual fluency in a standard language may be lower.

4.3.2 Ideologies of Language as a Core Value

In contrast to findings from the English Canadian newspapers that privileged the instrumental role of languages in society, findings from the French Canadian newspapers suggest that the French language serves as a fundamental component of Quebec's culture and value system. The belief in the intrinsic value of language will be referred to as "ideologies of language as a core value". According to Smolicz (1999: 105), core values are one of the most fundamental components of a group's culture:

> They generally represent the heartland of the ideological system and act as identifying values which are symbolic of the group and its membership. Rejection of core values carries with it the threat of exclusion from the group. Indeed, the deviant individual may himself feel unable to continue as a member. Core values are singled out for special attention because they provide the indispensable link between the group's cultural and social systems.

The role of French as a core value is historic in Quebec. The leaders of the Quebec nationalist movement, Jean Lesage and René Lévesque, both contended that language was central to Quebec identity. Jean Lesage once declared: "Of all the languages currently spoken in the world [...] the French language is the one that fits us best because of our own characteristics and mentality" (cited in Stark 1992: 133). During the height of the Quiet Revolution in 1968, René Lévesque declared: "Being ourselves is essentially maintaining and developing a personality that has existed for three and a half centuries. At the heart of this personality is the fact that we speak French. Everything else is linked to this essential element" (Lévesque 1968 [1997]). Still today, Gérard Bouchard (1997: 120) argues that French is "vested with all the French Canadian cultural heritage", and has become the benchmark of the status and vitality of French speakers in Canada (Beauchemin 2006; Bouchard 2002: 8).

```
une Acadienne prônant la beauté de notre langue et de notre culture. Je suis con
 chef de notre gouvernement ravale notre langue nationale au rang de langue régi
ur rapport à l'anglais. Où s'en va notre langue, où s'en va notre culture... Des
ous devons nous battre et protéger notre langue et notre culture... Le gouvernem
vernement que nous désirons garder notre langue et notre culture. ASSEZ, C'EST A
 chef de notre gouvernement ravale notre langue nationale au rang de langue régi
es réflexions sur notre culture et notre langue, ces derniers mois ont été parti
ne, de notre patrimoine et même de notre langue. Une telle mission ne se calcule
  de contribuer à la protection de notre langue; un récent sondage a pourtant mo
reconnaît comme peuple avec notre propre langue, notre propre culture, notre ide
fort soutenu pour améliorer notre propre langue, tant parlée qu'écrite? Aux jeun
s nous exprimons par notre culture et la langue française, sans exclure l'anglai
```

Fig. 4.4 French concordance lines with NOTRE and LANGUE

In the French Canadian newspapers, one way that language is marked as a core value of the Quebec nation is through references to "our" (*notre*) and "their" (*leur*) language (see Fig. 4.4).

Expanded concordance lines show that *NOTRE LANGUE* refers exclusively to the French language (12 occurrences), whereas *LEUR LANGUE* can refer to French, English, or other languages (20 occurrences). Moreover, *NOTRE LANGUE* is strongly linked with culture (58 % of occurrences, seven occurrences) and heritage and nationalism (16 % of occurrences, two occurrences). Unlike *NOTRE LANGUE*, discussions of *LEUR LANGUE* tend to refer to anglophones (17 occurrences), or individuals' specific language choice or particularities (3 occurrences). For example, an article in *L'Acadie nouvelle* from June 2009 quotes a health official as saying "we offer patients in all our establishments equivalent services and excellence in the language of their choice" (*nous offrons aux patients de tous nos établissements des services égaux et de qualité dans la langue de leur choix*). While discussions of *LEUR LANGUE* sometimes refer to French *and* French, these are also used to refer to Franco-Ontarians (one occurrence), Acadians (one occurrence), and generic francophones (seven occurrences), rather than to French speakers in Quebec.

Further evidence emerges from a downsampled text (Havrankova 2009). This letter to the editor argues that immigrants to Quebec should feel privileged to learn French. While other languages, such as Swedish and Dutch, are geographically limited, Havrankova argues that "knowledge of French opens the door not only to Quebec culture—already rich—but also to the immense culture of international Francophonie" (*la connaissance du français ouvre la porte non seulement sur la culture québécoise, déjà riche, mais aussi sur l'immense culture francophone mondiale*). French is also described as a "beautiful" (*belle*) language that inspires pride and joy. Havrankova evokes the prestige of French by referring to it as "the language of Anne Hébert" (*la langue d'Anne Hébert*), which parallels the expression "the language of Molière", a common substitution for reference to "the French language". Since Molière is a French cultural icon, Anne Hébert, a French-language Quebec author and poet, is attributed equivalent iconic status, and by association Quebec French acquires prestige. Since French has such value, there is little reason for immigrants to not learn and use it. Indeed, the topoi (see Sect. 3.2) underlying

Havrankova's argument are that immigrants should learn French because the French language has a central role in life in Quebec.

Another downsampled article (Cornellier 2009) indicates that the French language is central to Quebec national culture. In an interview, Quebec nationalist Pierre Falardeau lambasts Quebec filmmakers who make English films because he implies that they are foreign and disloyal to the nation (see Example 4.9).

Example 4.9 (Cornellier 2009)

La culture, selon Falardeau, doit incarner un parti pris, une fidélité à soi-même, donner du sens à la vie. C'est la raison pour laquelle le pamphlétaire rage encore une fois contre la culture de divertissement—«Pierre Lapointe, c'est en français, mais c'est comme rien»—ou, pire encore, de la défection. «C'est comme si on se fabriquait notre propre culture américaine, pour consommation locale», lance-t-il au sujet de Pascale Picard et des cinéastes québécois qui tournent en anglais.

"According to Falardeau, culture must incarnate a preconception, a loyalty to oneself, giving meaning to life. It's for this reason that the pamphleteer rages once again against entertainment culture—"Pierre Lapointe, it's in French, but it's like nothing"—or worse still, against defection. "It's as though we create our own American culture for local consumption", he hurls out on the subject of Pascale Picard and Quebec filmmakers who shoot in English".

In a similar way, the downsampled article that was discussed in Sect. 5.3 (Rioux 2009) also alluded to the pivotal role of the French language in Quebec society, which is partly why it was argued that it should be promoted by Quebec's representatives in international forums.

4.3.3 Ideologies of Standardised Language

Ideologies of standardised language are assumptions about how language should be used "correctly" in order to maintain the "quality" of a language. These ideologies tend to be conservative and prescriptive, advocating a singular "best practice" wherein optional variability should be suppressed (Milroy 2001). As noted in Chap. 1, standard language ideologies are often at play in media discourse. This is because the media are not only sites where public figures engage in debates over language but also because as literal texts they embody "a particular ideology of orthography, syntax, and usage" (DiGiacomo 1999: 105).

In the French Canadian newspapers, there seemed to be a particularly high likelihood of standard language ideologies emerging in the data because of previous research that has suggested that a lengthy history of language debates has contributed to present-day ideologies of standardised French. French is one of the most standardised languages in the world, and French speakers internationally have developed strong representations of a singular, unified language (Eloy 1998; Francard 1998; Kasuya 2001; Jaffe 1999; Lodge 1993; Moïse 2007; Pöll 2005; Schieffelin and Doucet 1998). One important myth associated with French is that there is a "centre", that is, a standard or a norm, which derives from the territory of the French state. Around this centre circulate various regional and international French "peripheral" varieties (Bouchard 2002: 137–145; 244–245; Eloy 1998; Lodge 1993; Lüdi 1992; Oakes and Warren 2007: 112). Boudreau and Dubois (2007: 105) cite numerous studies showing that a French "standard" is not a reality; rather, it forms part of the linguistic imagination of francophones all over the world, including in Canada.

Research has suggested that many Canadian French speakers developed insecurities about their language variety (for overviews, see Boudreau and Dubois 2007: 105; Bouchard 2002: 135). Associations such as the *Société du parler français du Canada*, founded in 1902, worked to raise the profile of Canadian French (see Bouchard 2002: 115–150; Oakes and Warren 2007: 110–111) and contributed to the redefinition of the Canadian variety of French. Debates are still ongoing about the standardisation of French in Quebec, with different groups advocating different benchmarks of quality French: some feel that French from France should be the benchmark and some contend that it should be French in North America (see Lockerbie 2005: 16–17).

Given this context, it was presumed that ideologies of standard language would surface in the newspaper data. However, in the French newspapers, there were no references to some of the most commonly used labels that refer to standard or non-standard varieties of French in

Canada, including *français standard, français international, français d'ici, bon usage,* and *canadianisme* (see e.g. Bouchard 2002: 245). There were very infrequent references to *joual* (three occurrences) and *patois* (one occurrence), and these were not used uniformly within discussions about or comparisons with a standard language. For example, the reference to *patois* occurs in a discussion of a mother's desire to send her child to Saturday schools in the same way that ethnic minority children in Quebec are sometimes sent to Saturday schools to learn and practise their heritage culture. As can be seen in Example 4.10, her concern is that in multicultural Montreal, children may lose sight of their "patois" alongside the rest of their culture and heritage.

Example 4.10 (Blanchette 2009)

Songé: à inscrire mon B à l'école du samedi. Sans blague, faudrait peut-être s'y mettre et leur donner des cours de «québécois», leur patois, leur culture, leurs ancêtres, leur cuisine, leur religion, leur faune et leur flore. Des fois qu'ils l'oublieraient en chemin.

"Considered: signing my B up for Saturday school. All joking aside, maybe it would be best to get to it and give "Quebecois" classes, their patois, their culture, their ancestors, their food, their religion, their flora and their fauna. Sometimes it can be lost in the street".

In this case, then, patois is not derided or contrasted with a standard language; rather, it is part of heritage and has the privileged status of being first among the list of assets that Blanchette considers attributes of Quebec identity.

Another way of approaching this subject is by examining the "standard" against which Quebec or Canadian French is compared. In many cases, the standard that is used is the variety of French that is used in France, commonly known as *français de France.* In the French corpus, there are only three references to *français de France*, all of which are compared with the variety of French spoken in Quebec. One of the three instances to *français de France* occurs in the headline, which highlights a Quebec television show that has met with success in France. The headline ("*Minuit, le soir*" *en français de France*) refers to the programme (*Minuit, le soir*) being aired in France, but notably in the variety of French spoken in France (*en français de France*). The article notes that when aired in France, the "original Quebecois version" of the programme was supplemented by French subtitles (see Example 4.11).

Example 4.11 (Cloutier 2009)

Après avoir remporté 17 prix Gémeaux au Québec et quatre autres à l'étranger, la version originale québécoise, sous-titrée en français, avait été présentée sur les ondes de Cinécinéma Culte, en France, à l'automne 2007, recevant des critiques élogieuses.

"After having won 17 Gémeaux Awards [prizes in French Canadian achievements in Canadian television] in Quebec and four other awards internationally, the original Quebecois version, with French subtitles, had been broadcast on Cinécinéma Culte, in France, in autumn 2007, with glowing approval from the critics".

Example 4.11 shows that despite the acclaim for the programme, its language variety is still compared against a standard defined in France. The fact that the journalist highlights that the subtitling for screenings in France suggests that standard language ideologies were at play in the comparisons between varieties of French from France and Quebec. Nevertheless, because it was met with "glowing approval from the critics", it would seem that no language or varietal barrier is sufficient reason to overlook its quality.

With regard to the second reference to *français de France*, this occurs in the context of an article (Sarfati 2009) that discusses new Canadian additions to the *Le Petit Larousse* dictionary (2010 edition), published in France. These include references to Quebec author and playwright Marie Laberge, the Canadian filmmaker David Cronenberg, the French branch of the Canadian Broadcasting Corporation Radio-Canada, and some *québécismes*. The latter refers to vernacular features of Quebec French, in this case, singular words that are unique to Quebec. Notably, there are only two references to *québécismes* in the entire French corpus, and both occur in the context of this article. The *québécismes* referred to by this journalist include words such as *motton*, *gomme*, *saucette*, and *comptoir*, all of which have been included in the new French dictionary (see Example 4.12).

Example 4.12 (Sarfati 2009)

Pour ce qui est des québécismes, on écrit que dans la Belle Province, un comptoir est une "surface plate, sur un meuble fermé, dans laquelle un évier, un lavabo est souvent encastré"; un motton, une "petite masse de matière compacte et durcie" mais que, dans l'expression "avoir le motton", il signifie "avoir la gorge serrée" ou, comme dans "faire le motton", "posséder, gagner beaucoup d'argent"; un hameçonnage, une "technique de fraude par courriel" et une saucette, une "petite baignade" ou un "court séjour quelque part". Et puis, on indique qu'au Québec, le mot "gomme" est utilisé pour nommer ce qu'en "français de France" on appelle... chewing-gum.

"As for *québécismes,* the Le Petit Larousse writes that in La Belle Province a *comptoir* is "a flat surface, on a closed unit, often with an in-built sink". A *motton* is a "small mass of compact and hardened material" but in the expression *avoir le motton* it means "to have a closed throat" and in *faire le motton*, "to have or win lots of money". A *hameçonnage* is a "tactic for fraud by email" and a *saucette* is a "little swim" or a "short trip somewhere". Finally, the dictionary writes that in Quebec the word *gomme* is used for what the French [i.e., *en français de France*] call... *chewing-gum*".

Example 4.12 contains a number of interesting nominational strategies (van Leeuwen 2003 [1996]: 66) to refer to local and foreign terms. In the original French text, all *québécismes* (*motton, gomme, saucette,* and *comptoir*) are given in regular font. They easily might have been highlighted as technical terms or as items of interest by the use of italics or inverted commas; however, these terms are not marked in any way in the text. Journalists tend to use quotation strategies to highlight specific passages or words of interest and to dissociate themselves from the content of quotes (Cotter 2010: 148–149; Simpson 1993: 142). Since in this case the journalist opted not to highlight the terminology under discussion through quotation or emphasis strategies, they are normalised as regular lexicon in the text of the article. Indeed, these are words that the intended audience (i.e. Quebec French speakers who may use *québécismes*) are presumed to understand. Even the term *québécisme* is not emphasised in the text or highlighted with inverted commas, suggesting that it too is a normal and natural term.

Rather than highlighting local lexicon, then, the journalist highlights references to and uses of *français de France*. All definitions provided by

Le Petit Larousse are placed in inverted commas. Since these are direct quotations, perhaps this is unsurprising; however, since the only other reference in inverted commas is the reference to "français de France", this reference is marked. Finally, the single reference to the French term *chewing-gum* is not marked by inverted commas or by italics; however, it is marked by the suspension point (…), which functions to emphasise the term. Since *chewing-gum* is clearly a loan word from English, the effect is such that the authority of the international prestige language (i.e. the variety of French spoken in France) is noted with some irony—hence, it would seem, the inverted commas ("*français de France*").

The third reference to *français de France* occurs in an article that discusses a Quebecois actor, Marc-André Grondin, working in France (Lussier 2009b). The relocation of this actor to France is the pretext for the interview: Quebec actors are often "lost" to France because it is "practically impossible" for actors to make a living in Quebec cinema (*La réalité, c'est qu'un acteur désirant se consacrer exclusivement au cinéma ne peut pratiquement pas vivre de son métier au Québec*). When Quebec actors move to France, some "zealous zealots" (*zéalotes zélés*) consider this national betrayal, in part because actors are obliged to adopt the French that is used in France (*français de France*). While the relationship between Quebec and France is described as "sometimes a bit twisted" (*nos rapports avec la France sont parfois un peu tordus*), France is not explicitly evaluated negatively in the article. What is negatively portrayed is French cultural dominance, and this is notable through discussions of language varieties. Although the journalist notes that Marc-André is obliged to master "French from France" (*Marc-André doit évidemment maîtriser le "français de France"*), he also observes that the Quebecois are not the only French speakers forced to adapt while working in the French capital. Indeed, just as Belgian actors "erase" their accent (*gomment leur accent*), Swiss actors "lose all traces of a Swiss accent" (*perd toute trace d'accent suisse*), and all actors from regional France "adjust their language" (*doivent adjuster leur langage*), so too Quebec actors are obliged to master *le français de France*. The journalist notes that this is sensitive territory for the Quebecois (*nous avons collectivement l'épiderme plutôt sensible à cet égard*), but the Quebecois are not presented as isolated in this regard. Indeed, French cultural superiority is derided by the journalist, who claims that even actors originating from outside Paris must "sell their soul to camembert" (*ceux ayant vendu leur âme au camembert*) when they move to the capital.

Another way that ideologies of standardised language become manifested is through remarks about local or foreign accents. For example, in one case an accent is described as "French mixed with Québécois" (*accent français mâtiné de québécois*), another is a "broad" Acadian accent (*accent chiac bien assumé*), and another accent is "thick Québécois", which is difficult to understand (*un gros accent québécois. Même moi, je ne les comprends pas toujours*/ "a thick Quebec accent. Even I didn't always understand"). Other times a Canadian French accent is sufficient to identify an individual (*un serveur d'origine québécoise que vous reconnaîtrez par son accent*/ "a server from Quebec who you will recognise by his accent"), or the accent is remarked because it is "so Canadian" (*tellement canadien!*).

In conclusion, although there are very few examples that suggest ideologies of standard language in the French newspapers, it is notable that there are more examples of these ideologies in this data set than there were in the English data set. It was also somewhat unexpected that there was so little evidence of standard language ideologies when previous research has suggested that issues concerning standard language are long-standing in Quebec history.

4.3.4 Ideologies of Language Endangerment

Finally, the French corpus proved to be unique in comparison with the English corpus because it contained ideologies of language endangerment. As noted in Sect. 4.3.3, the history of the French language in Canada is interwoven with concerns over its status in comparison with both the so-called "international standard" in France and its international competitor—the English language. Because the French language has an important role as a core value in Quebec, concerns over its status are often rife. "Ideologies of endangerment" refer to the ways in which concerns over the future or status of a language are embedded in discussions of other (and perhaps unrelated) topics (Heller and Duchêne 2007: 4). Data from the French Canadian newspapers suggest that these concerns continue to be rife.

In both the English and the French corpora, there is explicit mention of the French language being "threatened" (eight occurrences, *menacé,* five occurrences, respectively), but language endangerment is also discussed in more subtle ways in the French corpus. References to the need to "promote" (*promouvoir*), "defend" (*défendre*), and "strengthen" (*renforcer*) French suggest an underlying assumption that Quebec needs to be "more French" (*plus français*). Individual articles describe French as a "minority language in North America" (*Extrêmement minoritaire en Amérique du Nord*) and the "Francophone space" in the Americas as "shrunken" (*rétréci*). The blame is almost inevitably placed on the English language because it is argued that English, and no other language, threatens French (see Example 4.13).

Example 4.13 (Dubuc 2009)

c'est cette langue [l'anglais] qui constitue une menace. Aujourd'hui encore [...] ni le chinois, ni le portugais, ni les autres langues parlées au Québec, sauf l'anglais, ne menacent le français.

"It is this language [English] that constitutes a threat. Still today [...] neither Chinese, nor Portuguese, nor any other language spoken in Quebec, except English, threatens French".

In Montreal, the city with particular symbolic value in the struggle for French predominance, French is seen to be ceding to English (*le français s'est mis à reculer à Montréal au profit de l'anglais*). The effect is such that anglicisms and French–English bilingualism are seen as posing a threat to the French language. Examples show that bilingualism is referred to as a process imposed on French speakers against their will. This is achieved by transforming the adjective (*bilingue*) into verbs (*bilingualiser,* "bilingualise"; *rendre bilingue,* "make bilingual") and by presenting bilingualism as a process with various stages ("a step towards anglicisation", "bilingualism is 'inevitable'", "the antechamber to assimilation") and a negative outcome (*assimilation, conséquences*). One example refers to bilingualism as the Trojan horse that "conquered" Louisiana, the Canadian West, Ontario, and the Acadian region of Eastern Canada, suggesting that bilingualism is part of a colonial-style conquest by English speakers.

However, discussions of endangerment do not only place the blame on the English language. French articles also stress the need for immigrants to learn French. While one example cites this as important for the integration of immigrants (*la pièce maîtresse de l'intégration des immigrants, c'est le français et l'emploi*), it is widely accepted that immigrants' adoption of French has been crucial for the survival of the language since the decline in francophone birth rate in the mid-twentieth century (Oakes and Warren 2007: 126). Thus, a large number of articles in the French corpus do seem to be united in the consensus that French is endangered in part because of the strength of English and immigrants' failure to adopt the French language.

One way to corroborate these findings is through the analysis of downsampled articles. In one aforementioned downsampled article (Rioux 2009), it is argued that because French is language of Quebec, it must be defended and promoted: "If Quebec does not show an essentially French face in international organisations every time it can, we should ask who will do it instead" (*Si le Québec ne présente pas un visage essentiellement français dans les organisations internationales chaque fois qu'il le peut, on se demande bien qui le fera à sa place*). Another article (Bélair-Cirino 2009) also reveals ideologies of language endangerment in a more explicit way by reporting on the results from a Leger Marketing survey on perceptions of language endangerment in Montreal.

Although the explicit topic of the Bélair-Cirino article is perceptions of language endangerment, the article contains a number of nominational strategies that provide insight into the explicit and covert ways in which social actors are included and excluded from categories according to the language they speak. Moreover, when this article is compared with an English newspaper article that deals with the same survey, the differences between the two suggest underlying ideologies that may exist in and differ between the French-speaking and English-speaking communities.

Bélair-Cirino's article uses the three usual categories for referring to people in Quebec: francophones, anglophones, and allophones. However, there are more references to French speakers (15 occurrences) than English speakers (10 occurrences) and non-English, non-French speakers (allophones) (four occurrences). Notably, the discursive amalgamation of English speakers and allophones occurs several times throughout the article, with references to *non-francophones* or "Quebecers whose first language is not French" (*Québécois dont la langue maternelle est différente du français*). In total, there are nine linguistically ambiguous references.[4]

Although the dominant trend throughout the article is to juxtapose French speakers with anglophones and allophones, there are several occasions when allophones are subsumed within discussions of anglophones, reducing the linguistic complexity (i.e. multilingualism) to a binary between English and French. The beginning of the article, for example, opens with the statement that, according to a recent survey, 90 % of francophone Quebecers believe that the French language is threatened, but this opinion is shared by only 25 % of anglophones and allophones. This survey, Bélair-Cirino continues, "brings to light an important gap between French-speaking and English-speaking Quebecers' perceptions of the language" (*Le sondage met en lumière un fossé important entre les perceptions des Québécois d'expression française et ceux d'expression anglaise sur la vitalité de la langue*). What is notable, then, is that this "important gap" was revealed through survey data elicited not only from francophone and anglophone sources but also from allophones. However, the perception gap that Bélair-Cirino highlights is instead one existing between francophones and anglophones.

A similar reduction of multilingualism to bilingualism presents itself midway through the article, where again anglophone and allophone survey results (*un point de vue que partagent 20 % des anglophones et allophones questionnés*) are reduced within a subsequent sentence to only anglophones: "Probably because [anglophones] do not understand the extent to which the French language is threatened" (*«Probablement parce que [les anglophones] ne comprennent pas à quel point la langue française est menacée», suppose Jack Jedwab*). Here again, the linguistic complexity of Quebec's population, and moreover the linguistic complexity of the survey data, is reduced to a binary juxtaposition between anglophones

[4]The differences in frequency between these references to identity categories are similar to the differences in frequency between identity categories across the French corpus more generally, where references to French-speaking identity (e.g. FRANCOPHONES and FRANCOPHONE, 313 occurrences and 238 occurrences, respectively) are more frequent than references to English-speaking identity (e.g. ANGLOPHONES and ANGLOPHONE, 87 wpm and 23 wpm, respectively), and far more frequent than references to the identity of speakers of other languages (e.g. ALLOPHONES, 5 wpm).

and francophones. Although it is the information source (Jack Jedwab) who states "anglophones" rather than "anglophones and allophones", it is the journalist who presents Jedwab's quote in such a way that it seems to reduce anglophone/allophone complexity to anglophone homogeneity.

Although Quebec has never been inhabited only by English speakers and French speakers, these are the principal categories used to represent social actors in the text. French speakers and English speakers are foregrounded and other language groups are backgrounded. The only token references to allophones occur in conjunction with references to anglophones (*anglophones et allophones,* three occurrences; *anglophone ou allophone,* one occurrence). Since discussions of allophones do not occur on their own, these references serve only to increase the numerical presence of anglophones rather than to include allophones' perspectives within the survey report. Indeed, it would seem that allophones are treated merely as statistics that are used to support—if not enhance—a line of reasoning that uses "English" as a label for all those who are antagonistic to French language maintenance. In van Leeuwen's (2003 [1996]: 49) terms, "allophone" is an aggregate category used to "regulate practice and manufacture consensus opinion". In this case, the consensus opinion concerns not only the role of language in society but also more specifically the inclusion and exclusion of social actors and the binary reductionism of linguistic and perspectival complexity in Quebec. In other words, the categorisation conflation of allophones with anglophones serves to draw boundary lines between those who feel French is threatened (French speakers) and those who do not (everybody else, who also tend to speak English). It also enhances the argument for why the *francisation* of immigrants (i.e. allophones) is so important (see above): if immigrants spoke French and were integrated into the dominant French-speaking community of Quebec, then they would not naturally align with the English perspective; instead, like other French speakers, they would understand that French is threatened.

The function of the English language is crucial when the linguistic labels are under consideration. Bélair-Cirino uses slightly less variable expressions to discuss English speakers in comparison with French speakers. As mentioned, while there are many labels for French speakers, only four labels are used to refer to English speakers:

1. *Francophones* (six occurrences)
2. *Québécois francophones* (three occurrences)
3. *Québécois d'expression française*/ "French-speaking Quebecers" (two occurrences)
4. *les personnes qui s'expriment en français* "people who speak French" (one occurrence)
5. *moins de 54 % de la population montréalaise parle français à la maison* "less than 54 % of the Montreal population speaks French at home" (one occurrence)
6. *Québécois dont la langue maternelle est le français* "Quebecers whose first language is French" (one occurrence)
7. *francophones du Québec* "francophones from Quebec" (one occurrence)

1. *Anglophones* (seven occurrences)
2. *anglophones du Québec* "anglophones from Quebec" (one occurrence)
3. *la communauté anglophone majoritaire hors Québec* "the majority anglophone community outside Quebec" (one occurrence)
4. [*Québécois*] *d'expression anglaise* "English-speaking Quebecer" (one occurrence)

Given the variety of these alternatives, it is notable that twice throughout the article still other terms are used to imply "French-speaking". In these cases, the term *Québécois* is used in such a way to refer to only French-speaking Quebecers, but this is not stated explicitly (see Examples 4.14 and 4.15).

Example 4.14 (Bélair-Cirino 2009, emphasis added)

Le gouvernement de Jean Charest «donne le sentiment à l'ensemble de la population québécoise qu'il n'est pas véritablement prêt à agir. Il y a un sentiment d'inaction, et ça inquiète beaucoup les Québécois», explique Alain-G. Gagnon, directeur du Centre de recherche interdisciplinaire sur la diversité au Québec (CRIDAQ).

"Jean Charest's government "gives the entire Quebec population the feeling that he's not really ready to act. There is a feeling of inaction, and that worries Quebecers a lot," explains Alain-G. Gagnon, director of the Centre for Interdisciplinary Research on Diversity in Quebec (*CRIDAQ*)".

Example 4.15 (Bélair-Cirino 2009, emphasis added)

«Il y a un sentiment peut-être d'inquiétude, mais que 90 % des Québécois pensent véritablement que le français soit véritablement menacé, ça m'apparaît un peu élevé», ajoute-t-il.

""There is maybe a feeling of concern, but if <u>90 % of Quebecers</u> really think that French is really threatened, that seems a bit high to me," he added".

In these examples, Gagnon's use of the term *Québécois* hides the fact that the survey found that 90 % of *francophone* Quebecers believed French to be threatened. Thus, Gagnon's omission allows for the representation of Quebec as a monolingual French-speaking territory to be naturalised (cf. Lisée 2007: 98). In addition, this labelling strategy also serves to make language endangerment not only an issue for French speakers (who, internationally, also have concerns over their language; see e.g. Moïse 2007); it also suggests that language endangerment is a national issue for all Quebecers.

At this point, it is useful to compare the French-language article to an English-language article reporting on the same Leger Marketing survey.[5] In the English corpus, three major city newspapers and one national newspaper—all owned by the CanWest media conglomerate—published nearly identical articles on 22 June, with the byline of Marion Scott in all cases save one (which is anonymous) (Anonymous 2009b; Marian Scott 2009a, b, c). The Montreal *Gazette* edition (Marian Scott 2009c) is the example that is chosen for analysis here. This edition is parallel to the other three (*National Post, Ottawa Citizen,* and *Vancouver Sun*) but is the longest version. The comparison of this English article with the French article (Bélair-Cirino 2009) will include the representation of social actors and strategies of collectivisation and perspectivation. Through this comparison, it becomes apparent that the French- and English-speaking journalists have reported the survey findings differently, in different languages, to different audiences.

[5] Although the French-language article (Bélair-Cirino 2009) was obtained through downsampling procedures detailed in Sect. 4.3.3, the English-language articles were specifically selected from the English corpus for comparison rather than by using downsampling procedures.

The English article (Marian Scott 2009c) includes references to social actors who are classified according to language: French speakers ("French-speaking Quebecers", "francophones", "French Canadian"), English speakers ("English-speakers", "anglophones"), those who do not speak French ("non-francophones"), and those whose mother tongue is neither French nor English ("allophones"). There is also mention more generally of immigrants, Quebecers and Montrealers. In terms of collectivisation, this article uses language as the primary criterion of social categorisation. However, in contrast to the French article where English speakers were categorised alongside allophones (*anglophones et allophones/anglophone ou allophone*), in Scott's rendition English speakers are categorised alongside immigrants ("English speakers and immigrants"), suggesting that both language and citizenship are meaningful group indicators.

The term "allophone" by definition is not synonymous with "immigrant": while "allophone" refers to someone whose first language is neither English nor French, this person is not necessarily an immigrant to Canada. Interestingly, Scott first uses the term "immigrant" but later uses the terms "non-francophone(s)" and "allophone(s)". Her interchangeable use of these terms implies that they refer to one and the same group. The effect of Scott's nominational strategy makes the interpretation of the survey findings notably different (see Example 4.16).

Example 4.16 (Scott 2009, emphasis added)

That [francophones'] concern has intensified as *allophones*—residents whose mother tongue is neither French nor English—have increased.

Had Scott continued to use the term "immigrants" in Example 4.16, the effect of the statement would have been considerably different. It is likely that Scott opted for "allophones" rather than "immigrants" because linguistic labels (i.e. "allophones") are more politically correct than ethno-cultural labels (i.e. "immigrants"). Indeed, had Scott continued to use the term "immigrants" in Example 4.16, she arguably would have portrayed francophones as intolerant, if not xenophobic. Still, Scott's representation of the situation is such that intolerance is precisely the representation that is achieved: according to her rendition, there are two polarised camps, one comprised of francophones/French-speaking Quebecers and the other comprised of everyone else (English speakers and allophones/immigrants). Furthermore, in Scott's text, the francophones' "concern" is somewhat ambiguous because the anaphoric reference to "the future of French in the city" (i.e. the subject of their concern) is interrupted by a vague quote from Lysiane Gagnon (see Example 4.17).

Example 4.17 (Scott 2009)

A 2008 survey found 79 per cent of francophones worried about the future of French in the city.

Quebecers have long been suspicious of "the cosmopolitan metropolis ... represented in the collective imagination as a threat to French Canadian survival," La Presse columnist Lysiane Gagnon wrote last month.

That concern has intensified as allophones—residents whose mother tongue is neither French nor English—have increased.

In Example 4.17, Scott switches from concerns over language according to survey findings to concerns over immigration (i.e. concerns over "allophones"). Furthermore, rather than citing the number of fluent French speakers or the level of French used at work (common benchmarks for language status), Scott cites findings on the mother tongue of Montreal residents. The effect is such that readers have no access to information concerning whether or not French is endangered (i.e. the subject of the Leger Marketing survey) and no access to information about why French speakers would believe French is threatened (i.e. the findings from the Leger Marketing survey). Furthermore, and perhaps most importantly, Scott provides no information source to confirm the connection between the rise in the "allophone" population and the rise in concern over language endangerment. It is, then, an assumption and implicature on the part of the journalist that the level of immigration affects francophones' concerns over language status; the swiftness of the switch between survey findings and demographics suggests that this may be assumed common and shared knowledge in the newspaper readership.

One final comparison of the English and French stories on the Leger Marketing survey is relevant to a discussion of ideologies of language endangerment: a comparison of the perspectival strategies employed. Perspectival strategies involve the expression of perspectives of the relevant interlocutor. This often involves intertextuality and interdiscursivity through the use of words or phrases (i.e. quotations) that are central to that perspective; systematic or lengthy quotations may indicate reliability of sources (van Dijk 1991; Wodak, 2009: 320). Both the English and the French articles quote Jack Jedwab, who commissioned the Leger Marketing survey, at length, suggesting his credibility and reliability as a source of information. However, the quotations from Jedwab are notably different in English and French. While in English Jedwab is predominantly used as a source for determining the implications of these results and suggesting solutions, in French, Jedwab is primarily used as a source for explaining and interpreting the survey results.

Both the English and French articles use quotes from Jack Jedwab to summarise the survey findings. Although in the English quotation Jedwab highlights the "gigantic gap between francophones and non-francophones" and in the French quotation he notes the "unanimity among francophones", both summarise the different perspectives and ultimately convey the same information. However, in the French article, four different quotes from Jedwab are used to explain, rationalise, and interpret the survey findings in terms of both why French speakers are concerned about their language and why the perspectives of francophones and anglophones differ. With regard to the former, Jedwab cites two specific sources (Marc Termote's study and the "offensive" by the *Office québécois de la langue française*) that have had an "unquestionable impact" on public opinion (Example 4.18). With regard to the latter, Jedwab contextualises the different perspectives of anglophones and francophones (Examples 4.18–4.20).

Example 4.18 (Bélair-Cirino 2009)

«Les non-francophones ne voient pas la situation de la même manière. Dans leur esprit, le français progresse à travers la province [parce que la proportion de] non-francophones qui apprennent le français comme langue seconde [croît]», ajoute-t-il.

""Non-francophones don't see the situation in the same way. From their perspective, French is progressing across the province [because the proportion of] non-francophones learning French as a second language [is growing]," he added".

Example 4.19 (Bélair-Cirino 2009)

«Probablement parce que [les anglophones] ne comprennent pas à quel point la langue française est menacée», suppose Jack Jedwab.

""Probably because [anglophones] do not understand the extent to which the French language is threatened," assumes Jack Jedwab".

Example 4.20 (Bélair-Cirino 2009)

«Les anglophones ont le sentiment d'être minoritaires vis-à-vis de la situation de la langue française. Les francophones, eux, ont l'air de croire que les anglophones ne comprennent pas la situation de la langue française», fait savoir M. Jedwab.

""Anglophones have the feeling of being a minority when faced with the French language situation. Francophones, for their part, seem to believe that anglophones do not understand the French language situation," Mr. Jedwab explains".

In addition to the quotes from Jedwab, Bélair-Cirino provides five additional explanations for the survey results according to Alain-G. Gagnon of the *Centre de recherche interdisciplinaire sur la diversité au Québec*. Gagnon argues that francophones' perspectives on their language have been affected by the "weakness" (*mollesse*) of the Charest government and its inactivity on the language front, the failure of the Bloc Québécois to adopt certain language policies, the Harper government's apathetic approach to court challenges, culture funding cuts, and cuts to Radio-Canada. In sum, then, the French article includes information from two separate external sources to explain why French speakers might be concerned about their language and why the perspectives of francophones and anglophones differ.

In contrast, in the English article Jedwab is used only to provide one interpretation of the survey findings. This interpretation closely parallels Jedwab's summary of the survey findings and provides no new information or perspective on the situation. Rather, the quote from Jedwab simply restates that English speakers and French speakers have different perspectives (see Example 4.21).

Example 4.21 (Scott 2009)

The conflicting perceptions of the status of French reveals [sic] fault lines remain between language groups, Jedwab said.

This quote from Jedwab is the only approximation to an explanation by a substantiated source that English readers are provided. There are no other explanations, rationalisations, or interpretations—apart from the implication that French speakers become more concerned as the allophone population increases. Since the connection between francophone linguistic insecurity and the allophone population is unsubstantiated (see discussion above), and because Scott does not refer to any source for the claim, the data is questionable in terms of both its relevance and its origin. In sum, then, English readers are not provided explanations for the results of the Leger Marketing survey either in terms of why French speakers might be concerned about their language or in terms of why the perspectives of francophones and anglophones differ. In contrast, French readers are provided explanations for both.

The English article continues to cite Jedwab extensively, but the quotations are used to determine the implications and suggest solutions rather than explain the findings. Indeed most of his suggestions for solutions are uninventive (e.g. Jedwab calls for dialogue between anglophones and francophones) and repetitious, and the implications are simply predictions of future language tensions. Thus, even though Scott draws on Jedwab as a source extensively, there are no explanatory or interpretative statements, unlike in the French article where quotations serve to summarise, explain, contextualise, and interpret survey findings. Moreover, these quotations do not indicate that French is endangered.

Perhaps the most notable Jedwab quotation that is missing from the English article is Example 4.19: "[anglophones] do not understand the extent to which the French language is threatened". This quote explains that francophones and anglophones have different perspectives because anglophones do not understand the situation of the French language. Since this explanation is notably missing from the English article, and because there are no explanations for French linguistic insecurity apart from the increase in the allophone population, the effect of Scott's construal is such that francophones appear wary of, if not xenophobic towards, non-francophones. It is notable that Jedwab, who states in the French article that anglophones do not understand French language endangerment, is not solicited for similar comment in the English article.

Indeed, French language endangerment tends not to be presented as a credible issue in the English article, which begins with the lead "Is French threatened in Montreal?". Since the lead contains the most essential information of an article, it determines to some extent how article content is meant to be understood (Cotter 2010: 170; van Dijk 1991: 118). The function of this particular lead is that doubt is cast on the issue of French language endangerment. In addition, "the survival of French in Montreal" is described as "a perennial concern"—a description that arguably diminishes the impact and the importance of endangerment by presenting it as a regular affair. In sum, language endangerment is not presented as a pressing issue but rather as a perennial concern that francophones face alone—anglophones and immigrants/allophones do not believe the French language is threatened.

Attempts to discredit French language endangerment are not limited to this single article. Support for this finding can be found across the English corpus. For example, an editorial in *The Record* uses quotation strategies to question, if not deride, the very idea that the use of English at the St Jean Baptiste celebrations might constitute a "threat" (see Example 4.22).

Example 4.22 (McDevitt 2009)

A prime example of this has occurred as the sponsor of an "alternative" St-Jean-Baptiste Day celebration has decided that two English-language acts, scheduled to appear, may not do so because their presence might confuse people and pose a "threat" to the French language in Quebec.

The author of a letter to the editor in *The Gazette* also questions the idea of a threat to the French language, using modalisation, interjections, and rhetorical questions (see Example 4.23).

Example 4.23 (Moore 2009)

Did your article really say a bluegrass group and a country singer were banned from the St. Jean Baptiste Day celebrations because their singing in English would constitute a threat to the French language?

For crying out loud, the lyrics of bluegrass and country music are a threat to the English language. For that reason alone, they are wildly popular to English speakers.

In sum, two articles (Bélair-Cirino 2009; Marian Scott 2009c) provide different perspectives on language endangerment in Quebec and reflect ideologies of endangerment that appear to be reported in similar ways more widely throughout the English and French corpora. In the French article, the report of the Leger Marketing survey is used as a vehicle for the dissemination of ideologies of French language endangerment: French and English speakers' opinions on language endangerment differ because of recent events and findings that have revealed fractures in the French fabric of Montreal and also, at least in part, English speakers do not understand the extent to which French is threatened. In contrast, the English article begins by asking if French is threatened in Montreal, implying a binary, contestable outcome, and the question is never answered. French speakers' concerns over their language are not substantiated in the article, and instead they are framed as protectionist if not intolerant of speakers of other languages.

Importantly, the differences between these articles have serious implications: the English article (Marian Scott 2009c) is taken from *The Gazette,* one of the most widely circulated newspapers in Canada and the only English-language daily broadsheet published in Montreal, the second largest city in Canada. The perspective adopted in this article thus has a potentially wide audience. In addition, the three near-same versions were published on the same day elsewhere. At the time of publication (2009), all four newspapers were owned by the CanWest media conglomerate, which shared resources and wire stories. The other three newspapers besides *The Gazette* include a national newspaper (*National Post*), the only English daily broadsheet in the national capital (*Ottawa Citizen*), and the only daily broadsheet published in Vancouver—Canada's third largest city (*Vancouver Sun*). In other words, three of these newspapers are "hegemonic" dailies (i.e. with no direct or comparable competition in their immediate location), and the other is one of only two national newspapers. All four have large readerships, and thus the perspective of the single article just examined has a much wider audience than it would initially seem. Thus, while English readers may have their suspicions about Quebec confirmed in their newspapers, French readers in Quebec might find the *Le Devoir* article and its assumptions unproblematic—indeed, French readers may be reassured in their perspective on language endangerment, or even have their linguistic concerns heightened by the article.

As a result, these differences between French and English Canadian newspapers suggest "how newspapers with different audiences, identities, political commitments and hence editorial policies mediate the information they receive" (Richardson 2007: 106–107). The impact of this mediation is that newspapers publish a guided perspective. The articles can plausibly lead to misunderstandings between English speakers and French speakers or reinforcement of positions. Indeed, a report on the divide between anglophones' and francophones' perspectives on language may result in a deeper divide.

4.4 Conclusion

The aim of this chapter was to identify language ideologies emerging from English and French Canadian newspaper data. Findings demonstrated that, in English, language issues tended to not be discussed but when they were discussed, French was the focus not English. These findings seem to suggest the presence of monolingual ideologies, which contribute to naturalising an understanding of Canada as an English-speaking (and not bilingual) country. Such an understanding is underscored through discussions of immigration, wherein the importance of English, and not French (the other official language), is made explicit. When languages (and not just English or French) were discussed, it was most often with reference to fluency and education in languages, or with reference to languages being used in international contexts. These representations suggest the presence of instrumental language ideologies, that is, the belief that language(s) are assets or commodities to be deployed. The data did not indicate that languages were viewed as cultural entities valuable to specific social groups or that less "useful" languages should be protected or promoted. Instead, in several instances it seemed that the "usefulness" of languages was seen to trump other social functions.

Although the French newspapers showed some similarities to the English newspapers, there were also significant differences. First, there was some evidence of monolingual ideologies, but in a way very different from the English Canadian newspapers. While in the latter case, monolingual ideologies tended to be unmarked and the importance of English appeared to be presumed, in the case of French Canadian newspapers, the importance of French tended to be explicit throughout. However, the importance of French was particularly salient with reference to the province of Quebec and not the entire country. Similarly, there appeared to be some presence of instrumental language ideologies, but only with reference to the English language; these were also not as salient as in the English Canadian newspapers. Instead, what tended to predominate were ideologies of language as a core value, which foregrounded the importance of the French language as an identity pillar, and ideologies of endangerment, which underpinned concerns over the status and future of the French language in the province. The salience of these language ideologies, which rely on the premise that the language is symbolic of the group and its existence and therefore must be protected, is markedly different from the English Canadian newspapers, wherein instrumental language ideologies stressed the utilitarian value of languages.

This divide between language ideologies in the English and French Canadian newspapers was particularly clear in the case of the English newspapers' representation of French language endangerment. This example indicated that doubt was cast on the veracity of concerns over endangerment, and there appeared to be little indication that research had been undertaken to verify whether the language was, indeed, under threat. This example, along with others within the corpus, suggests the incommensurability of instrumental language ideologies and ideologies of language endangerment. If language is valued because it is useful, then how can it be understood if it is under threat from lack of use? This gap between English and French Canadian newspapers' language ideologies suggests why the "two solitudes" may continue to persist in Canadian society. With a lack of exposure not only to languages but also to alternative language ideologies, for example, through the media system, groups may find it difficult to comprehend one another, not only literally but also culturally. Since the Canadian print media systems have long existed in parallel in English and French with little interaction and exchange (see Chap. 2), we will explore the potential for overcoming the solitudes with the media system in the online world in subsequent chapters.

References

Anonymous. (2009a, 4 July). Divine liturgy to be held tomorrow. *Moncton Times & Transcript*, p. E6.

Anonymous. (2009b, 22 June). Francophone Montrealers fear loss of their language. *Vancouver Sun*, p. B4.

Anonymous. (2009c, 1 July). Vigilance essential for French. *Toronto Star*, p. A17.

Aubry, J. (2009, 19 June). Le plus grand vin canadien? *Le Devoir*, p. B6.

Baker, P. (2010). *Sociolinguistics and corpus linguistics*. Edinburgh: Edinburgh University Press.

Beauchemin, J. (2006). La protection de la langue et de l'identité collective comme enjeu au sein de la conscience historique québécoise. In M. Pagé & P. Georgeault (Eds.), *Le Français, langue de la diversité québécoise: Une réflexion pluridisciplinaire* (pp. 131–151). Montréal: Québec Amérique.

Bélair-Cirino, M. (2009, 22 June). Le français à Montréal: 90% des francophones sont inquiets. *Le Devoir*, p. A1.

Blackledge, A. (2000). Monolingual ideologies in multilingual states: Language, hegemony and social justice in Western liberal democracies. *Estudios de Sociolingüística, 1*(2), 25–45.

Blackledge, A. (2002). The discursive construction of national identity in multilingual Britain. *Journal of Language, Identity and Education, 1*(1), 67–87.

Blanchette, J. (2009, 19 June). Deux longs mois à tuer. *Le Devoir*, p. B10.

Blatchford, C., & Leeder, J. (2009, 20 June). Did we push her too much? *The Globe and Mail*, p. A1.

Blommaert, J., & Verschueren, J. (1998). The role of language in European nationalist ideologies. In B. B. Schieffelin, K. A. Woolard, & P. V. Kroskrity (Eds.), *Language ideologies. Practice and theory* (pp. 189–210). Oxford: Oxford University Press.

Bouchard, G. (1997). Ourvrir le cercle de la nation. Activer la cohésion sociale. *Réflexion sur le Québec et sa diversité. L'Action nationale, 87*(4), 107–137.

Bouchard, C. (2002). *La langue et le nombril: Histoire d'une obsession québécoise.* Montreal: Fides.

Boudreau, A. (2011). La nomination du français en Acadie : parcours et enjeux. In J. Morency, J. de Finney, & H. Destrempes (Eds.), *L'Acadie des origines: mythes et figurations d'un parcours littéraire et historique* (pp. 71–94). Sudbury: Éditions Prise de parole.

Boudreau, A., & Dubois, L. (2007). *Français, acadien, acadjonne*: Competing discourses on language preservation along the shores of the Baie Sainte-Marie. In M. Heller & A. Duchêne (Eds.), *Discourses of endangerment: Ideology and interest in the defence of languages* (pp. 99–120). London: Continuum.

Boudreau, A., & Urbain, É. (2014). La presse comme tribune d'un discours d'autorité sur la langue: représentations et idéologies linguistiques dans la presse acadienne, de la fondation du Moniteur Acadien aux Conventions nationales. *Francophonies d'Amérique, 35* (*Les journaux des communautés francophones minoritaires en Amérique du Nord*, Ed. D. Laporte), 23–46.

Boyer, H. (2001). L'*unilinguisme* français contre le changement sociolinguistique. *Travaux neuchâtelois de linguistique, 34*(35), 383–392.

Bucholtz, M. (2003). Sociolinguistic nostalgia and the authentification of identity. *Journal of Sociolinguistics, 7*(4), 399–416.

Cardinal, L. (2008). Linguistic peace: A time to take stock. *Inroads, 23*, 62–70.

Cloutier, M. (2009, 3 July). Minuit, le soir en français de France. *La Presse*, Arts et spectacles, p. 10.

Corbella, L. (2009, 4 July). No surprise burka-clad women didn't write in. *Calgary Herald*, p. A8.

Cornellier, L. (2009, 27 June). Pierre Falardeau et son Elvis. *Le Devoir*, p. E5.

Cotter, C. (2010). *News talk: Investigating the language of journalism.* Cambridge: Cambridge University Press.

Delaney, G. (2009, 17 June). New Canadians sworn in. *The Chronicle-Herald*, p. A12.

DiGiacomo, S. M. (1999). Language ideological debates in an Olympic city: Barcelona 1992–1996. In J. Blommaert (Ed.), *Language ideological debates* (pp. 105–142). Berlin: Mouton de Gruyter.

Dubuc, P. (2009, 22 June). La victoire des maîtres chanteurs. *Le Devoir*, p. A7.

Eloy, J.-M. (1998). Légitimité et légitisme linguistique: Questions théoriques et pratiques d'idéologie linguistique. *Révue québécoise de linguistique, 26*(2), 43–54.

Ferenczy, M. (2009, 3 July). Broader opportunities. *Ottawa Citizen*, p. A9.

Fralic, S. (2009, 30 June). O Canada, our home and disparate land. *Vancouver Sun*, p. A1.

Francard, M. (1998). La légitimité linguistique passe-t-elle par la reconnaissance d'une variété "nationale"? Le cas de la communauté française de Wallonie-Bruxelles. *Révue québécoise de linguistique, 26*(2), 13–23.

Garvin, P. (1993). A conceptual framework for the study of language standardization. *International Journal of the Sociology of Language, 100*(101), 37–54.

Havrankova. J. (2009, 22 June). Apprendre le français, un privilège. *Le Devoir*, p. A6.

Heller, M. (1990). French immersion in Canada: a model for Switzerland? *Multilingua, 9*(1), 67–85.

Heller, M. (1995). Language choice, social institution, and symbolic domination. *Language in Society, 24*(3), 373–405.

Heller, M. (2003a). Actors and discourses in the construction of hegemony. *Pragmatics, 13*(1), 11–31.

Heller, M. (2003b). Globalization, the new economy, and the commodification of language and identity. *Journal of Sociolinguistics, 7*(4), 473–492.

Heller, M., & Duchêne, A. (2007). Discourses of endangerment: Sociolinguistics, globalization and social order. In A. Duchêne & M. Heller (Eds.), *Discourses of endangerment: Ideology and interest in the defence of languages* (pp. 1–13). London: Continuum.

Howlett, K. (2009, 17 June). French schools will be available to more students. *The Globe and Mail*, p. A12.

Jaffe, A. (1999). Locating power: Corsican translators and their critics. In J. Blommaert (Ed.), *Language ideological debates* (pp. 39–66). Berlin: Mouton de Gruyter.

Jaspers, J., & Verschueren, J. (2011). Multilingual structures and agencies. *Journal of Pragmatics, 43*, 1157–1160.

Kariel, H. G., & Rosenvall, L. A. (1983). Cultural affinity displayed in Canadian daily newspapers. *Journalism Quarterly, 60*(3), 431–436.

Karim, K. H. (1993). Construction, deconstructions, and reconstructions: Competing Canadian discourses on ethnocultural terminology. *Canadian Journal of Communication, 18*(2). Retrieved from http://www.cjc-online.ca/index.php/journal/article/viewArticle/744/650

Kasuya, K. (2001). Discourses of linguistic dominance: A historical consideration of French language ideology. *International Review of Education, 47*(3–4), 235–251.

Kulyk, V. (2010). Ideologies of language use in post-Soviet Ukrainian media. *International Journal of the Sociology of Language, 201*(1), 79–104.

Kymlicka, W., & Patten, A. (2003). Language rights and political theory. *Annual Review of Applied Linguistics, 23*, 3–21.

Lawrence, G. (2009, 20 June). De l'évanescence à l'efferevescence. *Le Devoir*, p. D1.

Le Bouthillier, C. (2009, 25 June). Le Grand Caraquet—suite. *L'Acadie Nouvelle*, p. 13.

Lévesque, R. (1968[1997]). *René Lévesque: Mot à mot* (Citations colligées par Rémi Maillard). Montreal: Les Éditions internationals Alain Stanké.

Lisée, J. F. (2007). *Nous*. Montreal: Boréal.

Lockerbie, I. (2005). The debate on l'amenagement du français in Québec. In I. Lockerbie, I. Molnaro, K. Larose, & L. Oakes (Eds.), *French as the common language in Québec: History, debates and positions* (pp. 15–65). Québec: Éditions nota bene.

Lodge, R. A. (1993). *French, from dialect to standard*. London: Routledge.

Lüdi, G. (1992). French as a pluricentric language. In M. Clyne (Ed.), *Pluricentric languages: Differing norms in different nations* (pp. 149–178). Berlin: Mouton de Gruyter.

Lussier, M. A. (2009a, 4 July). De père en flic. *La Presse*, p. Cinema 2.

Lussier, M. A. (2009b, 5 June). L'appartement de Marc-André. *La Presse*, Arts et spectacles, p. 5.

Mazerolle, B. (2009, 25 June). The quintessential Canadian. *Moncton Times & Transcript*, p. A1.

McDevitt, M. (2009, 16 June). For all the world to see. *The Record*, p. 6.

Meurice, P. (2009, 7 July). Pauvres touristes. *La Presse*, p. A13.

Milroy, J. (2001). Language ideologies and the consequences of standardization. *Journal of Sociolinguistics, 5*(4), 530–555.

Moïse, C. (2007). Protecting French: The view from France. In M. Heller & A. Duchêne (Eds.), *Discourses of endangerment: Ideology and interest in the defence of languages* (pp. 216–241). London: Continuum.

Moore, D. (2009, 17 June). Threat to whom? *The Gazette*, p. a20.

Nolen, S. (2009, 19 June). India's gay community fights for 'dignity'. *The Globe and Mail*, p. A16.

Oakes, L. (2010). Lambs to the slaughter? Young francophones and the role of English in Quebec today. *Multilingua, 29*, 265–288.

Oakes, L., & Warren, J. (2007). *Language, citizenship and identity in Quebec*. Basingstoke/England/New York: Palgrave Macmillan.

Pacini-Ketchabaw, V., & de Almeida, A. E. (2006). Language discourses and ideologies at the heart of early childhood education. *International Journal of Bilingual Education and Bilingualism, 9*(3), 310–341.

Pöll, B. (2005). *Le français langue pluricentrique? Études sur la variation diatopique d'une langue standard*. Berlin: Frankfurt am Main.

Ravindran, M. (2009, 30 June). How to speed immigrants' entry into the workforce. *Vancouver Sun*, p. A10.

Rea, J. M. (2006). *Ideologies of language: Authority, consensus and commonsense in Canadian talk about usage* (Unpublished PhD Thesis, Simon Fraser University). Retrieved from: Summit.sfu.ca/system/files/iritems1/2863/etd2355.pdf

Richardson, J. E. (2007). *Analysing newspapers: An approach from critical discourse analysis*. Basingstoke: Palgrave.

Rioux, C. (2009, 3 July). Full bilingue. *Le Devoir*, p. A3.

Sarfati, S. (2009, 8 July). Marie Laberge dans le Larousse. *La Presse,* Arts et spectacles, p. 6. Available http://www.cyberpresse.ca/arts/livres/200907/08/01-882260-marie-laberge-dans-le-larousse.php

Schieffelin, B. B., & Doucet, R. C. (1998). The "real" Haitian creole: Ideology, metalinguistics, and orthographic choice. In B. B. Schieffelin, K. A. Woolard, & P. V. Kroskrity (Eds.), *Language ideologies. Practice and theory* (pp. 285–316). Oxford: Oxford University Press.

Scott, M. (2009). In search of a bad reference corpus. In D. Archer (Ed.), *What's in a word-list? Investigating word frequency and keyword extraction* (pp. 79–92). Oxford: Ashgate.

Scott, M. (2009a, 22 June). French threatened in Montreal, poll finds. *National Post*, p. A6.

Scott, M. (2009b, 22 June). Quebecers split over threat to French in Montreal. *The Ottawa Citizen*, p. A5.

Simpson, P. (1993). *Language, ideology and point of view*. London: Routledge.

Smolicz, J. J. (1999). In M. Secombe & J. Zajda (Eds.), *J. J. Smolicz on education and culture.* Albert Park: James Nicholas Publishers Pty Ltd.

Stark, A. (1992). English-Canadian opposition to Quebec nationalism. In R. Kent Weaver (Ed.), *The collapse of Canada?* (pp. 123–157). Washington: The Brookings Institution.

Valpy, M. (2009, 27 June). The emperor and the tennis pro. *The Globe and Mail*, p. A1.

Van Dijk, T. A. (1991). *Racism and the press*. London: Routledge.

Van Leeuwen, T. (2003[1996]). The representation of social actors. In C. R. Caldas-Coulthard & M. Coulthard (Eds.), *Readings in critical discourse analysis* (pp. 32–70). London: Routledge.

Vigor, J. C. (2009, 20 June). Cet art qu'est la composition florale. *Le Devoir*, p. D6.

Vipond, M. (2008). One network or two? French-language programming on the Canadian Radio Broadcasting Commission, 1932–36. *The Canadian Historical Review, 89*(3), 319–343.

Wai, V. (2009, 18 June). Discrimination and Asian actresses. *National Post*, p. A21.

York, G. (2009, 15 July). Sterilized, stigmatized. *The Globe and Mail*, p. A7.

5

Language Ideologies in Online News and Commentary: The Case of the Vancouver Olympics

In the previous chapter, we examined language ideologies in Canadian newspapers within a period of relative "linguistic peace", which established the ideologies that tend to be embedded in quotidian Canadian discourse. However, ideologies are sometimes inflamed and exaggerated during times of national and linguistic crisis (Cardinal, 2008: 63; cf. Billig, 1995: 109), particularly in countries like Canada, where beliefs about language, the nation, and the state are firmly intertwined. According to Blommaert (1999b: 1), language ideological debates are "debates … in which language is central as a topic, a motif, a target, and in which language ideologies are being articulated, formed, amended, enforced". In other words, these are situations that have been transformed into public forums wherein languages serve as contested or contestable subjects.

As we recall from Chap. 2, Canada is an officially bilingual country. While this status reinforces English and French at the federal level, both languages do not necessarily have equal status at the provincial level from coast to coast. Most provinces and territories are English-dominant, with the exception of Quebec, where 78 % of the population has French as a first language and the official language is French, and New Brunswick,

R. Vessey, *Language and Canadian Media*,
DOI 10.1057/978-1-137-53001-1_5

whose population is approximately 30 % French-speaking and is officially bilingual (see Sect. 2.1). The status of French in Canada and its unequal distribution across the country mean that bilingualism in Canada often raises issues of regional identities. More specifically, given that Quebec is the heartland of Canadian French speakers, it—and French—is often marked as different from the rest of the country. Indeed, although French has only ever been spoken in large numbers in Central and Eastern Canada, federal bilingual policies ensure its privileged status across the country, which has led some Western Canadians—in addition to those of non-English and non-French descent—to feel that they are not adequately represented in the Canadian Federation.

This type of regionalism is both a fundamental defining feature of Canadian identity and a powerful dividing element (Taylor 1993: 104); crucially, regionalism can be directly linked to issues pertaining to official languages. For example, Vipond (1996: 190) notes that Western Canada historically opposed bilingualism policies in Canada, and Nurse (2003: 54) observes a rising tide of Western Canadians in favour of separatism:

> Current studies indicate that a sense of regional alienation and frustration has increased in Western Canada over the last few years and journalistic reports suggest that some measure of this frustration is leading some Western Canadians to consider separatism as a potential political option.

Thus, although the objective of the bilingualism policies was to create a national allegiance that was unconditioned by membership in any single community, it could be that many Western Canadians are unable to "see themselves" in the bilingual image that Canada projects to the world.

In 2010, Canada hosted the Winter Olympics in Vancouver, a city perched on the edge of the Pacific Ocean and far removed from the historic political and geographic hub of the country—Ontario and Quebec. When Vancouver was chosen to host the Olympics, the Canadian government agreed to contribute financially through the Ministry of Canadian Heritage, and a clause in the financial agreement ensured that the opening ceremony would take into account the obligations set out in the Official Languages Act (Office of the Commissioner 2010: 42). However, immediately after the event, members of the public, politicians, and officials alike noted an insufficient amount of French during the ceremonies.

These were not the first Olympic Games to face criticisms over language, nor the first in which such criticisms were aired in the media. DiGiacomo (1999) illustrates the language ideological debates surrounding the 1992 Olympic Games in Barcelona and the "sequels" of debates that lasted into 1996. As in Barcelona, the debate in Canada focuses on the question of "[w]hose Olympic Games were these?" (DiGiacomo 1999: 106). In the same way that Catalan is a symbol of Catalonian identity, French, alongside English, is a symbol of Canadian identity. Commentators saw the Vancouver Olympics as an opportunity to show the world "what Canada is all about" (CTVMontreal 2010).

This chapter examines the perceptions of and responses to the Vancouver Olympics opening ceremonies of 2010 according to accounts and opinions published in national newspapers. More specifically, it aims to investigate how English and French Canadian journalists and commentators reported on and/or responded to this language ideological debate. The chapter proceeds as follows: Sect. 5.1 presents the data used for this particular study and provides details about how they were analysed, Sect. 5.2 presents the findings (first from the articles under examination and then the commentaries), and then Sect. 5.3 summarises the findings.

5.1 Data and Methods

In order to continue with the aims presented in Chap. 1 (i.e. comparing and contrasting French and English Canadian language ideologies), English and French national newspapers were both selected as data for analysis. As noted in Chap. 2, the English newspaper *The Globe and Mail*, published in Toronto, is Canada's most widely read national newspaper with the second highest circulation in the country after the Toronto-based *Toronto Star* (Newspapers Canada 2010). It is widely recognised as liberal and left wing in its political orientation and a supporter of Canadian federalism (Gagnon 2003: 78; Retzlaff and Gänzle 2008: 84). In addition to the four articles from *The Globe and Mail*, one article was taken from CTVMontreal, which in 2010 was a branch of the CTV-Globemedia media company alongside *The Globe and Mail* newspaper. Much of the content was shared across branches, for example, through the website http://ctv.theglobeandmail.com. Five articles were also taken from the French newspaper *Le Devoir*, based in Montreal. Although distributed mostly in Quebec, here *Le Devoir* is considered a national newspaper due to its content, perspective, and the fact that it has been argued to promote Quebec nationalism (Gagnon 2003: 78).[1]

Crucially, the data for this chapter differ from the articles examined in Chap. 4, which were taken from print versions of newspapers. Here, the articles were collected from the relevant online news websites, which allow for greater interaction with readers through, for example, commentary. Online commentary can usefully serve as a "supplement" to original texts (e.g. newspaper articles) that can help to situate them within larger discourse contexts (O'Halloran 2011). A study of a text's situatedness can help to clarify the tension within and between discourses on certain topics. Analysing the similarities and differences between an original text and its "supplement" can also help to explain how meanings continue to be "hidden" within texts and may be remarked or unremarked upon by readers, depending on the discourse context (see O'Halloran 2011: 800). The use of corpus linguistics to study a text's "supplement" can also help circumvent the subjectivity of a researcher's individual "logico-rhetorical" module in analysis (O'Halloran 2011). In other words, any person making an argument may presume a certain degree of shared knowledge with his/her interlocutor. By comparing the way a topic is formulated in the original argument with the way it is constructed within a response from the reader or listener, we can start to understand what has been included or excluded (or repressed or marginalised) from the original or from mainstream discussions about this topic.

The selection criteria for articles included (1) the time period and (2) demonstrable public interest. The first criterion involved choosing five articles in each language that were published soon after the opening

[1] The editorial standpoint of these newspapers (Canadian federalism in *The Globe and Mail* and Quebec nationalism in *Le Devoir*) should be borne in mind with regard to findings. The largest French Canadian daily newspaper (*La Presse*) is federalist-leaning but was not selected because access to online comments was unavailable.

ceremonies, which took place on 12 February 2010. The second criterion involved establishing which articles sparked the most reactions in the online reader commentary. The five English articles sparked 1046 comments from readers, with the most (474) posted in reaction to a single text (Gagnon 2010). The French articles sparked fewer comments (95), likely due to the relatively smaller readership of *Le Devoir* (189,517 weekly circulation average compared to 1,906,686; Newspapers Canada 2010). In total, the corpus of English commentaries consists of over 106,000 words, while the corpus of French commentaries consists of just over 14,000 words.

The ten French and English articles were compared and contrasted using a combined corpus and discourse approach to the study of language ideology (see Chap. 3). Specifically, identity labels, social categorisation, perspectival strategies, intertextuality, cohesion, and topoi were compared and contrasted across the articles. In addition, the commentaries were also analysed using the same methods, and these were then compared against the findings from the articles.

5.2 Results

Results show a number of similarities and differences between representations of the opening ceremonies in English and French. We begin by presenting the differences between the English and French articles and then turn to the similarities between them. In Sect. 5.2.2, we turn to the small number of similarities between the English and French news commentary before turning to the differences between them. Section 5.2.3 summarises these findings and assesses the consistency of findings across the articles and their related news commentary.

5.2.1 Articles

Two of the ten selected articles, published on the same day (15 February), served as platforms for individual speakers, whose privileged positions enabled them to serve as "ideology brokers"—that is, social actors who claim authority in the field of debate (Blommaert 1999b: 9). In French, one article summarised an interview with then-Parti Québécois leader Pauline Marois (Canadian Press 2010). In English, an article summarised statements made by then-Canadian Heritage Minister James Moore (Taber 2010). These different individuals were the central focus of the articles and were cited extensively, and in the French article, no one but Marois was cited. Notably, each individual had different vested interests in language issues. While in 2010 Moore was a Cabinet minister of the Canadian federal government whose ministry contributed financially to the opening ceremonies, Marois' party is a separatist political party and, in 2010, the official provincial opposition.

In the articles, the messages from these public figures are diametrically opposed: while Moore is cited as arguing that it is time to "move on" from debates about French and the Olympics, Marois argues at length that both Canada and the Quebec Premier (Jean Charest) failed French speakers during the ceremonies. The contrast between the two is evident in the headlines, which distil the most important message of each article (Bell 1998: 83; van Dijk 1991: 51). In French, Marois is cited as accusing Canada of showing unacceptable scorn for francophones (*"Le Canada a affiché tout son mépris envers les francophones", accuse Marois*), whereas the headline in English article cites Moore's claim that the "[l]ack of French at [the] Olympic opening [was] 'no big deal'".

In the Canadian Press article, Marois refers to concerns over the future of French (*l'avenir du français au Canada*), and argues that the Quebec Premier should have defended French. These arguments pertain to another theme across three of the five French articles: language endangerment (see Heller and Duchêne 2007; Sect. 4.3.4). Similar to Marois' call for the defence of French, in another article, the Secretary General of the International Organisation of la Francophonie Abdou Diouf is cited as calling for unyieldingness in the "protection" of French (*son appel à l'intransigeance [...] pour protéger le français*) (Boileau 2010a). The same article evokes fears of decline through reference to Quebecers' ever decreasing proportion of the Canadian population and a comparison of the status of French in Vancouver with the status of French in the former French colony of Louisiana (*Cela n'a-t-il pas* [...] *des airs de Louisiane?*). In another article, French is described as a "dead language" in Vancouver (*Vancouver, où le français est une langue morte*) (Boileau 2010b).

Language endangerment is also evoked through linguistic battle metaphors, which occur in both of the aforementioned articles. It is argued that Diouf's "call to not wave the white flag" (*[s]on appel à ne pas baisser les bras*) must be heard because "in this bilingual country, it was a hard battle for French to have its place" (*dans ce pays bilingue, il fallait batailler ferme pour que le français ait sa place!*) (Boileau 2010a). The "continuous conflict" is described as "petty" (*la mesquinerie de cette lutte continuelle*) (Boileau 2010a). Another article (Boileau 2010b) describes the eventual inclusion of the French song in the opening ceremonies as an achievement that was "hard-fought" (*de haute lutte*) and "the kind of battle that makes one tremble" (*ce genre de bataille qui fait frémir*) (Boileau 2010b). Although ideologies of language endangerment permeate three of the five French articles, this is not the case in any of the English articles.

Another difference between the English and French articles consists of the use of first-person plural deictics "we", "our", and "us" in the English articles and the use of the equivalents *nous, notre,* and *nos* in the French articles. Deictics such as these are important in considerations of group identities and "in-group" and "out-group" boundary markers (De Cillia et al. 1999: 163–166) in part because they enable authors to "genericise" and "collectivise" above and beyond intragroup differences (van Leeuwen 2003 [1996]: 46–50). In English, there is an average of two first-person plural deictics per article as compared to an average of four in the French articles. While these numbers reflect the small data set, it is notable that most English deictics occur in statements given by people from Quebec. For example, Quebec Premier Jean Charest is reported as saying that "everyone would have liked to see more French in the ceremony [...] that [is] what *we'd* like to see during the rest of the Games" (CTVMontreal 2010, emphasis added). The same article also quotes talk radio host Benoît Dutrisac as saying to federal Liberal critic for official languages Denis Coderre, "They don't give a damn about *us*. That's *your* Canada" (CTVMontreal 2010, emphasis added). Finally, *La Presse* sports columnist Réjean Tremblay is quoted as writing that "*we* were not where *we* belong; it was *their* party" (Anderson 2010, emphasis added). In addition, in the French articles most deictics are used to refer to Quebecers.

Pauline Marois uses five deictics to refer to French-speaking Quebecers. For example, she is quoted as saying "That means that [...] *we* are a negligible quantity, that *we* are unimportant or even that *we* are a weight" (emphasis added) ("*Cela veut dire que [...] nous sommes une quantité négligeable, que nous ne sommes pas importants et à la limite, que nous sommes un poids*") (Presse Canadienne 2010). In other examples, it is argued that Abdou Diouf need not tiptoe around "our" political dynamics when discussing the Olympics (*Abdou Diouf [...] n'a pas à ménager les susceptibilités propres à notre dynamique politique quand il parle des Jeux olympiques*) (Boileau 2010a). The same article continues, "here, this reality [of linguistic inequality] surprise[d] no one: *we* all know that a French reflex [...] can never, ever be taken for granted" (emphasis added) (*[i]ci, cette réalité ne surprend personne: nous savons tous que le recours au français [...] ne va jamais, jamais de soi*). In this instance, the deictic "here" refers to a place where people ("we") are conscious of the real status of French, which is certainly Quebec, home of French language advocates in Canada. In another article (Boileau 2010b), a similar deictic is used to discuss Quebecers, who are called "people from here" (*les gens d'ici*). There is only one English example of a first-person plural deictic being used outside of a quotation to refer to social groups: in the *Globe* editorial, French and English are described as "both *our* official languages" (emphasis added). In sum, then, most first-person plural deictics in the English and the French articles originate in quotations from Quebecers. The pervasiveness of deictics to index French-speaking Quebecers suggests the discursive construction of a homogeneous French-speaking Quebec collective, to which no parallel seems to exist in terms of an English-speaking or bilingual collective.

Related to this point is the issue of homogeneity and heteroglossia across the articles (on heteroglossia in the media, see Busch 2006). The relatively homogeneous version of Quebec that is suggested by the use of first-person plural deictics is in fact consistent with the content of the articles. All five French articles are consistent in terms of arguing that not enough French was spoken. Three of the five articles allude to language endangerment and most portray a lack of surprise that French was forgotten. For example, one article reports that the Bloc Québécois were "extremely shocked" by the opening ceremonies, but "not surprised" (*Au Bloc québécois, on se montre "extrêmement choqué" par la situation, mais "pas surpris"*) (Bourgault-Côté 2010). In contrast, the English articles are divided both in terms of the assessment of the French content and in terms of French speakers' reaction to the opening ceremonies. For example, while one article focuses on the fact that the lack of French was "no big deal" (Taber 2010), another consistently mocks reactions to the opening ceremonies in the French press (Anderson 2010). The latter, entitled "Vancouver Games quickly turn sour for Quebec", contrasts the Olympic spirit "alive and well" in Vancouver with the "altogether different story in the Quebec press" (Anderson 2010). The reaction to the "not-quite-French-enough" ceremony is described as "immediate outrage" and "a collective uproar". The article contains predominantly negative evaluative lexis throughout to describe the lack of French and also French speakers themselves. Beyond the demands and fury cited in the article, French speakers and the French media are "concern[ed]", "worried", "quick to criticize", "disappointed", and "shocked". This trend of representing French speakers as emotional—and moreover, unhappy—is consistent with another article, the focus of which is the dissatisfaction reported by French speakers (CTVMontreal 2010). Indeed, the text is cohered by echoes of the same refrain of people talking about their feelings—which are predominantly negative (see Fig. 5.1).

These consistent reports of French speakers' unhappy emotions portray the issue of French during the Olympic opening ceremonies as

"say they feel slighted"
"said he enjoyed"
"was disappointed"
"said he felt"
"said they felt left out"
"can't say I felt included"
"expressed dissatisfaction"
"It was a big disappointment [... said Veronique]"
"echoed those sentiments"

Fig. 5.1 Expressions of disappointment from CTVMontreal (2010)

emotional—rather than political, or a question of rights. Furthermore, the depiction of French speakers as vocally emotional contributes to an overall negative image. Rather than being politically engaged Canadian citizens concerned over the content of a taxpayer-funded event, they are depicted as individuals who complain about hurt feelings, rejection, exclusion, and dissatisfaction. Since an important news value is objectivity and emotions are inherently subjective, the representation of French speakers as emotional arguably detracts from or misrepresents the newsworthiness of the Olympic language issue (on newsworthiness, see Cotter 2010: 68–70).

Although there are some consistent negative representations amongst three English articles, there are also positive representations in the two other English articles. These advocate the role of French in Canada and lament its relative absence during the opening ceremonies. The headline of the *Globe* editorial, for example, is “Les jeux du Canada”. This use of French in the headline foreshadows the advocacy of French throughout the article. French is described as “one of Canada’s two official languages”, “one of the official languages of the Olympic movement”, and importantly, the coexistence of the two languages is described as “a basic, continuing reality in Canadian life”. There is no doubt placed on the status of French; rather, it is described as “Canada’s French fact”. The argument is that “any celebration of Canadian history, identity and nationhood must give equal pride of place to French”. Similarly, another article advocates the role of French in Canada and describes French as “the other language of an officially bilingual country”, citing the Prime Minister as saying that “Canada as we know it was born in French” (Gagnon 2010). In sum, although three of the five English articles downplay the issue of French during the opening ceremonies and negatively represent French speakers as vocally emotional, two other articles advocate the use of French and its role in Canada. In contrast, the French articles are unanimous about the need for French during the ceremonies.

Despite the important differences noted so far, there are also similarities between the English and French articles. For example, nearly all articles in both languages privilege discussions of French but rarely discuss English. While this might seem understandable in a debate over the adequacy of French content at the Vancouver opening ceremonies, there is little discussion of which language *was* used in the ceremonies. For example, the opening sentence of one article discusses how the federal government was "disappointed" (*déçu*) by the weak presence of French during the opening ceremonies, but it is not stated until nearly halfway through the article that "the majority of the ceremony took place in English" (*l'essentiel du spectacle s'est déroulé en anglais*) (Bourgault-Côté 2010). Similarly, other articles refer to the lack of French but imply rather than state explicitly that the ceremonies took place in English: the ellipsis suggests the normative status of the English language. Throughout all five English articles, while there are 58 references to French ("French", "francophone/s"), with an average of 12 references per article, there are only 11 references to English ("English", "anglophone/s"), with an average of two references per article. In the 5 French articles, while there are 51 references to French (*français/e/s, francophone/s*), with an average of 10 per article, there are only 7 references to English (*anglais/e/s, anglophones*), with an average of 2 per article. English is only mentioned in four out of the five English articles and only three out of the five French articles. The implication is that even though a "lack of French" entails a "surplus of English", English is not discussed: its status is naturalised and embedded throughout all articles, suggesting not only monolingual ideologies but also what might be a larger issue of widespread anglonormativity (see Mackey 2002).

Another similarity in both the English and French articles is that bilingualism is an inconsistent theme. In one French article (Boileau 2010a), bilingualism is discussed in three instances; in another (Bourgault-Côté 2010), it is a major theme. In the other three French articles, though, there are no mentions of bilingualism at all. In contrast, no single English article has "bilingualism" as a major theme, but four of the five articles mention bilingualism at least once. Bilingualism is also discussed in different ways in most articles. While it provides the backdrop in terms of Canada's official languages for the linguistic provisions in the Olympics, it is often discussed in terms of its artifice because in most cases people, places, and events are not bilingual like they officially "should" be. Indeed, Canada's official bilingualism is contrasted in numerous articles with the country's linguistic reality (see Box 5.1).

Box 5.1: Discussions of the "Reality" of Canadian Languages in Boileau (2010a)

1. *Un pari bien ambitieux au regard de la **réalité**, comme s'en inquiète avec justesse le secrétaire général de la Francophonie*

   "An ambitious wager with regard to the **reality**, which worries the Secretary General of La Francophonie"

2. *"je me suis trouvé confronté à une **réalité** à laquelle je ne m'attendais pas"*

   "I found myself confronted with a **reality** I didn't expect"

3. *Ici, cette **réalité** ne surprend personne: nous savons tous que le recours au français dans ce grand Canada ne va jamais, jamais de soi*

   "Here, this **reality** surprises no one: we all know that a French reflex can never, ever be taken for granted"

4. *Mais pour le moment, il y a loin de la coupe aux lèvres. Le commissaire Fraser craignait, de façon **réaliste**, le "manque de réflexe" en faveur du français sur le terrain*

   "But for the moment, there's many a slip twixt cup and lip. [Official Languages] Commissioner Fraser feared, **realistically**, the 'lack of a French reflex' on the ground"

In sum, bilingualism does not seem to serve a stable role across English or French articles. While at times Canada's official bilingualism is used as a *topos* for the use of French at the Olympics (Bourgault-Côté 2010; *Globe* editorial 2010), in other cases (e.g. Boileau 2010a; Gagnon 2010) bilingualism is represented as a façade presented to the world that disguises the monolingual reality beneath.

The final finding that will be discussed pertains to similarities in the argument structure across all of the articles. Each article that was selected discussed, albeit to varying extents, the use of French at the Vancouver Olympic opening ceremonies. However, in many cases this topic becomes conflated with other topics of Canada–Quebec relations and French in

Quebec. As discussed in the introduction, although Canada is officially bilingual, most of Canada is English-dominant and Quebec is the area of the country in which French is predominantly spoken. Due to this linguistic polarisation, "Canada" is often used to refer to Englishness, whereas "Quebec" is used to refer to Frenchness. Sometimes this polarisation is explicit through reference to "English Canada" and "French Quebecers"; other times, this polarisation is less explicit, through reference to "the rest of Canada", which often means English-speaking Canada (Heller 1999b: 15; Kymlicka 1998: 10; Taylor 1993: 102), or discussions of French speakers "outside Quebec" (which is implied but not overtly stated to be the French-speaking heartland).

Perhaps unremarkably, many of the French and English articles that begin as discussions of the Olympic language ideological debate turn into discussions of Canada and Quebec. In some cases, the switch is explicit: in the Canadian Press article, Pauline Marois is cited as condemning "Canada" for its scorn of francophones. Later in this article, this is rephrased into a reproach of "English Canada" for its "indifference tainted with scorn" (*Mme Marois a reproché au Canada anglais de faire preuve d'une indifférence teintée de mépris*). The "Englishness" is later backgrounded, when Marois argues that "Canada [...] has demonstrated that without a doubt it considers the French-speaking minority to be a negligible quantity without importance, or worse, a ball and chain for the *anglophone majority*" (emphasis added) (*Le Canada [...] a démontré hors de tout doute qu'il considérait la minorité de la langue française comme une quantité négligeable sans importance, ou pire, un boulet pour la majorité anglophone*).

In other articles, the conflation of French issues and Quebec is more deeply embedded, and particularly in the English articles. For example, the title of one article is "Vancouver Games quickly turn sour for Quebec" (Anderson 2010). Although the article focuses on reactions to the opening ceremonies in the Quebec press, the fact is that reactions were not limited to Quebec, nor did only Quebec French speakers condemn the lack of French. The headline does not explain that debates about French were arguably (according to Taber 2010) "set off" by federal Heritage Minister James Moore—who is not from or a representative of Quebec. The focus on Quebec arguably polarises the language issue by focusing on Quebec and Quebecers rather than French in Canada more generally.

In a similar vein, another headline is "The big snub tarnishes Quebec gold" (Gagnon 2010). This relates to the fact that Canada's first gold medal won on Canadian soil was achieved by a French speaker. Remarkably, though, Gagnon refers to this as *Quebec's* gold, rather than *Canada's* gold: the connection between Quebec and French in the Olympics is only clear if it is understood that Quebecers are French-speaking, and this is only made explicit near the end of the article when Gagnon mentions "French-speaking Quebeckers". One article (CTVMontreal 2010) makes no attempt to explicitly connect the French language and Quebecers: the article lead states that "[s]ome Quebecers say they feel slighted after watching the Olympic opening ceremonies [...] and hearing very little French". The assumption is that Quebecers are French-speaking; because no other groups are cited as concerned by the opening ceremonies, it is also implied that only Quebecers were affected by the lack of French.

Among the French articles, one example focuses on French throughout and yet switches to a discussion of Quebec and Canada in the final two paragraphs (Boileau 2010b). Another French article (Boileau 2010a) relies on assumptions about the linguistic composition of Quebec and Canada in the statement "Quebecers will understand the need for this [linguistic] activism" (*Les Québécois comprendront ce nécessaire activisme*). Since this is the only mention of Quebec or Quebecers in the article, it is assumed that the reader understands that Quebecers are French-speaking. In summary, then, most French and English articles reveal essentialised assumptions about the linguistic composition of Canada and Quebec, which reduce the topic of French in the opening ceremonies from a national to a provincial issue, and in some cases conflate language issues with political Canada–Quebec relations.

5.2.2 Commentaries

Having presented the main findings from the English and French articles, we now turn to the commentaries in order to establish what readers assessed to be relevant to or missing from the journalists' account of the Olympics opening ceremonies.

In the Canadian Press article (2010), Pauline Marois is cited as condemning comments about Quebec and the French language posted on anglophone news websites, which she describes as "unimaginable, terrifying, and unacceptable" (*des commentaires anonymes 'inimaginables, effrayants et inacceptables' contre le Québec et le fait français*). Indeed, Marois observes an important fact: the subject of French during the Vancouver Olympics sparked a great deal of comments from online news readers, especially English readers. In the data sample used here, more than 67 English comments (6 %) were removed by website moderators with the explanation that they were deemed "not consistent with guidelines". Since comments are normally removed if they have been reported as "abusive" by another reader, this suggests the extent to which English comments contain disputed viewpoints and perspectives.

Due to the abundance of English commentaries posted in response to the five selected articles, frequent three-word clusters (compiled with WordSmith) serve as a useful site for the analysis of major themes. Some of the most frequent clusters are THE REST OF (94), REST OF CANADA (59), and IN THE ROC (7). Concordance lines reveal that most of these instances focus on a juxtaposition between Quebec and the "rest of Canada" (see Fig. 5.2). These examples suggest that language issues tend to be conflated with political issues in which Quebec figures as distinctively separate.

Other frequent clusters include THE LACK OF (40) and A LOT OF (39). When these clusters are expanded into concordance lines, many reveal contested accounts of whether there was sufficient ("a lot") or insufficient ("lack of") French in the opening ceremonies. Two other top clusters include modals (WOULD HAVE BEEN, 38; SHOULD HAVE BEEN, 33) and

```
 Quebec (and Ontario… but I would expect the rest of Canada to skip over my home provinc
. here that sound? The sound of silence! The rest of Canada doesn't care about Quebec.
s a character thing - Quebecers have it; the rest of Canada doesn't, as demonstrated by
he opening featured a Quebec singer that the rest of Canada did not know is enough.
                  Quebec show respect for the rest of Canada? Thanks for my morning laugh
continue to force the language police on the rest of Canada, while Quebec enjoys it's la
an first ! Joanne C So people wonder why the rest of Canada gets fed up with Quebec...Th
hem now have we? It's very annoying that the rest of Canada; will judge us Quebecois bec
sh. Its too bad Quebec has to bring down the rest of Canada all the tie. rd Jean Charest
be no mistake. It would be preferable if the rest of Canada could simply visit Quebec to
```

Fig. 5.2 Sample English concordance lines with THE REST OF CANADA and Quebec/Quebecers/Quebecois

most express grievances or reflections on the amount of French in the ceremonies. The clusters FRENCH AND ENGLISH (26) and ENGLISH AND FRENCH (24) suggest the often contested subject of bilingualism. Indeed, the concordance lines containing the cluster A BILINGUAL COUNTRY (18) reveal the extent to which bilingualism is hotly debated (see Fig. 5.3 examples of opposition to bilingualism are underlined).

The clusters GET OVER IT (19), ENOUGH IS ENOUGH (11), SHAME ON YOU (10), SICK AND TIRED (8), GET A LIFE (8), GIVE ME A [break] (7), GET OVER YOURSELVES (5), SO TIRED OF (5), BLAH BLAH BLAH (5), and SO SICK OF (5) express the heightened emotional level of the debate. Many of these examples come from readers who express fatigue with hearing from proponents of French issues (see Fig. 5.4).

Indeed, a motif of "complaint" recurs throughout the English commentary. The cluster A BUNCH OF (10) reveals numerous representations of French speakers as "complainers" (see Fig. 5.5).

Throughout the corpus, the lemma "whine" (word forms: WHINING, WHINE, WHINERS, WHINY, WHINNING [sic]) occurs 149 times. There are

```
t is democratic isn't it. After all, we are a bilingual country. STOP WHINING!! Sebster
en enough). I respect that fact that we are a bilingual country. I have found it interes
ceremonies and that was unfortunate. We are a bilingual country and this was a national
                                   Canada is a bilingual countyr only in in the sense tha
d be given equal billing is because this is a bilingual country. When Quebec City gets t
et we're spoon-fed this myth that Canada is a bilingual country. All the announcements a
           Canadian Myth #18349 Canada is a bilingual country 9 3 Report Abuse  plefeb
 I don't know what they want. Canada is not a bilingual country. That was just another b
en't bilingual in Canada. therefore its not a bilingual country, but indeed Quebec shoul
```

Fig. 5.3 Sampled English concordance lines containing A BILINGUAL COUNTRY

```
hining grievances from La Belle Provence. I'm SO sick of Quebec I wish it would just go
arest should shut his mouth. Fool! Mrowka  Im so sick of this French language crap. Queb
                                         I am so sick of hearing this bunch of morons co
ench!! Find something else to complain about. So sick of this english this and french th
er games for being not enough in French. I am so sicj of hearing about this constant bic
```

Fig. 5.4 English concordance lines with the cluster SO SICK OF

```
ll but geeze louise! It sounds like there are a bunch of whiney spoiled brats out there
zabeth Manley. I don't hear her whining. What a bunch of losers. Canadian athletes are d
                          Geez, what a bunch of whiners. Why do the french in o
  a minority withing their own country. What a bunch of hypocrites! Ria  Actually, I wa
rs who in this column tell quebeckers they're a bunch of cry-babies while they get an or
```

Fig. 5.5 Selected English concordance lines with the cluster A BUNCH OF

only 11 lexical collocates (i.e. non-grammatical words) of this lemma, among which are QUEBEC (17) and FRENCH (5). The lemma "complain" (word forms: COMPLAIN/ED, COMPLAINING, COMPLAINT/S) occurs 145 times throughout the commentary corpus; among the 9 lexical collocates of this lemma are QUEBEC (12) and FRENCH (5). The strong emphasis on complaining suggests a negative representation of Quebec and the French language.

One individual who is represented as a "complainer" by English commentators is the former Quebec Premier, Jean Charest (e.g. "whining from Charest", "complaints by Charest"). Although Charest played at best a marginal role in the English articles, in the comments he is discussed more often (64 occurrences) than, for example, Heritage Minister Moore (37), Canadian Prime Minister Harper (36), Official Languages Commissioner Fraser (12), and Pauline Marois (3). English concordance lines show that condemnation of Charest is extensive and diverse. Although Charest is not a Quebec separatist, in several examples he is grouped together with Gilles Duceppe, then-leader of the Bloc Quebecois (a federal separatist party), and in three examples he is argued to be a separatist: "Charest becomes more PQ everyday"; "Charest is a closet separatist"; "hey charest [sic] Quebec is not a country". Some commentators say they are "ashamed" of Charest, and others use modals to give Charest unchecked recommendations (e.g. "Charest should shut his mouth", "Charest should worry about bigger problems"). Two examples even contest the journalists' claims that Minister Moore set off the debate and instead argue that the instigator was Charest. Some examples use insults to berate the politician ("Is Jean 'STUPID' Charest trying made [sic] sure Quebec City won't get the Olympics in 2022 …?", "Wonder what idiot Charest will have to say about that?"). In sum, while in the articles specific social actors serve privileged positions as ideological brokers, in the online commentary, another individual, Charest, serves a privileged negative position as a social actor whose role is both misrepresented and exaggerated.

In the French corpus of comments, there are some similarities with the English data. For example, Quebec and Canada tend to be contrasted. In English, this took shape in the frequent cluster REST OF CANADA. In French, some of these contrasts emerged from the cluster LE CANADA EST. One example argues that "Canada is without a future for Quebec" (*le Canada est sans avenir pour le Québec*) and another polarises language and geography, arguing that "Canada is as English as Quebec is French" (*le Canada est aussi anglais que le Québec est français*). Other contrasts emerged when the lemma "Canada" (word forms: *Canada, Canadien/ne/s*) was explored. The most frequent lexical collocate of [Canada] is *anglais,* suggesting the potential for polarisation in familiar debates focusing on (English) Canada versus (French) Quebec. The next most frequent lexical collocate of [Canada] is *Québec*, with 17 collocations between [Canada] and the lemma "Québec" (word forms *Québec, Québécois/e/s*).

There are also differences between the English and French commentaries. For example, while the English commentaries showed contested discussions of Canadian bilingualism, French commentaries showed unwavering denials of Canadian bilingualism. One emphatic concordance line argues "Canada is a unilingual country! How much longer will it take us to understand?" (*Le Canada est un pays unilingue! Combien de temps encore nous faudra-t-il* [sic] *le comprendre?*). Another argues "federalism is dead bilingualism too and Canada is a complete fraud and disgrace for Francophones" (*le fédéralisme est mort le bilinguisme aussi et le Canada est une véritable fraude et honte pour les Francophones*). Other important differences include the fact that while English commentaries contain heightened emotional language and privilege the negative position of Jean Charest, French commentaries do neither.

5.2.3 Summary

The analysis of the English and French articles uncovered several differences: different voices were privileged, only the French articles contained evidence of ideologies of language endangerment, more first-person plural deictics were used by French speakers (as cited in both English and French articles), and while the French articles were fairly homogeneous in their treatment of the issue, the English articles were quite diverse. There were also several similarities between the articles: ideologies of monolingualism and, moreover, anglonormativity was found to be pervasive across the data, bilingualism served an inconsistent role, and language issues often served as a springboard into essentialisation and national political issues. As for the commentaries, however, the findings are not entirely uniform with the articles. For example, there was no marked difference between the use of deictics in English and French commentaries (*we* comprises 0.41 % of all words in the English commentary compared to 0.56 % for *nous* in the French commentary), nor were there any clear indications of ideologies of language endangerment in either corpus. There was also little indication of anglonormativity in commentary in either language. There are, however, some interesting parallels between the commentaries and the articles.

Although different individuals were privileged in the English and French articles, no one was privileged in the French commentaries, and the English commentaries focused on Quebec Premier Charest rather than Heritage Minister Moore, who had been the focus of an entire article. Bilingualism served an inconsistent role in the English and French articles, and while in the English commentary bilingualism continued to serve this contested role, in French commentaries Canada was consistently represented as monolingual rather than bilingual. Related to this point, while the English articles were found to be heteroglossic, the French articles were found to be fairly uniform: the English commentary contained heated debate about whether there was a "lack of" or a "lot of" French, but the French commentaries were uniform in the understanding that there was not enough French. In addition, many English commentators represented French speakers and Quebecers as vocally emotional (i.e. complaining) in a way similar to the English articles (albeit more overtly). Finally, the articles' conflation of language debates into debates about Quebec and Canada is consistent with this trend in the English and French commentaries. Although the most frequent English clusters suggest that the dominant topic is the Olympics, other clusters such as REST OF CANADA show how Canada–Quebec relations are brought into the fore. In the French commentaries, too, the lemma "Canada" and its collocation with the lemma "Québec" indicate that Canada–Quebec relations have been firmly intertwined with language debates.

5.3 Conclusion

It is useful to consider debates about the Vancouver Olympics opening ceremonies through the theoretical lens of language ideologies. Since ideologies are normally embedded and naturalised, they are not usually openly contested. However, when they are manifested in "debates", they often become controversial subjects for speakers with different social positions and vested interests. The opening ceremonies were a highly public affair, and comments about language content were also public, occurring in public statements and posted on public news forums. Since the individuals who participated in these debates presumably hold different social positions, this could explain why there were such ideological clashes in the commentaries. Sociodemographic information about online commentators could be useful to contextualise their arguments; still, there is a great deal to be said for online anonymity enabling individuals to express feelings that are often socially discouraged (Crystal 2011).

Language ideology theory is also useful for explaining why both articles and commentaries essentialised the links between language, identity, nationhood, and the Canadian state. The conflation of a language debate and national politics (e.g. Canada–Quebec relations, Quebec separatism) can be explained by the perceived role that languages play in different parts of the country. If French is understood as a "Quebec issue" because it is not spoken by many in the rest of Canada, it follows that Canadian "official bilingualism" is not a plausible argument for why French should have had equal status in the Olympics, which took place in Western Canada where little French is spoken. However, if French and English are understood as equal official languages of the country, then denying equivalent roles to both languages in an event like the Olympics would seem unthinkable. If the Canadian nation is conceptualised differently by different individuals and social groups, challenges to the country's official languages may be a product of the conflicting national imaginaries. Canadian bilingualism and diversity may be an experience only lived by minorities (Boudreau 2008: 70).

Some of the criticisms of the official languages policy may result from the tension between Canada's official identity and the identity of individual Canadians. Since most Canadians (83 %) are not French–English bilingual, the identity of the nation as "bilingual" does not necessarily map onto the national identity of individuals. As a result, English speakers who deny the equality of French may be attempting to justify their identity as an "unhyphenated" (i.e. authentic) Canadian in a version of the nation wherein English is presupposed. In the same way, the inconsistent role of "bilingualism" suggests that the word may mean, at the same time for different readers and writers, the (desirable or undesirable) equality of languages, the (legitimate or illegitimate) privileging of French, and the (true or false) nature of official languages in Canada. Given the multiplicity of meanings, some—including the now Official Languages Commissioner of Canada—have moved away from the word "bilingual" as a descriptor of the country (Fraser 2006: 9).

The findings from the articles and commentaries suggest that English is not always presupposed—it often plays an explicit role in debates. While monolingualism and anglonormativity were embedded in the articles, both evaporated in the online commentaries where debates were explicit and ideologies manifest. Also, while the English articles negatively represent French speakers as emotional about language (i.e. rather than politically engaged in the issue), it is in fact English speakers rather than French speakers who display a more heightened emotional response in the news commentary. Even though some English commentators argue that they are "so sick" of the language debate, many exhibit strong engagement in language issues, while simultaneously glossing over the role that language plays in the very activity in which they are participating. When individuals fail to notice the numerous roles that languages play in everyday life, languages lose cultural value in society. Such appears to be the case in Vancouver, where Olympics organisers believed they were fulfilling contractual language requirements by including in the cultural section of the opening ceremonies one French song, French speakers who did not speak, and a French poem in English translation (Office of the Commissioner 2010: 42). In contrast, the francophone commentators demonstrate awareness of the role of English in Canadian society, arguing that Canada is not bilingual—it is a predominantly English-speaking country. In sum, the naturalised role of the English language in English commentary may be unfortunate fallout from federal policies, which intended to make Canadians of all linguistic and cultural backgrounds more equal but instead masked the basis of linguistic privilege.

This chapter investigated only five English and five French articles from two newspapers, and the corpora of commentaries were relatively small by corpus linguistics standards. Despite the small scale, the findings are consistent with the findings outlined in Chap. 4 in that they suggest fundamental differences between English and French articles. If Canadians are not French–English bilingual, they may not have access to ideologies of the other language group.

References

Anderson, K. (2010, 16 February). Vancouver Games quickly turn sour for Quebec. *The Globe and Mail*. Available http://www.theglobeandmail.com/news/politics/vancouvergames-quickly-turn-sour-for-quebec/article1470359/

Bell, A. (1998). The discourse structure of news stories. In A. Bell & P. Garrett (Eds.), *Approaches to media discourse* (pp. 64–104). Oxford: Blackwell.

Billig, M. (1995). *Banal nationalism*. London: Sage Publications.

Blommaert, J. (1999b). The debate is open. In J. Blommaert (Ed.), *Language ideological debates* (pp. 1–38). Berlin: Mouton de Gruyter.

Boileau, J. (2010a, 13 February). Jeux olympiques—en français, toute! *Le Devoir*. Available http://www.ledevoir.com/sports/jeux-olympiques/283029/jeux-olympiquesen-francais-toute

Boileau, J. (2010b, 16 February). Olympiques de Vancouver—Loin des promesses. *Le Devoir.* Available http://www.ledevoir.com/sports/jeux-olympiques/283164/olympiquesde-vancouver-loin-des-promesses

Boudreau, A. (2008). Le français parlé en Acadie: idéologies, représentations et pratiques. In *La langue française dans sa diversité* (pp. 59–74). Government of Quebec. Available http://www.spl.gouv.qc.ca/fileadmin/medias/pdf/actes_colloque_langue_francaise_2008.pdf

Bourgault-Côté, G. (2010, 16 February). Ottawa est 'déçu'. *Le Devoir.* Available http://www.ledevoir.com/politique/canada/283217/ottawa-est-decu-mais-n-exigera-pas-plusde-francais-pour-la-cloture

Busch, B. (2006). Changing media spaces: The transformative power of heteroglossic practices. In C. Mar-Molinero & P. Stevenson (Eds.), *Language ideologies, policies and practices: Language and the future of Europe* (pp. 206–219). Basingstoke: Palgrave Macmillan.

Canadian Press. (2010, 15 February). Le Canada a affiché tout son mépris envers les francophones. *Le Devoir,* Available http://www.ledevoir.com/politique/

quebec/283157/vancouver-le-canada-a-affiche-tout-son-mepris-envers-les-francophones-accuse-marois

Cardinal, L. (2008). Linguistic peace: A time to take stock. *Inroads, 23*, 62–70.

Cotter, C. (2010). *News talk: Investigating the language of journalism*. Cambridge: Cambridge University Press.

Crystal, D. (2011). *Internet linguistics: A student guide*. London: Routledge.

CTV Montreal. (2010, 15 February). Not enough French at Olympic opening ceremonies, critics say. *CTV Montreal*. Available http://ctv.theglobeandmail.com/servlet/an/local/CTVNews/20100215/mtl_french_olympic_ceremonies_100215?hub=WinnipegHome

De Cillia, R., Reisigl, M., & Wodak, R. (1999). The discursive construction of national identities. *Discourse & Society, 10*(2), 149–173.

DiGiacomo, S. M. (1999). Language ideological debates in an Olympic city: Barcelona 1992–1996. In J. Blommaert (Ed.), *Language ideological debates* (pp. 105–142). Berlin: Mouton de Gruyter.

Fraser, G. (2006). *Sorry, I don't speak French. Confronting the Canadian crisis that won't go away*. Toronto: McClelland and Stewart.

Gagnon, S. (2003). La construction discursive du concept de la souveraineté dans les medias canadiens lors du referendum de 1995. *Revue québécoise de linguistique, 32*(2), 97–116.

Gagnon, L. (2010, 19 February). The big snub tarnishes Quebec gold. *The Globe and Mail. Available* http://www.theglobeandmail.com/news/opinions/the-big-snubtarnishes-quebec-gold/article1475096/

Globe editorial. (2010, 16 February). Les jeux du Canada. *The Globe and Mail*. Available http://www.theglobeandmail.com/news/national/les-jeux-du-canada/article1469342/

Heller, M. (1999b). Linguistic minorities and modernity: A sociolinguistic ethnography. London: Longman.

Heller, M., & Duchêne, A. (2007). Discourses of endangerment: Sociolinguistics, globalization and social order. In A. Duchêne & M. Heller (Eds.), *Discourses of endangerment: Ideology and interest in the defence of languages* (pp. 1–13). London: Continuum.

Kymlicka, W. (1998). *Finding our way: Rethinking ethnocultural relations in Canada*. Oxford: Oxford University Press.

Mackey, E. (2002). *The house of difference: Cultural politics and national identity in Canada*. Toronto: University of Toronto Press.

Newspapers Canada. (2010). *About newspapers*. Retrieved from http://www.newspaperscanada.ca/daily-newspaper-paid-circulation-data

Nurse, A. (2003). A profile of Canadian regionalism. In K. G. Pyke & W. C. Soderlund (Eds.), *Profiles of Canada* (pp. 35–61). Toronto: Canadian Scholars Press.

Office of the Commissioner of Official Languages. (2010). *Beyond obligations: Annual report 2009–2010.* Volume II. Available http://www.officiallanguages.gc.ca/sites/default/files/ar_ra_2009_10_v2_e.pdf

O'Halloran, K. (2011). Limitations of the logico-rhetorical module: Inconsistency in argument, online discussion forums and electronic deconstruction. *Discourse Studies, 13*(6), 798–806.

Retzlaff, S., & Gänzle, S. (2008). Constructing the European Union in Canadian news. *Critical Approaches to Discourse Analysis Across Disciplines, 2*(2), 67–89.

Taber, J. (2010, 15 February). Lack of French at Olympic opening 'no big deal,' Moore says. *The Globe and Mail.* Available http://www.theglobeandmail.com/news/politics/ottawa-notebook/lack-of-french-at-olympic-opening-no-big-deal-moore-says/article1468980/

Taylor, C. (1993). *Reconciling the solitudes: Essays on Canadian federalism and nationalism*. Montreal: McGill-Queen's Press.

Van Dijk, T. A. (1991). *Racism and the press*. London: Routledge.

Van Leeuwen, T. (2003 [1996]). The representation of social actors. In C. R. Caldas-Coulthard & M. Coulthard (Eds.), Readings in critical discourse analysis (pp. 32–70). London: Routledge.

Vipond, R. C. (1996). Citizenship and the Charter of Rights: The two side of Pierre Trudeau. *International Journal of Canadian Studies, 14*, 179–192.

6

Language Ideologies and Twitter in Canada

The previous chapter explored language ideologies in Canadian online news media and comments on those articles. In this chapter, we turn to tackle a new data type: Twitter. Twitter is a type of social media, an Internet-based site that promotes social interaction between participants (Page et al. 2014: 5). More specifically, Twitter is a microblogging site that allows users to post messages of 140 characters or less either to a group of followers or to the Internet more generally (Zappavigna 2012: 3). Users can "follow" other users whose accounts are public (or users whose accounts are private, if request for followership is accepted), which means that they receive tweets from those accounts in their Twitter feed. They can also retweet, which means that a tweet is reposted verbatim (and often marked with "RT"), and they can "favourite" tweets, which are then stored as part of the user's profile. Users can also "reply" to tweets (i.e. @replies in which the original tweeter is tagged in the reply), which means that they enter into direct conversation with another user; and they can tag their tweets with a hash (#), which serves to make a lexical item searchable across Twitter and creates a system of "ambient affiliation" (Zappavigna 2011) through which interested parties can explore the evolution of the tagged topic through users' publically available tweets.

R. Vessey, *Language and Canadian Media*,
DOI 10.1057/978-1-137-53001-1_6

What is unique to Twitter, as a type of social media, is that it is generally produced by and for anyone and distributed across large-scale audiences. Thus, unlike news media, which were originally designed for local or national audiences (see Chap. 1), social media are more international and globalised in their scope. For this reason, it is more difficult to assess the extent to which such data are relevant to a national context. Nevertheless, data show that the percentage of Canadians using Twitter continues to grow exponentially: according to an Ipsos Reid survey (2011), while less than 1 % of Canadians used Twitter in 2009, by 2011 that number had grown to almost 20 % (cited in Small 2014: 91).

Twitter has been the site of numerous Canadian public and political debates (e.g. Dubois and Dutton 2012) and it is increasingly the site for political campaigning. Small (2010b) notes that in 2008 just over 4000 accounts followed Canadian political party leader feeds, but by the conclusion of the 2011 campaign that number had increased by 101 % to just over 400,000 followers. Although these numbers do not necessarily indicate that all of these tweets on this account are being read or taken up by readers, it does provide a rough estimate of a user's online presence and perhaps even his/her popularity. Small (e.g. 2010a) has examined tweets from various Canadian political party and leader feeds, and her research has shown the extent to which political parties and leaders engage with the Canadian public, for example, through the use of @replies and retweets that create a "conversational ecology as they imply listening" (Small 2014: 95). However, Small's (2010a) examination of 27 Canadian political party and leader feeds found that less than 16 % of tweets were conversations between politicians and followers.

The lack of conversational use of Twitter is not surprising. Many Twitter users are not interested in contributing original content but instead use the site to aggregate and streamline content from a variety of sources for their personal use. Indeed, social media like Twitter can serve as an echo chamber in which individuals are exposed only to information and communities that support their own views (Gruzd and Roy 2014: 30). It has been argued that although people are likely to be exposed to a variety of perspectives on Twitter, it is not an effective platform to carry out meaningful discussion (Gruzd and Roy 2014: 36). Therefore, in some cases Twitter can serve less as a social network than as a broadcasting channel

(Small 2014: 106). In fact, the broadcasting power of Twitter actually extends beyond the realm of the "Twitterverse", since the content of tweets is often reported in mainstream media, too (Small 2014: 98).

Despite the growing importance of Twitter in Canada, there has been little research on it specifically for the national context (for some exceptions, see Chen and Smith 2011; Dubois and Dutton 2012; Dubois and Gaffney 2014; Gruzd and Roy 2014; Gruzd et al. 2011; Small 2010a, b, 2014). Small's research in particular is a notable exception, but while it is cutting edge, it is undertaken within the field of Canadian politics (often with a media studies angle), and has not tended to focus on language issues in particular or to apply methods relevant to linguistics (e.g. corpus linguistics, discourse analysis). Indeed, there appears to be no research on Canadian Twitter from a linguistics angle—and no research comparing English and French Canadian uses of Twitter. Although Gruzd and Roy (2014) examine "cross-ideological connections" in Canadian Twitter data with the aim of establishing the extent to which users become exposed to alternative political perspectives on the platform, their data appear to be entirely English medium, which means that there is no exposure to French-medium ideological alternatives.

Although there has been little work in this area, the relevance of Twitter to Canadian bilingualism is clear. In early 2015, a preliminary report from the Commissioner of Official Languages concluded that federal ministers should tweet in both English and French (Canadian Press 2015; Office of the Commissioner of Official Languages 2015). The conclusions, which were reported in national and international news, met with uproar in some parts of Canada, suggesting the extent to which official language issues have not been adequately considered in social media contexts (cf. Senate Committee 2012). It is the aim of this chapter to tackle the issue of studying similarities and differences in language ideologies across English and French Canadian Twitter data by addressing the following research questions:

1. How are languages represented in the Twitter accounts of Canadian political party leaders?
2. How are assumptions about languages embedded in the Twitter accounts of Canadian political party leaders?

3. What are the similarities and differences between representations of and assumptions about languages in the Twitter accounts of Canadian political party leaders?
4. How do the leaders' representations of and assumptions about languages compare to representations and assumptions in general tweets containing #cdnpoli and #polcan?

The chapter proceeds as follows: Sect. 6.1 presents the data under consideration, Sect. 6.2 presents the findings, and Sect. 6.3 discusses these with relation to findings from previous chapters.

6.1 Data

In order to explore Canadian Twitter, data were collected from several different sources. First, the verified Twitter accounts of the leaders of Canada's three major political parties were mined for data. These leaders include Stephen Harper, then Prime Minister of Canada and Leader of the Conservative Party of Canada; Thomas Mulcair, then Leader of the Official Opposition in Canada and Leader of the New Democratic Party of Canada (NDP); and Justin Trudeau, then Leader of the Liberal Party of Canada.

The politicians have rather different user profiles. First, the Twitter accounts date from different periods of time. Stephen Harper's English Twitter account was created in July 2007, but his French account was created in August 2008. Justin Trudeau's account was created in March 2008, but Thomas Mulcair's account was created only in August 2011. These different periods of membership are to some extent reflected in the number of tweets that exist in each account. On 11 July 2014, the date of data collection, Stephen Harper's English account listed 2540 tweets, whereas his French account listed only 2261 tweets. Justin Trudeau's account listed 5376 tweets, whereas Thomas Mulcair's account listed only 1805 tweets. Notably, though, Trudeau and Mulcair's accounts are bilingual and often contain similar messages in English and in French. In contrast, Harper has two separate Twitter accounts and therefore, combined, his accounts contain the most tweets.

Also, the Twitter accounts have considerably divergent followerships and differ in their use of other media. On the date of data collection (11 July 2014), Harper's English account (@pmharper) had over 485,000 followers but followed only 223 other Twitter accounts; the account contained 313 photos and videos. Harper's French account (@premierministre) had nearly 15,000 followers on the date of data collection but followed only 234 other Twitter accounts; the account also contained 302 photos and videos. Although Thomas Mulcair is the Leader of the Official Opposition of Canada, on the date of data collection his account (@thomasmulcair) had a comparatively small following, with only 71,100 followers; the account followed 1194 other Twitter users and contained 175 photos and videos. On the date of data collection, Justin Trudeau's Twitter account had a comparatively larger following, with 395,000 followers; the account also followed 746 other Twitter users and contained a large number of photos and videos (673) (see Table 6.1).

Unfortunately, not all tweets were accessible for data collection. Twitter does not normally allow access to users' entire Twitter history, especially if accounts contain large numbers of tweets. Twitter data were collected by scraping them from the politicians' Twitter account websites: https://Twitter.com/pmharper (Stephen Harper, English), https://Twitter.com/premierministre (Stephen Harper, French), https://Twitter.com/thomasmulcair (Thomas Mulcair), and https://Twitter.com/justintrudeau (Justin Trudeau).

Table 6.1 User profiles

Full name	Date of data collection	Date joined Twitter	Total number of tweets (as of 11/07/2014)	Following	Followers	Photos and videos
Stephen Harper @pmharper	21/07/2014	01/07/07	2540	223	485 K	313
Stephen Harper @premierministre	21/07/2014	01/08/08	2261	234	14.9 K	302
Justin Trudeau @justintrudeau	21/07/2014	01/03/08	5376	746	395 K	673
Thomas Mulcair @thomasmulcair	21/07/2014	01/08/11	1805	1194	71.1 K	175

Data were saved as Word Document files (.doc), complete with active hyperlinks, and then they were converted to text-only format (.txt) for compatibility with the corpus suite WordSmith Tools (Version 6) (Scott 2014). In the text files, metadata including usernames, dates, and response options (e.g. retweet, reply) were either stripped or tagged with headers (e.g. <header></header>) in order to not be included in corpus analysis. However, in all cases these metadata remained available in the Word Document files for consultation if required. In all cases, metadata for the labelling of hashtags (#) and usernames (@) were added to the files (hashtags (#) were changed to <hashtag> and @ symbols were changed to <at>) to ensure that these important functions were readable within automated corpus analysis.

Although in July 2014 Harper's English account listed 2540 tweets, only 1028 (40 %) were accessible for data collection, with the earliest tweet dating from 13 August 2013. As a result, the Harper English Twitter corpus, PmHarper, comprises 1028 tweets and 20,518 words. Also, these tweets include 107 verbatim retweets from other Twitter users. It was decided that since these tweets form part of the @pmharper account, they should be considered as regular tweets (albeit "conversational" tweets, cf. Small 2014). Therefore, 10.4 % of the tweets in the PmHarper corpus are retweets from other users. Similarly, although Harper's French account listed 2261 tweets, only 1073 (47 %) were accessible for data collection, with the earliest tweet dating from 1 July 2013. As a result, the Harper French Twitter corpus, Premierministre, comprises 1073 tweets and 21,676 words. These tweets include 54 verbatim retweets; therefore, 5 % of the tweets in the Premierministre corpus are retweets from other users.

Trudeau, being a frequent tweeter, had 5376 tweets listed on his account on 11 July 2014 (the date of data collection), but only 3426 (64 %) were accessible for data collection, with the earliest tweet dating from 24 September 2012. The Trudeau Twitter corpus therefore comprises 3426 tweets and 65,264 words. These tweets include 143 verbatim retweets; therefore, 4 % of the tweets in the Trudeau corpus are retweets from other users. Finally, Mulcair, a less frequent Twitter user, had only 1805 tweets listed on his account on 11 July 2014 and 1798 (99.6 %) were accessible for collection, with the earliest dating from 26 September

2011, just one month after the account was opened. The Mulcair Twitter corpus therefore comprises 1798 tweets and 36,440 words. These tweets include 42 verbatim retweets; therefore, 2 % of the tweets in the Mulcair corpus are retweets from other users (see Table 6.2).

Finally, it is important to note that, given the anonymous nature of the Internet, "there is no way to determine who is actually doing the tweeting—the leader or a staff person" (Small 2014: 98). These differences could potentially lead to differences in the content and style of tweets even within each account. Therefore, conclusions drawn based on these data are not argued to reflect the language, style, or agenda of the individual politicians; instead, they are taken to be examples of the variety of ways in which language ideologies are embedded and/or manifested in social media in the Canadian context.

In addition to the data drawn from the Twitter accounts of the federal party leaders, data were also drawn from tweets containing the hashtags #polcan and #cdnpoli. These are hashtags that refer to Canadian politics: #polcan tends to be used in French-medium tweets and is an abbreviation of *la politique canadienne* whereas #cdnpoli tends to be used in English-medium tweets and is an abbreviation of "Canadian politics". These are widely used on Twitter and, crucially, are widely used by the federal party leaders in their tweets. For example, while #polcan is the most frequently used hashtag in the (French) Premierministre corpus, #cdnpoli is the most frequently used hashtag in the (English) PmHarper corpus. Similarly, #polcan tends to be used in French-medium tweets in the Trudeau and Mulcair corpora, whereas #cdnpoli tends to be used in the English-medium tweets in these corpora.

In order to avoid predominantly time-sensitive findings, 200 tweets were collected once per day, one day per week over a seven-week period. The first date of data collection was Tuesday 6 May 2014 and the last date of collection Monday 23 June 2014. The tweets were collected by entering the hashtag #cdnpoli and #polcan in the Twitter search engine, choosing "all" (as opposed to "top") tweets, and scraping the first 200 from the site on each day of data collection. These hashtags were taken to indicate a Canadian focus—and to delimit the availability of Twitter data to a specifically "Canadian" context—because they are exclusively with

Table 6.2 Data summary

Full name	Verified account?	Dates included in data	Total number of tweets (as of 11/07/2014)	No. of tweets in corpus	% of total account tweets in corpus	Tokens in cleaned data	Type/token ratio (TTR; in cleaned data)	Retweets in corpus	% of corpus tweets that are retweets	Hashtags
Stephen Harper @pmharper	Y	13/08/13–11/07/14	2540	1028	40	20,518	17.63	107	10.41	1377
Stephen Harper @premierministre	Y	01/07/13–11/07/14	2261	1073	47	21,676	20.07	54	5.03	1349
Justin Trudeau @justintrudeau	Y	24/09/12–11/07/14	5376	3426	64	65,264	14.24	143	4.17	2903
Thomas Mulcair @thomasmulcair	Y	26/09/11–11/07/14	1805	1798	99.6	36,440	17.23	42	2.34	2209

relation to the Canadian context. Other researchers have used similar methods for collecting Canadian Twitter data; for example, Gruzd and Roy (2014) collected data based on the use of the hashtag #elxn41 for their study of the Canadian election.

Like the federal party leaders' corpora, tweets were saved as Word Document files (.doc), complete with active hyperlinks, and then they were converted to text-only format (.txt). In the text files, metadata including usernames, dates, and response options (e.g. retweet, reply) were tagged with headers (e.g. <header></header>) in order to not be included in the primary corpus analysis. Similarly, hashtags (#) were changed to <hashtag> and usernames (@) were changed to <at> to ensure that these functions were readable within automated corpus analysis; all original metadata remained available in the Word Document files for consultation if required. In the Cdnpoli corpus, this process produced an average of 4118 words per week and a total of 28,830 words over the seven-week period. For the Polcan corpus, this produced an average of 4163 words per week and a total of 29,147 words over the seven-week period (see Tables 6.3 and 6.4).

In this study, the unit of analysis is the individual tweet, which has a 140-character limit. These tweets often contain a considerable amount of verbatim repetition as users retweet stories and (in the case of Stephen Harper in particular; see Small 2014: 103) maintain a disciplined communication strategy and style that reduces creativity and improvisation in the tweets. This repetition largely compromises the possibility of analysing the data quantitatively using corpus linguistics: since corpus

Table 6.3 CDNPOLI corpus

Date		No. of tweets	Words	Types	Type/token ratio (TTR)	Standardised TTR
Tuesday	06/05/2014	200	4245	1451	36.33	46.55
Wednesday	14/05/2014	200	4214	1423	35.74	46.85
Thursday	22/05/2014	200	4073	1572	40.84	40.46
Friday	30/05/2014	200	4051	1485	38.64	52.92
Saturday	07/06/2014	200	3841	1425	39.68	46.58
Sunday	15/06/2014	200	4053	1565	41.38	53.03
Monday	23/06/2014	200	4353	1140	27.84	40.42
Totals		1400	28,830	5783	21.37	50.09

Table 6.4 POLCAN corpus

Date		No. of tweets	Words	Types	Type/token ratio (TTR)	Standardised TTR
Tuesday	06/05/2014	200	4115	1227	31.86	37.83
Wednesday	14/05/2014	200	4185	1230	31.24	38.05
Thursday	22/05/2014	200	4266	1118	27.65	34.1
Friday	30/05/2014	200	4147	1260	32.28	40.1
Saturday	07/06/2014	200	4042	1314	35.28	40.17
Sunday	15/06/2014	200	3979	1116	29.86	40.8
Monday	23/06/2014	200	4413	872	21.32	30.77
Totals		1400	29,147	4881	17.89	36.78

linguistics examines patterns in the data and patterns are based on repetition, the huge amount of repetition in the tweets mean that findings tend not to reveal "non-obvious meaning" (Partington 2010: 88) as is usually the case in corpus-assisted discourse studies of other data sets. However, a huge amount of detail can be contained within 140 characters, including images, URLs directing readers to other sites, @replies, and hashtags that group users' contributions (Small 2014: 95). Therefore, these components are studied at the discourse level as intertextual dimensions (and more specifically, hypertextual dimensions) of each tweet.

In the next section, findings are presented in the order of the research questions before finally summarising the findings in Sect. 6.3. The Cdnpoli and Polcan corpora were used primarily for comparison with the federal party leaders' corpora in order to answer research question 4.

6.2 Findings

Findings showed that languages were not, in general, a topic of discussion within the Twitter accounts of the federal party leaders. In fact, ENGLISH occurs only four times within all three accounts, and three of these refer to ENGLISH BAY, an area of Vancouver, British Columbia. The only instance where ENGLISH refers to language comes from a Trudeau corpus tweet, which comments on the death of Knowlton Nash, whose voice is described as that of "English Canada" (see Example 6.1).

Example 6.1

Justin Trudeau @JustinTrudeau

Deeply saddened to hear about the passing of Knowlton Nash. For so long, his voice was English Canada's voice. RIP

9:52 PM—25 May 2014

Since Trudeau tweets in both English and French, there is also a French version of the tweet, where Trudeau also describes Nash's voice as "that of Anglophone Canada" (*celle du Canada Anglophone*) (see Example 6.2).

Example 6.2

Justin Trudeau @JustinTrudeau

Profondément peiné d'apprendre le décès de Knowlton Nash. Sa voix a été celle du Canada anglophone si longemps. Qu'il repose en paix.

9:53 PM—25 May 2014

Notably, this is the only use of ANGLOPHONE/S in all federal party leaders' corpora.

There are two references to ANGLAIS/E/S in the federal party leaders' corpora, both of which come from the Trudeau corpus. In both these cases, though, Trudeau simply highlights the English language within his French tweets. For example, he highlights an English-medium speech (Example 6.3) and an English-medium article about running (Example 6.4).

Example 6.3

Justin Trudeau @JustinTrudeau

@Josee46 Vous êtes sérieuse?!? ça va sûrement donc vous frustrer encore plus quand vous voyez que son discours (à Las Vegas) fut en anglais…

2:04 AM—16 February 2014

Example 6.4

Justin Trudeau @JustinTrudeau

Super article en anglais sur la course #armyrun du weekend dernier par @CanadianRunning: http://runningmagazine.ca/22000-participate-in-army-run-5k-goes-off-course/….

11:45 PM—24 September 2013

This kind of metalinguistic flagging does not occur in the English versions of these tweets, usually because the English language dominates. For instance, Example 6.5 (the English version of Example 6.4) does not explain that the URL is for an English-language article and so it is implied that such a link would be understood by and relevant to followers who can read the English-medium tweet.

Example 6.5

Justin Trudeau @JustinTrudeau

Great article in @CanadianRunning on last weekend's #ArmyRun: http://runningmagazine.ca/22000-participate-in-army-run-5k-goes-off-course/ …

11:45 PM—24 September 2013

Metalinguistic flagging does occur in several tweets in the Mulcair corpus. For example, Mulcair tweets in English and in French that he has "always and will continue to defend the rights of linguistic minorities" (see Examples 6.6 and 6.7).

Example 6.6

Tom Mulcair @ThomasMulcair

Auj. nous fêtons la ténacité des Franco-Ontariens. J'ai tjr. défendu les droits des min. linguistiques et ne cesserai de les appuyer #onfr

4:34 PM—25 September 2013

Example 6.7

Tom Mulcair @ThomasMulcair

Today we celebrate the resilience of Franco-Ontarians. I have always and will continue to defend the rights of linguistic minorities #onfr

4:35 PM—25 September 2013

In Example 6.8, Mulcair explains again that the NDP "stands proudly with linguistic minorities", thus using metalanguage to make explicit a standpoint about language issues.

Example 6.8

Tom Mulcair @ThomasMulcair

Meeting with @ACFAAB, representing over 80,000 francophones in Alberta. The #NDP stands proudly with linguistic minorities in Canada

9:24 PM—2 October 2013

While metalanguage is not common in the other federal party leaders' tweets, metalinguistic flagging does occur in the URLs that are tweeted—especially the accounts of the Prime Minister, Stephen Harper. This is because all federal websites have (or should have) versions in both official languages; the language option means that the websites usually contain the fragments "eng" or "fra" to indicate the English or French version of the site in question. As a result, there are 69 instances of ENG in the federal party leaders' corpora, and 67 of these occur in the PmHarper corpus. Most of these URLs are sites from Prime Minister of Canada's news website, available at http://pm.gc.ca/eng/news. This site is, of course, available in French, at http://pm.gc.ca/fra/nouvelles, and for this reason the Premierministre corpus contains 71 instances of "fra". However, there is one exception where a Premierministre tweet refers readers to the English rather than the French version of the website (see Example 6.9).

Example 6.9

Stephen Harper @premierministre

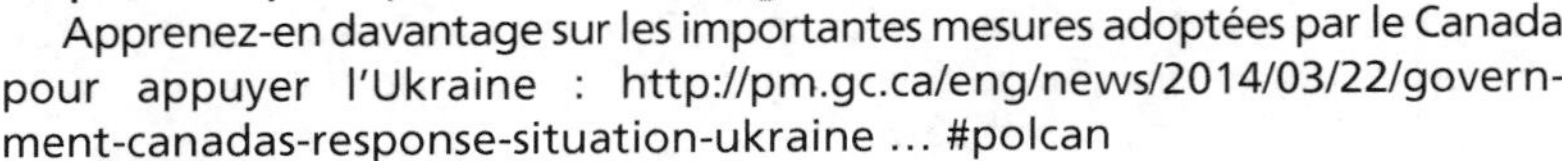

Apprenez-en davantage sur les importantes mesures adoptées par le Canada pour appuyer l'Ukraine : http://pm.gc.ca/eng/news/2014/03/22/government-canadas-response-situation-ukraine … #polcan

5:50 PM—22 March 2014

There is also a French version of the site (http://pm.gc.ca/fra/nouvelles/2014/03/22/reponse-du-gouvernement-du-canada-la-situation-ukraine), but the tweeting of the English rather than the French site—alongside other examples that are highlighted below—suggests the incremental use of English in the Premierministre corpus.

Although ENGLISH, ANGLOPHONE/S, and ANGLAIS/E/S were used only a very small number of times in the federal party leaders' corpora, there are comparatively far more references to the French language, culture, and French speakers. For example, there are three references to FRENCH, two of which again come from the Trudeau corpus (Examples 6.10 and 6.11) and the third from the PmHarper corpus (Example 6.12). These examples discuss the French language, culture, and people.

Example 6.10

Justin Trudeau @JustinTrudeau

Up in French in Qc first, but here's my @HuffPostCanada paper on why federal leadership on education is essential. http://huff.to/12TDjjY

2:15 PM—16 February 2013

Example 6.11

Justin Trudeau @JustinTrudeau

Today is International Day of La #Francophonie and a chance to celebrate the brilliance of the French language and culture @OIFfrancophonie

8:46 PM—20 March 2014

Example 6.12

Stephen Harper @pmharper

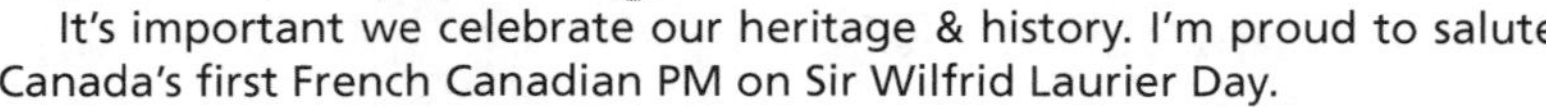

It's important we celebrate our heritage & history. I'm proud to salute Canada's first French Canadian PM on Sir Wilfrid Laurier Day.

1:10 PM—20 November 2013

Throughout the corpora, there are also references to FRANCOPHONIE, FRANCOPHONE/S, FRANCOPHILES, FRANCO-ONTARIEN/NE/S, FRANCO-MANITOBAN/E/S, and FRANÇAIS/ES (see Table 6.5).

These references to French issues occur in all federal party leaders' tweets. However, it is perhaps noteworthy that the PmHarper corpus contains the fewest references to French-language issues, with singular references to *francophonie*, *franco-Ontarian,* and *franco-Ontarians.* It would appear that the Premierministre corpus includes more discussions of French issues, with two references to *francophonie,* and singular references to *française, franco-ontariens,* and *français.* However, some of these differences may be the result of slight discrepancies in the availability of

Table 6.5 References to "franco*" in party leaders' corpora

		Users of terms			
Word	Freq.	Mulcair	Trudeau	Premierministre	PmHarper
FRANCOPHONIE	8	2	3	2	
FRANCOPHONES	6	3	4		
FRANÇAISE	4	1	3	1	
FRANCOPHONE	2	2			
FRANCO-ONTARIENS	3	1	1	1	
FRANCO-ONTARIAN	3	1	1		1
FRANÇAIS	3	2		1	
FRANCO-ONTARIANS	2	1			1
FRANCO-ONTARIENNE	2	2			
FRANCO-ONTARIEN	1	1			
FRANCO-MANITOBAN	1	1			
FRANCO-MANITOBAINE	1	1			
FRANCO	1	1			
FRANCOPHILES	1	1			
FRANCOPHIE	1	1			

data; for instance, Example 6.13 refers to the naming of Christian Paradis as Minister of International Development and La Francophonie, but this was posted on 15 July 2013, which was a date not available for data collection in the PmHarper corpus.

Example 6.13

Stephen Harper @premierministre

J'ai le plaisir de nommer @christianparad ministre du Développement international et ministre responsable de la Francophonie #remaniement13

3:42 PM—15 July 2013

Nevertheless, one instance of *française* that occurs in the Premierministre but not the PmHarper corpus pertains to congratulations to Canadian author Dany Laferrière, who was elected to the Académie française. Laferrière's election was celebrated in tweets in the Premierministre, Mulcair, and Trudeau corpora. Notably, though, while Trudeau tweeted the news in both English and French (Examples 6.14 and 6.15), Mulcair (Example 6.16) and Stephen Harper (Example 6.17) only tweeted the news in French.

Example 6.14

Justin Trudeau @JustinTrudeau

Congratulations to Dany Laferrière on being the first Quebecker, Haitian, and Canadian elected to the Académie française! #incrediblyproud

8:32 PM—12 December 2013

Example 6.15

Justin Trudeau @JustinTrudeau

Félicitations à Dany Laferrière, premier Québécois, Haïtien et Canadien à être élu à l'Académie française. #fiertéincommensurable

8:31 PM—12 December 2013

Example 6.16

Tom Mulcair @ThomasMulcair

Toutes mes félicitations à Dany Laferrière, le premier Québécois et Haïtien à se joindre au rang des immortels de l'Académie française.

4:11 PM—12 December 2013

Example 6.17

Stephen Harper @premierministre

Félicitations à l'écrivain canadien Dany Laferrière pour son élection à la prestigieuse Académie française.

4:29 PM—12 December 2013

Although references to French issues (i.e. items cited in Table 6.5) occur most often in the Mulcair corpus (19 occurrences), in most cases Mulcair, too, discusses French issues through the French language. For example, he wishes his followers "Happy International Day of La Francophonie"—but only in French (Example 6.18).

Example 6.18

Tom Mulcair @ThomasMulcair

Bonne journée internationale de la Francophonie à tous les francophones et francophiles!

4:13 PM—20 March 2014

However, other references to language issues or communities in the Mulcair corpus occur in tweets with both English and French versions.

Crucially, though, despite the occasional monolingual tweeting in the Mulcair corpus, due to the bilingual nature of the account, followers would arguably still gain exposure to French tweets, even if they do not fully understand the content. This is not the case, however, in the Premierministre corpus: the @premierministre account, with 15,000 followers (July 2014) is separate from the @pmharper account, which had 485,000 followers in July 2014. The different followership means that not everyone who follows one account necessarily follows the other, and therefore most followers of the @pmharper account would not gain exposure to the French-medium content or the French-focused topics of the @premierministre account.

In addition to the targeted searches for linguistic keywords (e.g. French/*français,* English/*anglais*), the WordSmith Tools KeyWords function was used to compare the frequencies in each corpus against one another. The Mulcair corpus was compared against the Trudeau, PmHarper, Premierministre, Polcan, and Cdnpoli corpora; the Trudeau corpus was compared against the Mulcair, PmHarper, Premierministre, Polcan, and Cdnpoli corpora; and the PmHarper and Premierministre corpora were compared against the Mulcair, Trudeau, Polcan, and Cdnpoli corpora. The Mulcair, Trudeau, PmHarper, and Premierministre corpora did not include any statistically significant words pertaining to linguistic issues, regardless of which corpus was used as the comparator corpus. Although French and English issues were not salient, it appears that they were the only languages mentioned at all. Searches were done for the terms ESPAGNOL/SPANISH, CHINESE/CHINOIS, JAPANESE/JAPONAIS, RUSSIAN/RUSSE, PORTUGUESE/PORTUGUAIS, GERMAN/ALLEMAND, and SWEDISH/SUÉDOIS, and even when these terms did appear, none of them referred to language or even cultural issues (some referred to associations or foreign countries or individuals).

Thus, although languages tend not to be explicitly represented as such in the Twitter accounts of the federal party leaders (at least not frequently), assumptions about languages nonetheless became manifested in some cases. Most notably, assumptions about languages became embedded in the federal party leaders' tweets because some leaders (e.g. Mulcair, Trudeau) use bilingual Twitter accounts and others (e.g. Stephen Harper) use monolingual Twitter accounts (@pmharper and @premierministre).

The Trudeau corpus is bilingual in that tweets tend to occur in both English and French. More specifically, tweets in one language also tend to be loosely translated into the other language. "Loose" translation is notable because in the PmHarper and Premierministre corpora, tweets tend to be rather more formulaic transliterations of one another, as in Examples 6.19 and 6.20.

Example 6.19

Stephen Harper @pmharper
Best wishes to Muslims here at home & around the world as they prepare to observe the holy month of Ramadan. http://bit.ly/1yUHUkm #cdnpoli
5:09 PM—27 June 2014

Example 6.20

Stephen Harper @premierministre
Nos meilleurs vœux aux musulmans d'ici et du monde entier qui se préparent à souligner le mois du ramadan. http://bit.ly/1yUHSZI #polcan
5:09 PM—27 June 2014

This transliteration strategy is in keeping with the "disciplined" communications strategy of the Conservative Party. According to former Conservative campaign manager Tom Flanagan, the leader should never improvise, candidates should never speak about personal beliefs, and electronic communication must be "careful and dignified" (cited in Small, 2014: 103).

In contrast, although Trudeau's English and French tweets tend to contain the same content (e.g. photos, links, message), they are less formulaic and tend not to be transliterations, as in Examples 6.21 and 6.22.

Example 6.21

Justin Trudeau @JustinTrudeau
Go behind the scenes with me on a busy by-election long weekend! #hopeandhardwork http://bit.ly/1rYqSjy
12:46 AM—11 July 2014

Example 6.22

Justin Trudeau @JustinTrudeau

Élections partielles : suivez-moi dans les coulisses d'une longue fin de semaine très chargée. #travailacharné http://bit.ly/1rYzUwW

12:46 AM—11 July 2014

The Trudeau corpus contains approximately equal proportions of English and French tweets, but there are cases where tweets exist only in one language and not the other. For example, when tweets are retweeted verbatim, they are not translated into the other language. That means that at least 143 tweets in the corpus occur only in one language. There are additional quoted tweets (non-verbatim retweets) that also tend not to be translated. Notably, most of the retweets in the Trudeau corpus are in English.

Also, there is considerable outreach in the Trudeau corpus through the use of the @username function, which tags other users in tweets. The Trudeau corpus contains 2323 uses of @, with an average of 43 % of tweets containing at least one @username outreach. Notably, most outreach is done in either one language or the other—not both. See, for instance, Examples 6.23 and 6.24, which occur only in one language and not the other.

Example 6.23

Justin Trudeau @JustinTrudeau

Enjoy your first #July4th in Ottawa, @BruceAHeyman. Don't worry; we have no designs on your flavors or colors. http://bit.ly/1ouz9rH

7:30 PM—4 July 2014

Example 6.24

Justin Trudeau @JustinTrudeau

Bonne conversation avec double médaillée @DodoMaltais de l'équipe @ OlympiqueCanada à Ottawa aujourd'hui! #ÉquipeCanada pic.Twitter.com/ C4wiQs8Fhj

10:34 PM—4 June 2014

However, there are some exceptions. When Trudeau reaches out to prominent public figures—and especially those with bilingual accounts—it is often done both in English and in French, as with Examples 6.25 and 6.26, where the username @pmharper is used in the English Tweet and @premierministre is used in the French tweet but the same picture exists in both cases.

Example 6.25

Justin Trudeau @JustinTrudeau

Nice to introduce Xavier to the Prime Minister. Good of @pmharper to say hello. Enjoy #Stampede2014 pic.Twitter.com/y8Ue794gv0

5:59 PM—4 July 2014

Example 6.26

Justin Trudeau @JustinTrudeau

Plaisir de présenter Xavier au @premierministre. Très gentil de la part du PM de lui dire bonjour. Bon #Stampede2014 pic.Twitter.com/o0ARKW8ZYh

5:59 PM—4 July 2014

Similar to the Trudeau corpus, the Mulcair corpus comprises the English and French tweets from Thomas Mulcair's bilingual Twitter account. As with Trudeau, most of Mulcair's tweets occur in both English and French and they tend to be loose translations of one another. However, as with the Trudeau corpus, retweets tend not to be translated and most outreach tends to be done in one language or another—not both. For instance, Examples 6.27 and 6.28 do not have translation equivalents.

Example 6.27

Tom Mulcair @ThomasMulcair

Merci @myriamfehmiu, excellente entrevue sur @rc_cb http://bit.ly/ugQOQl #Phareouest #radiocanada

7:08 PM—27 October 2011

Example 6.28

Tom Mulcair @ThomasMulcair
Thanks @alferraby, excellent interview on #cfax this morning http://bit.ly/sErfPk
7:08 PM—27 October 2011

The PmHarper and Premierministre corpora differ from the Mulcair and Trudeau corpora because these accounts are monolingual. In this case, "monolingual" means that the PmHarper corpus only contains English language and does not appear to contain any use of non-English terminology. The @pmharper account is entirely separate from the French Twitter account @premierministre and the only link between the two is in the @pmharper profile, which provides the option of following him in the French: "Suivez-moi en français à @premierministre". This is also the only French that would seem to exist as part of the account. In contrast, the Premierministre corpus is "monolingual" in that it contains only French tweets; the @premierministre account is entirely separate from the @pmharper account. Parallel to the @pmharper account, the @premierministre profile provides the option of following him in English: "Follow me in English: @pmharper". Although the @premierministre account and the resultant Premierministre corpus are predominantly "monolingual" in that they predominantly contain only one language (French), there are several instances of English words, websites, hashtags, and interactions with English Twitter users, suggesting a degree of code-switching and code-mixing within the tweets.

Although no use of code-switching or code-mixing was found in the PmHarper corpus, there are several instances in the French Premierministre corpus. Since the data were collected during the 2014 Olympics in Sochi, Russia, there are references to these events in all of the federal party leaders' corpora. However, in the Premierministre corpus, there are both English and French spellings of "Sochi" (French: Sotchi). This means that two hashtags are used to discuss this event: #Sochi2014 (5 occurrences) and #Sotchi2014 (35 occurrences). In a similar vein, the Canadian Olympic team was addressed in the Premierministre corpus; however, as a representative for the bilingual Canadian nation, the Olympic team had English and French accounts. Although the French version (@ OlympiqueCanada) was addressed in eight instances, the English version (@CdnOlympicTeam) was also addressed in two instances. Notably, neither French version (i.e. #Sotchi2014, @OlympiqueCanada) occur in the PmHarper corpus.

Other sports events were flagged through the use of English in the Premierministre corpus: for example, the English-medium hashtag #GoHabsGo (13) was used to cheer on Canada's Montreal Canadiens National Hockey League (NHL) hockey team, and #GoCanadaGo (5) was used to cheer on the Canadian Olympians in Sochi. Similarly, the hashtag #GoLions (1) was used to cheer on the BC Lions Canadian football team, #Canadadraft (2) was used in tweets about the 2014 National Basketball Association (NBA) draft, and #NorthernUprising (1) and #NothernUprising (1) were used to support the Toronto Raptors basketball team. The hashtag #NHLPlayoffs (1) was used to flag a tweet about hockey and #TeamUSA was used in a tweet about a Canada–USA hockey match. In addition to tweets discussing sports, other English-medium hashtags are used such as #citystorm, #royalbaby, #cdntrademission, #wethenorth, and #marketingfreedom. Furthermore, the hashtags #ABFloodAid, #ABFloods, #HellOrHighWater, and #TOFlood are used to discuss floods in Alberta and Toronto, but #MBInondations (2)—a French hashtag—is used to discuss floods in Manitoba. Finally, more widespread hashtags such as #FF ("Follow Friday") and #TBT ("Throw Back Thursday") are also used in the French corpus.

Perhaps most notably, there are 25 uses of the hashtag #cdnpoli in the Premierministre corpus. Although the French version of this hashtag (#polcan) occurs 631 times in the corpus, the instances of #cdnpoli arguably constitute a form of code-switching or code-mixing. Related to this, the politics of individual provinces are sometimes under discussion. These, too, often become flagged through the use of hashtags, and hashtags can occur in both English and French (i.e. with the French *pol-* prefix or the English *-poli* suffix) and, because the names of many provinces have English and French versions, with French or English names (see Table 6.6).

Table 6.6 Possible provincial hashtags in English and French

Province (English)	Hashtag	Province (French)	Hashtag
Newfoundland and Labrador	#NLPOLI	Terre-Neuve-et-Labrador	#POLTN
Nova Scotia	#NSPOLI	Nouvelle-Écosse	#POLNE
Prince Edward Island	#PEIPOLI	L'Île-du-Prince-Édouard	#POLIPE
New Brunswick	#NBPOLI	Nouveau-Brunswick	#POLNB
Ontario	#ONPOLI	Ontario	#POLON
Quebec	#QCPOLI	Québec	#POLQC
Manitoba	#MBPOLI	Manitoba	#POLMB
Saskatchewan	#SKPOLI	Saskatchewan	#POLSK
Alberta	#ABPOLI	Alberta	#POLAB
British Columbia	#BCPOLI	La Colombie-Britannique	#POLCB

Table 6.7 English and French provincial hashtags in the PmHarper and Premierministre corpora

Hashtag	Freq.	Source	Hashtag	Freq.	Source
#NLPOLI	0		#POLTN	0	
#NSPOLI	0		#POLNE	0	
#PEIPOLI	0		#POLIPE	0	
#NBPOLI	0		#POLNB	0	
#ONPOLI	0		#POLON	0	
#QCPOLI	1	PmHarper (1)	#POLQC	2	Premierministre (2)
#MBPOLI	0		#POLMB	0	
#SKPOLI	0		#POLSK	0	
#ABPOLI	0		#POLAB	0	
#BCPOLI	2	PmHarper (1) Premierministre (1)	#POLCB	0	

While all of these hashtags are possible (indeed, practically any hashtag is possible on Twitter), not all of them are used. For example, in the PmHarper and Premierministre (combined), only some examples exist (see Table 6.7).

These findings indicate that, first, provincial politics are not a topical issue for the Prime Minister of Canada. Second, we can also see that an English hashtag (#BCPOLI) was used instead of the French version (#POLCB) in the Premierministre corpus, but the French hashtag #POLQC was used in the Premierministre corpus whereas the English hashtag #QCPOLI was opted for in the PmHarper corpus. Although these findings are of very low frequency, they suggest that while both

English and French hashtags might be used in the French @premierministre account, only English hashtags tend to be used in the English @pmharper account.

In summary, despite the possibility of using or creating French equivalents or alternatives, the Premierministre corpus contains several instances of English hashtagging and outreach. Although there are arguably no French alternatives for such widespread hashtags as #FF and #TBT, other hashtags used in the Premierministre corpus are user-generated and therefore could easily include French rather than English words. Thus, despite the fact that the PmHarper corpus contains no foreign language hashtags, the Premierministre corpus contains a high proportion of English hashtags.

In the Trudeau corpus, the use of code-switching and code-mixing is more difficult to establish due to the bilingual nature of the account and the tweets. Nevertheless, it was found that there was some degree of code-switching in ways similar to the Premierministre corpus. For example, the Trudeau corpus contains many retweets and often RT ("retweet") is used to mark these retweets; also, the hashtag #FF occurs 16 times and 7 of these occur in French tweets. The English hashtag #GoHabsGo also occurs 31 times in both English- and French-medium tweets. Although the Trudeau corpus contains some French tweets with English hashtags and even some tweets where hashtags are used in English but not French versions of tweets, in most cases different hashtags are used in English and French (see Example 6.29).

Example 6.29

Justin Trudeau @JustinTrudeau

#CPC cuts to refugee healthcare go against basic Canadian values, and unnecessarily harm the most vulnerable. #WorldRefugeeDay

1:02 AM—21 June 2014

Justin Trudeau @JustinTrudeau

Coupes du #PCC dans les soins pour les réfugiés=contraire aux valeurs canad. + touchent les plus vulnérables. #JournéeMondialedesRéfugiés

1:01 AM—21 June 2014

Notably, different hashtags are used in English and French tweets pertaining specifically to the Liberal campaign. While #realpriorities was the

English hashtag, #unpaysplusfort ("a stronger country") was the French hashtag used in the equivalent cases, as in Example 6.30.

Example 6.30

Justin Trudeau retweeted

RAPPEL: le #PLC embauche! La date limite pour postuler est le 10 janv. Plus d'info ici : http://ow.ly/smcUb #PolCan #UnPaysPlusFort

11:45 PM—7 January 2014

Justin Trudeau retweeted

REMINDER: #LPC is hiring! Deadline to apply is Jan. 10. Have a look here for more info: http://ow.ly/smcMV #cdnpoli #RealPriorities

11:45 PM—7 January 2014

Since "a stronger country" is in no way the equivalent of "real priorities", this suggests that slightly different messages are being sent to the English- and French-speaking Twittersphere. Nevertheless, all tweeters are exposed to the same messages because the @justintrudeau account is bilingual and there is no way of filtering out tweets in the other official language.

Finally, the Trudeau corpus contains a diverse set of hashtags pertaining to provincial politics, but there is still a bias towards English hashtags. For example, there are no uses of French hashtags for Newfoundland and Labrador, Alberta, or British Columbia but there are uses of the relevant English hashtags in French-medium tweets. Also, although there is one use of #POLNE (Nova Scotia politics) in a French tweet, there are six instances of #NSPOLI in French tweets. Similarly, there are two uses of #POLON in French tweets, but five uses of #ONPOLI in French tweets. These findings suggest the preponderance of English hashtags in French-medium Twitter (see Table 6.8).

Nevertheless, the Trudeau corpus also contains an interesting counter-trend: the predominant use of #POLQC in both English- and French-medium tweets about Quebec politics. Although there are two instances of #QCPOLI in English tweets, there are a further three English tweets containing the French hashtag #POLQC. No French tweets contain the

Table 6.8 Provincial hashtags and language usage in Trudeau corpus

Hashtag	Freq.	Language of tweet	Hashtag	Freq.	Language of tweet
#NLPOLI	6	French (3), English (3)	#POLTN	0	n/a
#NSPOLI	15	French (6), English (9)	#POLNE	1	French (1)
#PEIPOLI	0	n/a	#POLIPE	0	n/a
#NBPOLI	2	English (2)	#POLNB	1	French (1)
#ONPOLI	18	French (5), English (13)	#POLON	2	French (2)
#QCPOLI	2	English (2)	#POLQC	8	French (5), English (3)
#MBPOLI	1	English (1)	#POLMB	1	French (1)
#SKPOLI	1	English (1)	#POLSK	0	n/a
#ABPOLI	4	French (2), English (2)	#POLAB	0	n/a
#BCPOLI	6	French (2), English (4)	#POLCB	0	n/a

English hashtag #QCPOLI. These findings seem to indicate an alignment of English hashtags with English-dominant provinces such as Newfoundland and Labrador, Alberta, and British Columbia (even in French-medium tweets) and an alignment of French hashtags with the French-dominant province of Quebec (even in English-medium tweets). Although no conclusive findings could possibly be based on such small numbers, this does suggest the extent to which language ideologies are becoming manifested in online language, including, in a condensed way, in hashtags.

Finally, the Mulcair corpus is fully bilingual in a way similar to the Trudeau corpus. There are instances of marking English and French retweets with RT and using generic English hashtags such as #FF and #TBT in both English and French tweets. However, unlike the other federal party leaders' corpora, there are some tweets that are bilingual in that a single tweet contains both English and French, as in Examples 6.31 and 6.32.

Example 6.31

Tom Mulcair @ThomasMulcair

I basically haven't aged a day… Right…? Je n'ai pas pris une ride… N'est-ce pas…? #TBT #cdnpoli #polcan

11:40 PM—29 May 2014

Example 6.32

Tom Mulcair @ThomasMulcair

Follow our #NDP candidates / Suivez nos candidats #NPD @S_Moraille @LindaMcQuaig @Corythewelder @Natalie_NDP #FF #polcan #cdnpoli #byelxn41

4:46 PM—8 November 2013

Table 6.9 Provincial hashtags and language usage in Mulcair corpus

Hashtag	Freq.	Language of tweet	Hashtag	Freq.	Language of tweet
#NLPOLI	3	English (3)	#POLTN	0	n/a
#NSPOLI	0	n/a	#POLNE	0	n/a
#PEIPOLI	0	n/a	#POLIPE	0	n/a
#NBPOLI	0	n/a	#POLNB	0	n/a
#ONPOLI	7	English (6), French (1)	#POLON	0	n/a
#QCPOLI	2	English (1), French (1)	#POLQC	2	French (2)
#MBPOLI	0	n/a	#POLMB	0	n/a
#SKPOLI	2	English (1), French (1)	#POLSK		n/a
#ABPOLI	0	n/a	#POLAB	0	n/a
#BCPOLI	2	English (2)	#POLCB	0	n/a

Notably, these examples are not just bilingual in their lexical content; they also include both English and French hashtags (#polcan, #cdnpoli). Indeed, unlike the other corpora, there are five instances in which the hashtags #polcan and #cdnpoli collocate, suggesting an appeal to both English and French speakers within a single tweet. To flag provincial politics, the Mulcair corpus contains a set of hashtags that are not particularly diverse. For example, he only uses one French hashtag (#POLQC, two occurrences), and this occurs only in French tweets. He also uses the English version (#QCPOLI) in both English- and French-medium tweets. The rest of his provincial politics hashtags are English-only, and these occur in both English- and French-medium tweets (see Table 6.9).

Finally, when we turn to the CDNPOLI and POLCAN corpora to see how languages figure there, we see that there is little explicit discussion of languages; also, language ideologies tend to be embedded differently from the party leaders' corpora of tweets.

First, frequency lists and hashtags from the Cdnpoli corpus indicate that this data set almost entirely comprises English tweets whereas frequency lists and hashtags from the Polcan corpus indicate that this data set only predominantly comprises French tweets. This is in keeping with the federal party leaders' corpora, where #cdnpoli was used in English tweets (and in some French tweets), but #polcan was used in French tweets and not in English tweets. In other words, the hashtags are by and large indicators not only of the topic of the tweet (i.e. Canadian politics) but also of the medium of the tweet.

Nevertheless, there are some exceptions to this general rule. For example, there are 73 instances of #cdnpoli occurring in the Polcan corpus, indicating that #cdnpoli and #polcan collocate in 5 % of tweets within the Polcan corpus. Notably, though, 20 of these tweets (27 %) are English medium and 3 are bilingual with English and French equivalent content and hashtags. This kind of code-mixing within a tweet was only found in three instances in the Mulcair corpus (see Examples 6.31 and 6.32). However, in the Polcan corpus, the only examples found with intra-tweet code-mixing also mention the NDP or its leader Thomas Mulcair; as a result, it seems that this style of code-mixing in tweeting may be specific to this political party (see Examples 6.33, 6.34, and 6.35).

Example 6.33

Guy Caron @GuyCaronNPD

About 5 min before my set of questions to FinMin Oliver/Encore 5 min avant mes questions au MinFin Oliver. #cotw #npd #ndp #polcan #cdnpoli

1:30 AM—15 May 2014

Example 6.34

Alexandre Huet @Alex_Huet

The #NDP leader is ready for game 7 #gohabsgo #cdnpoli Le chef du #NPD, prêt pour la 7e partie! #polcan pic.Twitter.com/hqCt93d8rK

9:47 PM—14 May 2014

Example 6.35

CPAC @CPAC_TV
LIVE ONLINE/EN DIRECT EN LIGNE—Thomas Mulcair—http://www.cpac.ca/en/direct/cpac2/ … #cdnpoli #polcan
4:43 PM—5 June 2013

Nevertheless, this also means that the remaining 50 (68 %) tweets that contain English hashtags are French-medium, suggesting that it is still French Twitter users who tend to demonstrate metalinguistic awareness through their combined use of English and French hashtags. Indeed, #polcan is used only twice in the Cdnpoli corpus (0.1 % of all tweets), and both of these tweets are English medium. Overall, then, the use of the hashtags #cdnpoli and #polcan is in line with findings from the federal party leaders' corpora, where English hashtags were sometimes used in French tweets but French hashtags were not found in English tweets.

In terms of representations, languages are rarely represented in the Cdnpoli corpus. In fact, apart from usernames and URLs, FRENCH and LANGUAGE do not occur at all; ENGLISH only occurs once (see Example 6.36).

Example 6.36

always vote @always_vote
@thomsonian Wish there was English translation @CPAC_TV. Over 30 mins of open questions fr press! @ThomasMulcair did well explaining #cdnpoli
9:07 PM—14 May 2014

In this example, "fr" is used to refer to French; however, it is the only such instance in the Cdnpoli corpus, as no other abbreviations for French (e.g. Fre, Fren, Fran, franco) were found. This user's metalinguistic comment, which pertains to a lack of translation of French content, has some similarities with tweets in the Trudeau corpus, where examples note publications "up in French in Qc first" or "en anglais" (see Examples 6.3, 6.4, and 6.10). There is little metalinguistic commentary of this sort in the other federal party leaders' corpora. Moreover, it is not common within the Cdnpoli corpus itself, suggesting perhaps that there are few instances where English speakers would need to be aware of French (or indeed other language) content in their everyday experiences. Searches indicated that there were no references to other languages, either.[1]

Notably, there is considerably more metalinguistic commentary in the Polcan corpus than in the Cdnpoli corpus. For example, there are three references to LANGUE and four hashtags of #LANGUESOFFICIELLES. Notably, most of these references are calls for action in the defence or promotion of French, suggesting that there are—to some extent—ideologies of language endangerment underpinning the tweets (see Chap. 4). In other words, some French-medium Twitter users represent the French language as in need of protection and/or promotion and call on actors to take up this cause (see Example 6.37).

Example 6.37

Yvon Godin @YvonNPD

Joignez-vous à moi pour demander @JacquesGourde de voter pour juges bilingues à la Cour surpême! #languesofficielles #frcan #polcan #NPD

8:12 PM—6 May 2014

In addition to these general references to language, there are specific references to English: ANGLAIS/E/S occurs five times in the Polcan corpus. Three of the five instances comment on the unilingual nature of English use. For example, Example 6.38 notes that a poorly translated Tweet is responded to in English by Veterans Minister Julian Fantino. Example 6.39 posts news about not requiring English to do business, and Example 6.40 admonishes Stephen Harper (@pmharper) for his wife's monolingual English speech at the Beny-sur-mer Canadian War Cemetery in Normandy, France. In other words, these tweets take issue with the use

[1] CHINESE, RUSSIA/N, and GERMAN/Y were found in the corpus but without any relevance to language or cultural issues.

of English when French translations or equivalents are available—particularly when English is used by those in public office.

Example 6.38

Philippe-V. Foisy @pvfoisy

Le député du NPD lit un tweet du ministre des Vétérans. Très mal traduit. Fantino répond en anglais... #polcan

7:34 PM—14 May 2014

Example 6.39

Mathieu Bélanger @Belangmt

À ceux qui pensent qu'il faut apprendre l'anglais pour faire des affaires. Ce n'est plus le cas. #polQC #polCAN #PQ http://journalmetro.com/plus/techno/501984/demonstration-de-traduction-en-temps-reel-sur-skype/ ...

10:11 PM—29 May 2014

Example 6.40

Michel Dauphinais @micdau

@pmharper Le discours unilingue anglais de votre épouse à Beny-sur-mer est un total manque de respect pour tous les francophones. #polcan

5:16 AM—6 June 2014

There are also five references to FRANÇAIS/E/S, eight references to FRANCOPHONE/S, and 11 uses of the hashtag #frcan, referring to French Canada or French Canadians. First, in the tweets discussing French, it is worth noting that when the language is under discussion, it is often either alongside or with an implied reference to English. For instance, Example 6.41 explicitly discusses French alongside English with relation to languages spoken in Canada. In Example 6.42, Stephen Harper is cited as saying that Justin Trudeau contradicts himself "from one language to the other" (*d'une langue à l'autre*) and Trudeau replies that Harper does not understand French (*Harper comprend mal le Français*). Here, while French is made explicit, the "other" language is implied but not explicitly stated to be English. Finally, in Example 6.43, it is noted that the Auditor General of Canada (*vérificateur general du Canada*, or VG) began his speech in French. The fact that this was noteworthy suggests that normally French is not used, but another language is.

Example 6.41

Boris Proulx @borisproulx

La langue la plus parlée dans chaque province du #Canada, après l'anglais et le français http://imgur.com/mnIUW9d #polcan #polqc

4:02 PM—14 May 2014

Example 6.42

Raymond Filion @filionrayTVA

Stephen Harper dit que Justin Trudeau se contredit d'une langue à l'autre. Trudeau réplique que Harper comprend mal le Français. #polcan

7:33 PM—14 May 2014

Example 6.43

Philippe-V. Foisy @pvfoisy

Le VG débute sa conférence de presse en français #polcan

4:33 PM—6 May 2014

When francophones are discussed (eight instances), it tends to be within contexts discussing bilingualism. Indeed, five of these eight instances mention bilingualism explicitly (see Example 6.44).

Example 6.44

Alexandre Boulerice @alexboulerice

Les conservateurs représentant des Francophones doivent appuyer le bilinguisme à la Cour suprême http://ift.tt/1j8Gegx #NPD #polcan

5:15 PM—6 May 2014

Similarly, all 11 uses of #frcan, discuss bilingualism and/or official languages, suggesting that there is a persistent awareness of the wider linguistic context underpinning most French-medium tweets that discuss the French language or French speakers. All of examples call for more bilingualism at the federal level, for example, in the Supreme Court of Canada (*Cour supreme du Canada/ CSC*) (see Example 6.45).

Example 6.45

Marie-C. Monchalin @Mnchln

@Christianparad juges bilingues à #CSC égalité et justice pour francophones. Comme min du Québec, appuyez #C-208 #frcan #polcan #NPD

9:07 PM—6 May 2014

Therefore, French, English, and bilingualism are all more salient topics of discussion in the POLCAN corpus—and more specifically within the French tweets of the POLCAN corpus—than in the CDNPOLI corpus.

6.3 Discussion

As the findings have shown, language ideologies tend to play a role in Canadian Twitter in a variety of different ways. We can best review these by returning to the research questions posed in the introduction.

The first question asked how languages are represented in the Twitter accounts of Canadian political party leaders. Data from all of the federal party leaders' corpora suggest that English Canadian language, culture, and speakers are discussed less frequently than French Canadian language, culture, and speakers. The fact that English is not mentioned at all—save two occurrences in the Trudeau corpus—suggests that its status is largely taken for granted, indicating the monolingual ideologies underpinning English Canadian Twitter. Although numbers are small, the Trudeau and Mulcair corpora contain more references to language issues than the PmHarper and Premierministre corpora, and the Premierministre corpus contains slightly more discussion of language issues than the PmHarper corpus. Also, the Mulcair and Premierministre corpora both tend to discuss language issues slightly more often in French than in English. However, neither English nor French issues are salient in any federal party leader corpus (i.e. according to the raw frequency and statistical significance of lexical items such as French/*français*); furthermore, no other languages tend to be discussed either.

The second question asked how assumptions about languages were embedded in the Twitter accounts of Canadian political party leaders. Assumptions about languages became salient in a number of different ways, but perhaps most immediately through monolingual versus bilingual tweeting tendencies. While some leaders (e.g. Mulcair, Trudeau) use bilingual Twitter accounts (and the Mulcair corpus even contained bilingual tweets), others (e.g. Stephen Harper) use monolingual Twitter accounts (@pmharper and @premierministre). Also, while the tweets of Mulcair and Trudeau tend to be loose translations of one another, Harper's tweets tend to be formal and formulaic transliterations of one another. This arguably suggests a more naturalistic approach to bilingualism in the cases of Mulcair and Trudeau and a more formal approach in the case of Harper. The differences between English and French tweeting suggest a distinct audience design in the case of each party leader: while Mulcair and Trudeau arguably design their tweets for a bilingual public, Harper appears to design his tweets for two separate (and perhaps non-interacting) publics, one English-speaking and the other French-speaking. Notably, though, all party leaders seem to design their tweets slightly differently depending on the language of use. For example, French-medium tweets generally contained more discussion of language issues than English-medium tweets, perhaps suggesting an expectation that French Twitter users would be more interested in or concerned by language issues than English Twitter users. This finding is largely in keeping with findings from Chap. 4, where it was discovered that language issues are far more prevalent and wide-ranging in French Canadian newspapers than in English Canadian newspapers.

The leaders' corpora also demonstrate the important functional role of English. For example, all leaders engage with the public through retweets and @replies; however, these tend to occur only in one language and not the other (e.g. through translation). Perhaps because of the dominant role of English in online spaces, in most cases this language tends to be

English. Also, although the Premierministre corpus is arguably monolingual (French), it nonetheless contained some incremental uses of English in URLs, hashtags, and @replies, even when there were French alternatives available. Similarly, the use of English and French provincial hashtags by all leaders suggested the extent to which language ideologies are manifested in online language. Despite the availability of alternatives, most federal party leaders used English hashtags in French tweets to tag English-dominant provinces. The use of English rather than French hashtags might be due to the functional role of English; however, these instances could also suggest the extent to which naturalised assumptions about these provinces and the languages predominantly spoken there become embedded in language use, even in cases with a limit of 140 characters.

Question 3 asked about the similarities and differences between representations of and assumptions about languages in the Twitter accounts of Canadian political party leaders. Findings showed that there are a number of differences across the corpora. As with the answer to question 2 (above), the most salient differences are in the accounts themselves: while two separate accounts are maintained for Stephen Harper—one in English and one in French—the other leaders have only one account for both languages. The Mulcair corpus was unique in that it contained several instances of intra-tweet code-switching (Examples 6.31 and 6.32), but the Trudeau corpus contained some code-mixing (e.g. through English hashtags in French tweets) and the Premierministre corpus contained some code-mixing, too. In the latter case, however, the ostensibly monolingual nature of this corpus and the availability of French alternatives indicate not only that the code-mixing is unplanned but also that English is making incremental incursions into the French Twittersphere.

Finally, question 4 asked how the leaders' representations of and assumptions about languages compare to representations and assumptions in general tweets containing #cdnpoli and #polcan. First, the CDNPOLI and POLCAN corpora contain mainly English-medium and French-medium tweets, respectively, but the POLCAN corpus contains far more code-switching and code-mixing than the CDNPOLI corpus. Also, the POLCAN corpus contains far more metalanguage than any other corpus, including references to language (*langue*), official languages (*langues officielles*), English (*anglais/e/s*), French (*français/e/s*), and francophone/s. Although the French language is discussed more than the English language, this is often because English is taken for granted and/or assumed.

Therefore, it would seem that the party leaders' increased discussion of French and language issues in French-medium tweets actually aligns with French Twitter users' metalinguistic discussions. In other words, if party leaders design their tweets specifically for French speakers not only by using the French language but also by discussing language issues, then this is based on an accurate assumption that these issues are more salient for French speakers themselves. Indeed, English tweeters express little concern with language issues—English, French, or other. English Canadian tweeters appear to have little need to engage with any language but English in social media unless they so choose. This is not the case in French Canadian Twitter, where language issues figure in metalinguistic discussions and also through English hashtags, @replies, retweeting, URLs, and other content.

These findings suggest some reasons why the Official Languages Commissioner Graham Fraser's conclusions that federal ministers should tweet in both official languages were so contentious, especially for English-speaking Canadians: given that English Twitter users are rarely confronted with other languages in their socially mediated lives, an enforcement of the presence of French seems like a deliberate incursion on their freedom to produce and consume exclusively English-medium material. However, for French Canadians whose Twittersphere undergoes incursions from English in nearly all respects with regular occurrence, such freedom seems nearly impossible to attain.

References

Canadian Standing Senate Committee on Official Languages. (2012). *Internet, new media and social media: Respect for language rights!* Available http://www. parl.gc.ca/Content/SEN/Committee/411/OLLO/rep/rep05oct12-e.pdf

Canadian Press. (2015, 12 February). Federal ministers must tweet in both English and French: Language czar. *CTV News*. Available http://www.ctvnews.ca/politics/federal-ministers-must-tweet-in-both-english-and-french-language-czar-1.2233799

Chen, P. J., & Smith, P. J. (2011). Digital media in the 2008 Canadian election. *Journal of Information Technology and Politics, 8*(4), 399–417.

Dubois, E., & Dutton, W. H. (2012). The fifth estate in Internet governance: Collective accountability of a Canadian policy initiative. *Revue française d'études américaines, 4*(134). Available https://www.cairn.info/revue-francaise-d-etudes-americaines-2012-4-page-81.htm

Dubois, E., & Gaffney, D. (2014). The multiple facets of influence: Identifying political influential and opinion leaders on Twitter. *American Behavioural Scientist, 58*(10), 1–18.

Gruzd, A., & Roy, J. (2014). Investigating political polarization on Twitter: A Canadian perspective. *Policy & Internet, 6*(1), 28–45.

Gruzd, A., Wellman, B., & Takhteyev, Y. (2011). Imagining Twitter as an imagined community. *American Behavioural Scientist, 55*(10), 1294–1318.

Office of the Commissioner of Official Languages. (2015). *Statement from the Commissioner of Official Languages about ministers' Twitter use.* Available http://www.officiallanguages.gc.ca/en/news/releases/2015/2015-02-20

Page, R., Barton, D., Unger, J., & Zappavigna, M. (2014). *Researching language and social media: A student guide*. London: Routledge.

Partington, A. (2010). Modern diachronic corpus-assisted discourse studies (MD-CADS) on UK newspapers: An overview of the project. *Corpora, 5*(2), 83–108.

Scott, M. (2014). *WordSmith Tools, Version 6*. Liverpool: Lexical Analysis Software.

Small, T. A. (2010a). Canadian politics in 140 characters: Party politics in the Twitterverse. *Canadian Parliamentary Review, 33*(3), 103–124.

Small, T. A. (2010b). Still waiting for an Internet prime minister: Online campaigning by Canadian political parties. In H. McIvor (Ed.), *Election* (pp. 173–198). Toronto: Emond Montgomery.

Small, T. A. (2014). The not-so-social network: The use of Twitter by Canada's party leaders. In A. Marland, T. Giasson, & T. A. Small (Eds.), *Political communication in Canada: Meet the press and tweet the rest* (pp. 92–110). Vancouver: UBC Press.

Zappavigna, M. (2011). Ambient affiliation: A linguistic perspective on Twitter. *New Media & Society, 13*(5), 708–806.

Zappavigna, M. (2012). *Discourse of Twitter and social media: How we use language to create affiliation on the web*. London: Bloomsbury Publishing.

7

Language Ideologies in Online News, Commentary, and Twitter: The Case of "Pastagate"

In previous chapters, language ideologies in Canadian news, commentary, and social media have been addressed. This chapter brings together all of these themes by investigating the role of language ideologies at the intersection of news, commentary, and Twitter. To tackle these diverse media types, this chapter focuses on a single issue which took place in 2013 known as "Pastagate".

On 19 February 2013, inspectors from the *Office québécois de la langue française* (OQLF) sent a letter of warning to Massimo Lecas, owner of the Buonanotte Italian restaurant in Montreal, objecting to the use of Italian words on its menu. Lecas promptly reported the letter on the microblogging site Twitter, with a link to an Instagram image of the menu's linguistic offences, which included the word "pasta". The story was immediately picked up by a local journalist who retweeted the photo and reported the story on his radio blog. The blog was then picked up by activist groups, which shared the story, related stories, and memes tens of thousands of times over social media. The story broke internationally and by 26 February had been chronicled in over 350 newspaper articles across 14 countries (Wyatt 2013).

The impact of this social media deluge was immediate in Quebec: by 8 March, the head of the OQLF had resigned, the OQLF warning to

R. Vessey, *Language and Canadian Media*,
DOI 10.1057/978-1-137-53001-1_7

Buonanotte had been declared "overzealous", and on 18 October it was announced that the OQLF would be "modernising" its approach in order to deal with complaints more efficiently and in order to better support businesses and citizens (OQLF 2013). In addition, the success of the so-called "Pastagate" affair has been linked to the provincial government's abandonment of the controversial Bill 14, which proposed amendments to Quebec's Charter of the French Language. In other words, the social media campaign appears to have had rather direct effects on language policy in Quebec.

While the OQLF conceded that it had been "overzealous", zeal also reverberated in the news and social media backlash. The international appeal of the story and its popularisation in social media suggest that the story touched a nerve internationally. Since the international response was largely unanimously disapproving, it may indicate that a loosely coherent set of beliefs and understandings about languages (i.e. language ideologies) permeate a range of different countries, cultures, and contexts. The aim of this chapter is not only to explore language ideologies in different media types, but also to compare language ideologies in national and international media in English and French. The following research questions guide these aims:

1. How are languages represented in the news, commentary, and social media that discuss Pastagate? What are the similarities and differences between these representations?
2. Do representations differ according to the country of origin (Canada, US, UK, France)?
3. Do representations differ across languages (English, French)?

This chapter proceeds as follows: Sect. 7.1 presents the theoretical framework, Sect. 7.2 presents the data and methods, Sect. 7.3 presents the findings, and Sect. 7.4 summarises the conclusions.

7.1 Theoretical Framework

The fact that Pastagate and Quebec's language policies were so widely condemned by an international audience suggests the extent to which the adoption of policy depends on "linguistic cultures" (Schiffman 2006).

Linguistic culture refers to the "sum totality of ideas, values, beliefs, attitudes, prejudices, myths, religious strictures, and all the other cultural 'baggage' that speakers bring to their dealings with language from their culture" (Schiffman 2006: 112). Linguistic culture does not imply that culture resides *in* language (e.g. in grammar) but rather that language tends to be used as a vehicle to communicate the beliefs of linguistic communities (i.e. communities delineated by language use) (Schiffman 2006: 121). In other words, policies may be understood and taken up to different extents if languages themselves are understood differently within communities, and especially if these communities tend not to share a common language.

In Canada, the coexistence of official language policies (i.e. the Charter of Rights and Freedoms (Constitution Act 1982, s. 33) and the Official Languages Act (R.S.C. 1985, c. 31 (4th Supp)), which institute the official status of English and French) and multiculturalism policies (i.e. the Canadian Multiculturalism Act, R.S.C. 1985, c. 24 (fourth Supp.)) explicitly denaturalises one-to-one relationships between languages and cultures. Nevertheless, as discussed in Chap. 2, the notion of "two solitudes" has been used to describe a Canadian divide based not only on language, but also on culture (e.g. Heller 1999a: 143). Thus, it is possible that Canada's language policies are implemented within distinct "linguistic cultures" and, within these, language ideologies may circulate through different mediums (i.e. English and French) and may affect the uptake of language policies.

As discussed in Chap. 1, the news media are particularly important sites for the study of ideological discourse. In fact, news media have been credited with the creation of "moral panics" (e.g. Cohen 1972) in society—and in particular moral panics focusing on language issues (e.g. Cameron 1995; Johnson 1999). Moral panics have been described as "supposedly emanating from the ever-increasing moral laxity within our society" and they tend to involve the following successive stages: (1) something or someone is defined as a threat to values or interests; (2) this threat is depicted in an easily recognisable form by the media; (3) there is a rapid build-up of public concern; (4) there is a response from authorities or opinion makers; and (5) the panic recedes or results in social changes (Johnson 1999: 2).

Moral panics in the news also relate to what Fowler (1994: 91) has called "hysteria": "behaviour which attains autonomy, which sustains itself as an expressive performance, independent of its causes". In other words, these are "pseudo-events"—events that are only real insofar as they become topics within the media (Boorstin cited in Cotter 2010: 111) that become real "discursive events" (Fairclough 2010: 94). When such discursive events focus on language and evolve into moral panics, these are forms of "language ideological debates" (Blommaert 1999a; see Chap. 5). In other words, the media become sites and platforms for individuals to voice their language ideologies, that is, make explicit beliefs and understandings about languages that more often tend to be taken for granted and understood as common sense.

When moral panics about language evolve, they often involve metaphoric arguments about language and society that draw on language ideologies (Cameron 1995; Johnson 1999). However, according to a constructivist approach, the extent to which ideologies can evolve into moral panics depends on the interests of a particular group in promoting a problem, the resources available to them, the ownership that they secure over the issue, and the degree to which their analyses of the issue are accepted as authoritative (Jenkins 1992: 3, cited in Johnson 1999: 21–2). Thus, the creation of a moral panic may be contingent on the extent to which branches of the media grant particular groups the time and space to air their views to specific audiences. Furthermore, in order for an issue to develop into a moral panic, a common language is arguably required to communicate the story to a wider audience.

In a globalised world, online transnational forums offer new and unprecedented opportunities for communication, interaction, and the development of minoritised and even endangered languages (see e.g. Leppänen and Häkkinen 2012: 18). Nevertheless, the English language continues to have an important role as a medium of communication in international media. Also, English is one of the official languages of Canada alongside French, and historically Canadian media developed along parallel lines in English and French (see Chap. 2). Web 2.0 provides affordances to minoritised languages and indeed more opportunities for

Canadian English and French speakers to bridge the previously established "two solitudes" gap that has been reinforced by the news media. However, it remains unclear if these affordances and opportunities are being drawn on by users. It also remains unclear the extent to which new and social media differ from traditional news media and whether these are simply being used to further the divide to a wider audience. Indeed, the fact that English Canadian media have ready access to an international English-speaking media audience suggests that English Canadians have greater capacity to propagate a "moral panic" about language. To explore the extent of this capacity, this chapter compares national and international, news and social, and English and French media focusing on "Pastagate".

7.2 Data and Methods

The data under analysis consists of two main sets: the Pastagate corpus and the news articles, commentary, and tweets focusing on the news stories.

First, the "Pastagate corpus" consists of 4795 tweets and retweets containing the word "Pastagate". Since tweets consist of only 140 characters, the Pastagate corpus comprises only 123,853 words. With this data set, the aim was to explore how the term "Pastagate" was being used by the online community rather than by Canadians specifically. To this end, tweets were collected based on their date of posting and content. In terms of date of posting, tweets were collected from the first occurrence of "Pastagate" on Twitter the day after the restaurant owner posted his original statement online (20 February 2013) until 21 August 2013, which is approximately when the alternative media sharing site www.pastagate.com was created and the term began to be used in URLs. Within this time period, all publicly available tweets containing the term "Pastagate" were included. Since data collection was not restricted to Canadian Twitter users, this data set allowed for some exploration of how the Canadian language context was being represented internationally on social media.

Second, another data set consisting of online news articles, commentary, and tweets focusing on the news stories was also collected. Online news articles were collected according to language (English and French), place of publication (Canada, USA, Britain, and France), scope of their readership (e.g. national and international news), and focus on the "Pastagate" story. More specifically, the *Globe and Mail* and the *National Post* newspapers are Canada's only two English-language national (i.e. national market) newspapers and in 2013 these were among the widest circulated newspapers in Canada according to weekday circulation figures (Newspapers Canada 2013; see also Chap. 2). In the USA, FoxNews.com is an English-language online news source linked to the Fox News cable and satellite news television network and is the sixth most frequently visited news website internationally (ebizmba.com). *National Public Radio* (henceforth *NPR*) is a national syndicator of public radio stations in the USA and ranks 669 on the Alexa Global Rank of most visited websites in 2014 (alexa.com). The *Guardian* is a British newspaper and its website is the tenth most popular news site internationally (ebizmba.com). Finally, the *Economist* is a news magazine based in London; its website had an average of 7,860,671 unique monthly visits in 2012 (Auditedmedia.com). In French, *La Presse* is the most widely read French newspaper in Canada, with an average weekday circulation of 241,659 (Canadian Newspapers 2013). *Le Devoir* is an elite Quebec newspaper with an average weekday readership of only 35,158 (Canadian Newspapers 2013). *Le Huffington Post Québec* is the French branch of the online news website of Huffington Post. *Radio Canada* is the French arm of the Canadian national public broadcaster. Finally, the *Nouvel Observateur* is a weekly French news magazine and the third most frequently consulted website for French information with 6,911,000 website hits in April 2014 (Mediaobs 2014). One article focusing on Pastagate was selected from each of these sites (see Table 7.1.).

In addition, all publicly available online comments on these articles were collected from the news websites. Also, the headlines generated by news websites through retweeting (i.e. the headline generated when the reader clicks the Twitter icon on a news story webpage to retweet) were entered into Twitter and all publicly available tweets citing these articles were collected for analysis (see Tables 7.2 and 7.3).

Table 7.1 Selection of international news articles

	Author	News source	Country	Date of publication	Web source
English data	Canadian Press	*The Globe and Mail*	Canada	08/03/2013	http://www.theglobeandmail.com/news/national/quebecs-language-watchdog-head-steps-down-after-pastagate/article9513486/
	Nelson Wyatt	*National Post*	Canada	26/02/2013	http://news.nationalpost.com/2013/02/26/quebecs-pastagate-pr-nightmare-story-gets-60-times-more-coverage-outside-province-than-marois-investment-trip/
	Bill Chappell	*NPR*	USA	26/02/2013	http://www.npr.org/blogs/thetwo-way/2013/02/26/172982758/pastagate-quebec-agency-criticized-for-targeting-foreign-words-on-menus
	(No author)	*Fox News*	USA	22/02/2013	http://www.foxnews.com/leisure/2013/02/22/canadian-restaurant-told-pasta-should-be-in-french/
	(No author)	*The Economist*	UK	11/03/2013	http://www.economist.com/blogs/johnson/2013/03/language-policy
	Allan Woods	*The Guardian*	UK	01/03/2013	http://www.theguardian.com/world/2013/mar/01/quebec-language-police-ban-pasta
French data	(No author)	*Huffington Post*	Canada	18/10/2013	http://quebec.huffingtonpost.ca/2013/10/18/oqlf-modernise-pratiques-plaintes_n_4122643.html
	Émilie Bilodeau	*La Presse*	Canada	20/02/2013	http://www.lapresse.ca/actualites/montreal/201302/20/01-4623777-le-mot-pasta-cause-un-exces-de-zele.php
	Guillaume Bourgault-Côté	*Le Devoir*	Canada	08/03/2013	http://www.ledevoir.com/politique/quebec/372805/presidence-de-l-oqlf-louise-marchand-quitte-son-poste
	(No author)	*Radio Canada*	Canada	21/02/2013	http://www.radio-canada.ca/nouvelles/societe/2013/02/21/002-oqlf-buonanotte-plainte.shtml
	Daniel Girard	*Nouvel Observateur*	France	26/02/2013	http://leplus.nouvelobs.com/contribution/789937-francophonie-quand-le-gouvernement-quebecois-fait-dans-l-exces-de-zele.html

Table 7.2 International English-language news articles, comments, tweets and word counts

Article	Number	Word count	Comments	Commentary word count	Tweets	Twitter word count
The Globe and Mail	1	732	92	3741	31	583
National Post	1	679	525	14,794	25	490
NPR	1	612	40	1795	99	1775
Fox News	1	262	4	81	9	192
The Economist	1	618	295	19,860	140	2627
The Guardian	1	764	539	14,525	247	4814
Totals	**6**	**3667**	**1495**	**54,796**	**551**	**10,481**

Table 7.3 International French-language news articles, comments, tweets, and word counts

Article	Number	Word count	Comments	Commentary word count	Tweets	Twitter word count
Huffington Post	1	450	24	553	11	248
La Presse	1	394	0	0	44	1005
Le Devoir	1	577	16	1051	21	484
Radio Canada	1	551	160	7349	12	247
Nouvel Observateur	1	843	10	1015	10	220
Totals	**5**	**2815**	**210**	**9968**	**98**	**2204**

Data were analysed using a form of cross-linguistic corpus-assisted discourse analysis (see Chap. 3) adapted for the different languages and genres within the data set.

The presentation of findings proceeds as follows: first, findings from the Pastagate corpus will be presented, then findings from the news articles, commentary, and tweets focusing on the news stories will be presented.

7.3 Findings

7.3.1 Pastagate Corpus Findings

One of the most immediate findings to emerge from the Pastagate corpus pertained to frequency. The most frequent lexical items (e.g. PASTAGATE, 5153; QUEBEC, 1779; LANGUAGE, 1260; OQLF,

1003; MONTREAL, 792; PASTA, 559) refer to the most repeated themes—language issues in Montreal, Quebec, and the word "pasta". However, non-content related words are also frequent: several items (e.g. HTTP, COM, WWW, and LY) suggest the extent to which websites—and in particular, news websites featuring stories about Pastagate—figured in the tweets. The frequency of HTTP (3575) suggests that at least 75 % of all tweets contain one website link.

Since URLs were not tagged in the corpus and punctuation was ignored, URL fragments occur as individual lexical items in the analysis. Thus, the most frequent clusters in the corpus tend to include these fragments (e.g. the cluster HTTP BIT LY consists of fragments containing http://bit.ly, a short URL redirection service). Other frequent clusters are fragments of headlines from these retweets of URL links. For example, all 170 instances of the cluster QUEBEC LANGUAGE OFFICE come from one of two verbatim retweeted headlines: "'Pastagate' prompts review at Quebec language office" (82) and "Head of Quebec language office resigns in wake of Pastagate" (87) (CBC 2013a, b). The frequent cluster HTTP YOUTUBE also highlights the role of other media (in this case, YouTube videos) in the dissemination and popularisation of this story. Alternative media were used to mock and parody the Pastagate context. For example, one user posted parody videos of actors enforcing "French Only zones" in Montreal by informing passers-by—in English—of the pretend rules and regulations that would require them to use French only. These examples suggest the diversity of ways in which Twitter was used as a nucleus for affiliation with a shared condemnation of the enactment (and possibly the very existence) of Quebec's language policy.

Another notable finding from the frequency lists was the presence of the French language as a medium of some tweets. English was the predominant medium within the corpus; nevertheless, French functional words occur frequently (e.g. DE, 1066; LE, 897; LA, 840) and the frequent cluster HTTP WWW LAPRESSE (166) refers to a French online news source (*La Presse*). Other frequent clusters such as DE LA LANGUE (93) and PRÉSIDENTE DE L (89) attest to the presence of the French medium within this data set. These instances suggest that the term "Pastagate" resonates within the French-speaking community; further investigation indicates that

French users engage with the term and contribute to and contest its evolving meaning.

Certainly, many instances of the term "Pastagate" occur in French tweets because they are used in news stories being retweeted (e.g. 52 retweets of "'Pastagate': la présidente de l'OQLF démissionne", Teisceira-Lessard 2013). However, numerous original French-medium tweets contain "Pastagate", and some of these express concern over what is seen to be an overreaction to the issue. For instance, one user laments that people so quickly jump to the conclusion that the OQLF should be abolished; she implies that its role is important but is often forgotten (*c'est dommage que certains crient à l'abolition de l'OQLF. On oublie facilement sa raison d'être...*). Another poster expresses frustration that the Buonanotte restaurant is profiting from the OQLF's actions, and calls for the restaurant owners to send their profits to the government (*Les proprio. devraient faire un chèque au gvt*).

There are many who express disgust with Pastagate, the actions of the OQLF, and Quebec's language laws more generally. In Example 7.1, the tweeter questions the real source of the scandal: is the problem a lack of judgement or intelligence on the part of the OQLF or on the part of the law?

Example 7.1

Judes Dickey @judes_dickey

Pastagate: Est-ce qu'on parle de manque de jugement/intelligence de l'OQLF ou d'une loi qui à la base manque de jugement/intelligence?

2:20 PM—22 February 2013

"Pastagate: Are we talking about the OQLF's lack of judgement/intelligence or about a law that fundamentally lacks judgement/intelligence?"

Some tweeters are more virulent, describing the OQLF as having an attitude of "zealots" and the recent practices as "linguistic Nazism". In Example 7.2, the tweeter explains that while she "adores" her language and wants to protect it, the "overzealous" actions of the OQLF are embarrassing and inappropriate.

Example 7.2

Patricia Doyon @DoyonPatricia
J'adore ma langue et veux bien la défendre, mais je trouve embarrassant et carrément déplacé cet excès de zèle de l'OQLF!!! #OQLF #pastagate
7:31 PM—2 March 2013
"I love my language and really want to defend it, but I find the OQLF's overzealousness embarrassing and completely inappropriate!!! #OQLF #pastagate"

Condemnation of former OQLF president Louise Marchand was particularly fierce. Many Twitter users took advantage of the opportunity to play on words with the term "noodle" (*nouille*). This term can serve as an adjective, meaning "dumb", or as slang for "penis" or "prick" (see Example 7.3).

Example 7.3

michel juneau @MichelJuneau
C vrai que le #PQ aime mieux voir le mot #Nouille au lieu de #Pasta ça reflète mieux leur image #Pastagate
2:38 PM—21 February 2013
"It's true that the #PQ prefers seeing the word #Noodle instead of #Pasta it better reflects their image #Pastagate"

Nevertheless, there was some support voiced for the former president through retweets of an article in which Marchand is described as the "victim of Pastagate" (see Example 7.4).

Example 7.4

Regine Pierre @ReginePierre48
Victime du "pastagate" Présidence de l'OQLF: Louise Marchand quitte son poste | Le Devoir http://www.ledevoir.com/politique/quebec/372805/presidence-de-l-oqlf-louise-marchand-quitte-son-poste … via @ledevoir
4:47 PM—8 March 2013
"Victim of "pastagate" Presidency of the OQLF : Louise Marchand leaves her post | Le Devoir http://www.ledevoir.com/politique/quebec/372805/presidence-de-l-oqlf-louise-marchand-quitte-son-poste … via @ledevoir"

Thus, although English was the dominant medium of this data set, the French language was also used to both condemn and defend the actions of the OQLF.

These preliminary findings suggest that raw frequency findings, which are often a useful starting point in corpus linguistic research (Baker 2006: 47), can prove less advantageous within a corpus of Twitter data (see Chaps. 3 and 6). Indeed, frequency was also not particularly useful here because some of the core lexical items of interest to this study (e.g. English/*anglais*, French/*français*) were not among the most frequent words. The words ENGLISH and ANGLAIS/E/S occurred 123 and 45 times, respectively, and the words FRENCH and FRANÇAIS/E/S occurred 277 and 141 times, respectively. The word FRENCH ranked 50 on the wordlist of most frequent words and only combined FRANÇAIS/E/S and FRANCAIS/E/S rank 98 on the wordlist.

Although FRANÇAIS/E/S occurs as a stand-alone hashtag (i.e. with no grammatical function) in 3 instances and within websites and usernames in 15 instances (e.g. *@Impératif Français*), it predominantly exists in nominal and adjectival forms. FRANÇAIS/E/S occurs as an adjective in 66 instances, but 56 % (37) of these occur in the semi-fixed phrase *Office [québécois/e] de la langue [français/e/francais/e]*. Most (40 %, or 15) instances of this semi-fixed phrase occur in the standard format (*Office québécois de la langue française*), but there are 12 references to the *Office de la langue française*. There are also eight erroneous uses of gender, accent, and capitalisation (e.g. *québécoise* instead of *québécois*), so this semi-fixed phrase does not emerge as a frequent cluster. References to *Office [québécois/e] de la langue [français/e/francais/e]* aside, only 21 % (29 occurrences) of all instances of FRANÇAIS/E/S occur as adjectives. Most (45 %) adjectival uses of FRANÇAIS/E/S refer to the French language (*la langue française,* 13). In particular, there are five specific references to protecting, defending, and the "combat" for the French language, as in the following examples (see Examples 7.5, 7.6 and 7.7).

Example 7.5

Anne-Gaëlle Metzger @AGMetzger
Pastagate : jusqu'où va la **défense de la langue française**... (En anglais !) @nprbusiness: http://n.pr/YVL2HE by @publicbill
10:37 PM—2 February 2013
"Pastagate: how far for the defence of the French language... (In English!) @nprbusiness: http://n.pr/YVL2HE by @publicbill"

Example 7.6

HuffPost Québec @HuffPostQuebec
Pastagate, ou de la nécessité de **reconcevoir le combat pour la langue française** au Québec ow.ly/jEfaW
2:41 AM—2 April 2013
"Pastagate, or the necessity to rethink the combat for the French language in Quebec ow.ly/jEfaW"

Example 7.7

CatherineMaisonneuve @cathmaison
C'est ok de protéger la langue française, mais là les zélés on se calme ...!!—@joebeef digs into "pastagate" http://www.montrealgazette.com/Beef+owner+digs+into+pastagate/8007898/story.html ...
2:55 PM—24 February 2013
"It's ok to protect the French language, but there the overzealous need to calm down ...!!—@joebeef digs into "pastagate" http://www.montrealgazette.com/Beef+owner+digs+into+pastagate/8007898/story.html ..."

Notably, these examples take issue with the actions of the OQLF while at the same time recognising the necessity of protecting French, thereby manifesting ideologies of language endangerment. For instance, Example 7.5 questions how far (*jusqu'où*) action should go to protect the French language, but does not suggest that French is not in need of protection. Example 7.6 retweets a news story about "the need to rethink the combat for the French language" (*la nécessité de reconcevoir le combat pour la langue française*), which also presupposes that the French language requires a battle. Example 7.7 argues that while the "overzealous [OQLF agents] need to calm down" (*là les zélés on se calme*), it is "ok" to protect the French language.

FRANÇAIS/E/S also occurs as a noun in 57 instances, of which 13 (23 %) refer to a person or people from France. All other nominal uses refer specifically to French as a language. Notably, a salient trend is for tweets to discuss things that exist or occur "in French" (13), or things being done *to* or *for* French (13) (combined, 46 % of occurrences). Notably, there are nine instances in which French is represented as a cause or something in need of defence and protection (*défendre [...] le français; protéger le français*). Similar to the examples listed above, none of these examples suggest that French should not be protected. Example 7.8 argues that Law 101 is meant to "protect us from the proliferation of English" (*nous protéger de la prolifération de l'anglais*), but explains that Italian does not threaten French. Thus, it seems clear that "we" are in need of protection. Similarly, Example 7.9 argues that Pastagate does not help "the French cause" (*la cause du français*), once again suggesting that French requires protection. Example 7.10 clearly advocates the need for French protection by exclaiming "Defend French yes! Defend French stupidly, no!".

Example 7.8

Mario Asselin @MarioAsselin

@CDubeCAQLevis La loi 101 vise à **<u>nous protéger de la prolifération de l'anglais</u>**; l'italien ne menace pas le français. @GilOuimet #pastagate

4:35 PM—1 March 2013

"@CDubeCAQLevis Bill 101 aims to protect us from the proliferation of English; Italian does not threaten French. @GilOuimet #pastagate"

Example 7.9

say_ouate @Say_Ouate

Pasta ou comment se mettre les pieds dans les plats!Ça n'aide absolument pas **la cause du français** au Quebec, amis anglos furieux! #pastagate

5:09 AM—21 February 2013

"Pasta or how to stick your foot in other people's food! This absolutely doesn't help the French cause in Quebec, Anglo friends furious! #pastagate"

Example 7.10

Emmanuel Scotto @emscotto

Défendre le français *oui! Défendre connement le français, non! #pastagate à #Montréal*

3:05 PM—5 March 2013

"Defend French yes! Defend French stupidly, no! #pastagate in #Montreal"

Another trend—albeit less salient—is for French literacy to be criticised (see Examples 7.11, 7.12 and 7.13).

Example 7.11

Nathaline Tremblay @NatTremb

@MarieBeamar @7PinkPanther7 **Je déplore que #OQLF fasse la guerre à l'anglais ou #pastagate mais rien contre** le mauvais français & fautes.

3:17 AM—29 July 2013

"@MarieBeamar @7PinkPanther7 I regret that the #OQLF is warring against English or #pastagate but not against poor French and errors"

Example 7.12

Kong @Wicker_Bin

*#ecoeuredepayer pour des zélés de l'#OQLF quand nos jeunes ne savent même pas **écrire et parler correctement le français** #pastagate*

2:19 PM—23 February 2013

"#disgustedtopay for the overzealous #OQLF when our youths don't even know how to write and speak French correctly #pastagate"

Example 7.13

Kong @Wicker_Bin

*Quand #OQLF s'attaquera-t-il aux vraies problèmes, comme celui de **la qualité du français de nos jeunes à l'école**? #pastagate #polqc*

1:20 PM—28 February 2013

"When will the #OQLF attack real problems, like the quality of French of our children in schools? #pastagate #polqc"

These instances condemn the OQLF for not addressing the diminishing quality of French in Quebec and allude to wider concerns about the standard of French in Quebec, a topic that has been debated for many decades (if not longer—see Bouchard 2002). In other words, these examples indicate the presence of ideologies of standardised language.

Finally, it is notable that while there are frequent references to the French language, there are few references to what French *is* or *does*. For example, there are no references to why French should be protected, spoken, or used more generally. Furthermore, there are few references to *using* French (e.g. speaking, learning, and teaching). In other words, the French language is predominantly represented as a passive recipient of action or as a circumstantial adjunct contextualising other action taking place.

When the French language is discussed in English tweets (e.g. FRENCH, 277), some of the most frequent clusters pertain to retweeted content. For example, the 76 references to FRENCH ONLY ZONE pertain to retweets of the aforementioned YouTube videos. Also, the 18 references to QUEBEC'S FRENCH HARDLINERS pertain to retweets of a *Globe and Mail* article, as in Example 7.14.

Example 7.14

The Globe and Mail @globeandmail
From @GlobeQuebec: 'Pastagate' reveals the hypocrisy of Quebec's French hardliners http://bit.ly/13QS7fm
6:04 PM—26 February 2013

Retweets aside, FRENCH occurs as an adjective in 75 (43 %) instances, and 20 of these refer to the OQLF (e.g. "French language office"). There are three references to the Charter of the French Language, and notably six references to French language endangerment (e.g. protect/promote/supporting/save the French language). These examples do not presuppose that French should be protected, as was the case with FRANÇAIS/E/S. For example, Example 7.15 declares that Quebec's promotion of French is discriminatory and creates apartheid in Canada.

Example 7.15

Promote-Blog.Com @PromoteBlogCom
RT @heritagektown http://www.nationalpost.com/m/wp/news/canada/blog.html?b=news.nationalpost.com/2013/02/23/following-pastagate-famous-montreal-restaurant-goes-public-about-its-own-language-police-run-in ... APARTHEID IN CANADA? Yes. Quebec and all levels of government promote... http://bit.ly/XMu0O0
12:55 AM—24 February 2013

Similarly, Example 7.16 argues that there is a "fine line" between protecting French and "whitewashing multiculturalism", suggesting that such protectionism is xenophobic and potentially racist.

Example 7.16

Jackson Bliss ジャブ @jacksonbliss
@nprnews I love Québec (avec tout mon coeur), but there's a fine line between **protecting French** + whitewashing multiculturalism. #Pastagate
9:26 PM—26 February 2013

Example 7.17 uses scare quotes to argue that "protecting" French is simply a guise for discrimination.

Example 7.17

Zappien @Zappein
#Quebec needs a #harlemshake to rid off the #oqlf and discrimination disguised as **"protecting" French** #pastagate bit.ly/YYQKdx
11:55 PM—6 March 2013

In a similar vein, there are also nine references to "French language police", a popular label in English-speaking Canada used to negatively evaluate OQLF agents investigating complaints. POLICE, which occurs 293 times in the corpus, collocates with LANGUAGE in 265 cases, but notably collocates with LANGUE in only nine cases.

FRENCH also occurs as a noun in 71 cases and 17 (24 %) of these discuss things taking place in French. However, unlike the uses of FRANÇAIS/E/S, 20 (28 %) references also discuss speaking and learning French (see Fig. 7.1). Thus, English tweeters place more emphasis on using (i.e. speaking, learning) languages than French tweeters, thus exhibiting instrumental language ideologies (a finding consistent with previous chapters, see e.g. Chap. 4).

Notably, ENGLISH and ANGLAIS/E/S occur considerably less frequently (123, 45, respectively) than FRENCH and FRANÇAIS/E/S (277, 141, respectively). These terms are also used rather differently, too. In French, *anglais* occurs most often as a noun (84 % or 38 instances), indexing things taking place "in English" (*en anglais*). The most salient trend in nominal uses (32 % or 12 occurrences) is to refer to the original complaint about the Buonanotte restaurant. It eventually transpired that the OQLF inspectors had misunderstood the original complaint that an individual had been given an English menu (with Italian) and not a French menu (Bourgault-Côté 2013). When the inspectors investigated the claim, they were given a French menu, where the inspectors noted the extent of Italian. Nevertheless, in the original complaint, the problem was not seen to be the use of Italian, but rather the use of English (see Examples 7.18 and 7.19).

```
olf and Pauline Marois got to DjokerNole who's speaking French at CoupeRogers bill1
13 Mar A Marie Antoinette moment in Quebec? Can't speak French? Walk! no metro for
bec ministers to speak to Canadian counterparts only in French http://natpo.st/Z2to
ues. Like pastagate. And people who don't care to learn French. http://instagram.co
e DJ_20_1003 Apr je veux ce t-shirt Keep Calm and Learn French #Pastagate ? Pfff. p
```

Fig. 7.1 Selected concordance lines discussing speaking and learning French

Example 7.18

Frédéric @quebeclibrefran

'Pastagate' (français au Québec) Une manipulation. **La plainte portait sur l'anglais**, pas l'italien… http://www.ledevoir.com/politique/quebec/372332/buonanotte-la-plainte-originale-ne-portait-pas-sur-l-italien …

7:00 PM—9 March 2013

"'Pastagate' (French in Quebec) A manipulation. The complaint was about English, not Italian. http://www.ledevoir.com/politique/quebec/372332/buonanotte-la-plainte-originale-ne-portait-pas-sur-l-italien …"

Example 7.19

Kim Crawford @KimCCrawford

le mensonge est la vérité! ***Le menu est entièrement en anglais*** *>>> FAUX! menu italien & francais OU italien & anglais #pastagate #ORWELL*

4:56 AM—10 March 2013

"the lie is the truth! The menu is entirely in English >>> WRONG! menu Italian & French OR Italian & English #pastagate #ORWELL"

In the rare cases where *anglais* occurs as an adjective, it is used to describe English menus, Canadians (*Canadiens anglais*), songs (*chansons anglaises*), terms (*terme/s anglais*), media (*Médias anglais*), and the "English minority" (*la minorité anglaise*). In contrast, *English* occurs equally as a noun and as an adjective, and it is predominantly discussed with reference to its uses (speaking, making, teaching/learning), and *prevention* of uses (ban, forbid, disallow), as in Examples 7.20 and 7.21.

Example 7.20

SocialRover @socialrover
In Quebec it is officially prohibited to speak English http://www.theworld.org/2013/03/is-french-still-vulnerable-in-quebec/ ... #pastagate
12:29 PM—29 March 2013

Example 7.21

Anika Heinmaa @MassBucketry
http://www.liveleak.com/view?i=529_1361049066 ... Raw vid of complete asshole screaming at person for speaking english in public in Montreal #pastagate #qcpoli
2:12 AM—3 March 2013

Notably, *English* is also used as an adjective to describe various items ranging from programmes (11 occurrences) to muffins (1 occurrence).

The difference between the uses of *ANGLAIS/E/S* and ENGLISH seem to suggest that French tweets were focused on establishing the facts about the original complaint (i.e. about English on the menu) whereas the English tweets pertain to wider issues about banning English in other contexts. Furthermore, the English-medium tweets seem to focus more on using (e.g. speaking, learning, writing) English and French rather than simply denoting things taking place in these languages, privileging an instrumental understanding of language. In contrast, there is hardly any reference to language use in the French tweets, which in some instances suggest that the OQLF's efforts would be better spent improving the quality of French, privileging ideologies of standardised language and ideologies of language endangerment. Also, while many French tweets presumed that French is threatened and requires protection, in English tweets this kind of protectionism is criticised.

The final step in the analysis of the Pastagate corpus was to examine hashtags. The most frequent hashtag in the corpus is #PASTAGATE and with 2829 instances it is five times more frequent than any other hashtag. However, other hashtags are also used. Since raw frequencies proved to be somewhat problematic (see discussion above), these hashtags were not analysed according to their frequency but rather according to the

Table 7.4 Ten most frequent news hashtags

Hashtag	Frequency
#CNN	49
#NEWS	42
#SUNNEWSNETWORK	40
#CJAD	28
#NBC	19
#CBC	17
#ABC	16
#BBCWORLD	13
#BAZZOTV	9
#BBCNEWS	8

following categories of emergent themes: (1) news outlets, (2) geography, (3) politics, (4) topic-specific items, (5) humour, (6) negative evaluation, and (7) hashtags linking the story to other contexts.

The first category of hashtags pertained to news outlets or news sources, and not just Canadian news sources, but also American, British, English, and French news outlets (Table 7.4). Notably, most of these hashtags occurred in tweets that contained numerous different news hashtags. It seems that Twitter users were hashtagging multiple news outlets in order to flag the story to the international community and to international news outlets more specifically, as in Example 7.22.

Example 7.22

Mike Kane @PBTFMedia
#OQLF is always backtracking. Don't be fooled #spoongate #spoonscandal #cjad #sunnewsnetwork #cnn #cbc #pastagate
1:38 AM—22 June 2013

Another category consisted of hashtags pertaining to geography (see Table 7.5). While Montreal is the most frequently cited location, other Canadian locations are mentioned and international sites, too. These instances seem to suggest an appeal to the international community or the international interest in this story.

A third large category of hashtags pertains to politics (see Table 7.6), including references to specific political parties such as the elected

Table 7.5 Ten most frequent geography hashtags

Hashtag	Frequency
#MONTREAL	281
#QUEBEC	211
#CANADA	57
#MONTRÉAL	11
#MTL	9
#TORONTO	7
#514 [Montreal area code]	6
#CANADIENS	5
#QUÉBEC	5
#FRANCE	4

Table 7.6 Ten most frequent politics hashtags

Hashtag	Frequency
#OQLF	555
#PQ	323
#POLQC	233
#ASSNAT	179
#BILL14	145
#QCPOLI	134
#CDNPOLI	78
#BILL101	70
#OLF	67
#LOI101	65

minority government of Quebec, the Parti Québécois (#PQ, 323), and opposing parties such as the Parti Libéral du Québec (#PLQ, 33).

Hashtags also refer to individual politicians (e.g. #MAROIS, 34) and to Canadian (e.g. #CDNPOLI, 78; #CANPOLI, 3; #POLCAN, 5) and Quebec politics (#QCPOLI, 134; #POLQC, 233). Notably, different hashtags are used in English and in French: while #CDNPOLI and #QCPOLI tend to be used in English to tag Canadian and Quebec politics, #POLCAN and #POLQC tend to be used to refer to the same topics in French (see Chap. 6). These hashtags only occur together in four instances within the corpus (see Fig. 7.2).

Similarly, #BILL14 and #LOI14 are English and French hashtags used refer to the same language policy document and #BILL101 and #LOI101 refer to Quebec's Charter of the French Language. Again,

```
#polqc #assnat #pq #pastagate #qcpoli
e=8870035 … #pastagate #polqc #qcpoli #pq
- http://bit.ly/YcCXSf #polqc #qcpoli #cdnpoli #pastagate #OQL
- http://bit.ly/YcCXSf #polqc #qcpoli #cdnpoli #pastagate #OQL
```

Fig. 7.2 Collocation of #POLQC and #QCPOLI

only in very rare cases do these occur as collocates. For example, #BILL14 occurs 145 times and collocates with #BILL101 in 40 (28 %) occurrences, but only collocates with #LOI101 and #LOI14 in fewer than 5 % of instances (eight and two, respectively). Similarly, #LOI101 occurs 70 times but only collocates with #BILL101 in two (3 %) instances. While these numbers cannot reveal anything in and of themselves, the collocation patterns suggest that little effort is being made to appeal to both English and French Twitter users at the same time. Instead, in most cases it seems that the exclusive use of monolingualism in hashtagging suggests an affiliation with *either* English Twitter users *or* French Twitter users. In other words, the use of these distinct hashtags suggests that different language groups are not only participating within the debate, but they are also appealing to distinct communities of ambient affiliation (Zappavigna 2011). This divide further enhances the potential for the "two solitudes" to be perpetuated in online spaces (see Chap. 6).

A fourth category of hashtags pertains specifically to the Pastagate controversy (see Table 7.7).

Table 7.7 Ten most frequent topic-specific hashtags

Word	Hashtag frequency	Raw frequency	% of raw frequency occurring as hashtag
#PASTAGATE	2829	5153	55
#PASTA	91	654	14
#LANGUAGE	54	1266	4
#BUONANOTTE	29	248	12
#COFFEEGATE	29	29	100
#SPOONGATE	26	28	93
#FRENCH	16	337	5
#CAFFEGATE	12	14	86
#TURBANGATE	10	12	83
#ENGLISH	9	151	6

Notably, most words that directly index the topic—for example, *pasta, language, French, English,* and *Italian*—are used less often as hashtags than more playful words or neologisms. For example, although PASTA occurs 654 times in the corpus, only 91 (14 %) occur as hashtags. Similarly, although the words LANGUAGE and ITALIAN occur 1266 and 339 times, respectively, only 4 % and 2 % of these instances occur as hashtags. In contrast, spin-offs of Pastagate—which included reports of OQLF investigations into coffee cups inscribed with *caffè* and spoons at a frozen yogurt venue with English catchphrases such as "this is my mix"—took on names such as *caffegate* and *spoongate* that only ever occur as hashtags within this corpus. Indeed, the items that occur predominantly as hashtags rather than as regular functioning words in the corpus include *coffeegate, spoongate, caffegate, turbangate, dildogate, spoonscandal, steakgate, redialgate,* and *strudelgate*—all items pertaining to stories related to the premise of Pastagate. Since these hashtags are all searchable, they function as a simple method of extending the scope of Pastagate to new and developing domains. In contrast, lexical items pertaining specifically to the actual Pastagate topic (e.g. language, French, English, and Italian) occur proportionally less often as hashtags. This suggests that the facts surrounding Pastagate were less salient than the more evaluative, sensationalist descriptors and labels that occurred proportionally more often as hashtags.

Another category of hashtags pertains to the humorous appeal of the story (Table 7.8). References to "comedy", "funny", "lol", "humor/humour", and "LMFAO" all suggest the extent to which a story about such language policing aroused incredulity. However, other readers did not evaluate the story as humorous and instead highlighted negativity and embarrassment with hashtags such as #helpme, #idiots, #laughingstock, #cretins, #honte ("shame") (see Table 7.9).

Table 7.8 Humour hashtags

Hashtag	Frequency
#COMEDY	49
#FUNNY	42
#LOL	10
#HUMOR	5
#HUMOUR	2
#LMFAO	1

Table 7.9 Negative evaluation hashtags

Hashtag	Frequency
#HELPME	8
#HONTE	8
#NOFRENCHZONE	6
#RACIST	5
#QUEBECBASHING	4
#DISCRIMINATION	3
#EQUALITY	3
#FRANCOFASCISTS	3
#ENOUGHISENOUGH	2
#ETHNOCIDE	2
#ZÉLOTE	1

More extreme negativity was expressed through the use of hashtags such as #racist (5), #francofascists (3), #ethnocide (2), and #anglophobes (1). These hashtags are used exclusively in English tweets and express a more extreme negative evaluation of Pastagate; they naturalise a link between linguistic protectionism (and language policy enforcement) and varying levels of xenophobia. Hashtags such as #zélote are used by French tweeters who also make links between Pastagate and extremism. However, the (English) hashtag #quebecbashing only occurs in tweets that are otherwise entirely written in French. The label "Quebec bashing" tends to be used to highlight English Canada's negative representation of events in Quebec—an issue discussed at length, for example, in the work of Barbeau (2013). Two of these four hashtags retweet the story that the original complaint against the Buonanotte restaurant did not pertain to the use of Italian on the menu, but rather the use of English on the menu.

Notably, the story about the original complaint seems to have been only reported in French, and not picked up in English. When English-language tweets refer to this story, the original complainant is described as a "[s]erial language complainer" and someone who "hates English" (see Examples 7.23 and 7.24).

Example 7.23

Steve Faguy @fagstein

OQLF Buonanotte complainant says doesn't hate Italian, just hates English. http://bit.ly/ZN0ZIC #pastagate via @finnertymike

6:01 PM—2 March 2013

Example 7.24

Don Macpherson @DMacpGaz

(FR) Serial language complainer behind #pastagate says he complained about menu in Eng, not Italian. http://bit.ly/ZYQ3Fv #qcpoli #oqlf

1:11 PM—3 March 2013

However, these descriptors were not used in the retweeted article (Bourgault-Côté 2013) and English hashtags are used to propagate this misrepresentation of the story to the wider English-speaking Twittersphere. In other words, even when the English tweeters do pick up the factual context of the original complaint, they misrepresent and propagate the misrepresentations to a wider public.

The final category of hashtags pertains to links made between Pastagate and other contentious or negative stories in and about Quebec (Table 7.10). These include the hashtags #CEIC and #CORRUPTION, which refer to the Charbonneau Commission, a public inquiry into corruption in the management of public construction contracts in Quebec. This Commission is irrelevant to Pastagate but the linkage serves to negatively evaluate Quebec more generally. Similarly, the hashtag #MAGNOTTA refers to Luca Magnotta, the Montrealer accused of (among other things) killing and dismembering an international student. This individual is also irrelevant to Pastagate but serves to perpetuate and extend the negativity to wider and more serious issues.

In summary, the Twitter data here showed that the French and English languages were represented rather differently depending on the medium of use (i.e. English or French). English-medium tweets tended to focus on language use and often mocked the situation in Quebec, whereas French-medium tweets were more diverse: while some expressed embarrassment

Table 7.10 Hashtags links Pastagate to other stories

Hashtag	Frequency
#CEIC	24
#CORRUPTION	2
#MAGNOTTA	2

and incredulity, others continued to advocate the need to protect French, sought to establish the truth behind the scandal, or cited the need to improve the quality of French in Quebec. Given that these trends were not linked to specific users in different contexts, in the next section we will explore the extent to which language ideologies such as these can be tied to news articles and readers using English and French in different locations internationally.

7.3.2 News Article Findings

In order to explore the way that language ideologies are linked to different languages and national contexts, the next step was to analyse news articles from different countries focusing on Pastagate (see Table 7.1). The analysis, which began with the discourse analysis of English articles, indicated that the themes of control, negativity, international contexts, and business permeate these data. For example, the *Globe and Mail* article uses adjectives such as *embarrassing, undesired, bitter, damning, [not] proud, aggressive,* and *dwindling* and nouns such as *ridicule, symptom, controversy, incidents, headache, problem, difficulty,* and *consequences.* The article also thematises control by repeatedly referring to the OQLF as the "language watchdog" (four instances), which "enforce[s] Quebec's language law". The OQLF is imbued with the more general themes of negativity and control, as in Example 7.25.

Example 7.25 (*Globe and Mail*)

The head of Quebec's language watchdog agency has resigned after a series of controversies that created embarrassing headlines at home and abroad.

Similarly, the *Fox News* article evokes a highly monitored society through the use of words such as *strict, rules, forced, enforces,* and *police;* these dimensions of control are mocked throughout the article, as in: "All this ribbing caused the language police to eat their words". *The Guardian* article also focuses on the controlling nature of Quebec, mentioning powerful social actors (e.g. *inspectors, police, transgressors, spy agency, top-court judge*), controlling actions (*protect, deploy, rein in, take on, conduct spot checks, break the law, force, undercut, order, wield the power, crackdown*), and general negativity (*scrutiny, complaints, picking a fight, outrage, unleash, tempest, outcry, frustrations, sinister, plot, perfect storm, failed, threatened, cacophony, severe*). The theme of control permeates *The Economist*, too, which uses negative adjectives (e.g. [not] *good, ridiculous, serious, not easy, bad*) and negative nouns (e.g. *ridicule, warning, violation, fine, incident, issue, distraction*) to thematise controlling actions (e.g. *forced, instructed, tussled, barraged, preserving, needed, toughen*). Finally, in *NPR*, the theme of control is again salient, with words such as *enforce, rules, guard, allowed, stricken, infractions, allowed,* and *police.* The negative depiction of such control becomes clear with nouns such as *criticism, disbelief, outrage, barrage, complaints, problem, flap,* and *debate* and adjectives such as *serious, sad, depressed,* and *wrong.*

The juxtaposition of local and international contexts is also an undercurrent in these articles. For example, the Buonanotte restaurant is represented as "trendy" (National Post) and popular with internationally renowned celebrities (e.g. Leonardo DiCaprio, Robert De Niro, Bono, Rihanna, and Jerry Seinfeld cited in *Fox News* and the *Guardian*). More generally, the OQLF—and Quebec more generally—tend to be juxtaposed with an international, English-speaking context, as in Example 7.25. Journalists from the *Globe and Mail, NPR,* and *National Post* all stress the impact of international reporting of this story. In fact, the *National Post* article focuses on this topic and repeats the international media figures three times. First, the figures are cited in the headline (see Example 7.26).

Example 7.26 (*National Post*)

Quebec's 'pastagate' PR nightmare: Story gets 60 times more coverage outside province than Marois investment trip.

Then, the figures are mentioned twice in the article. Also, the *National Post* reinforces the importance of the international context (e.g. "outside the province", "trip", "foreign", "out-of-province", "14 countries", and "160 countries"), naming specific international destinations (e.g. New York, Australia) and using lexical and numerical quantification that stress the impact of news reporting (e.g. *multiplied, 60 times, significantly, 350, all, 12, 160, a period of,* and *few months*).

Against such an influential international context, Quebec and its language laws seem rather marginalised. Indeed, the *Economist* seems to underscore this status, describing Quebec as "barraged with English from *the rest of Canada* and from *the United States*" (emphasis added). Quebec is depicted as marginalised not only within "a world where English is the language of business" but also within the country: "Quebec [is] a former French colony conquered by Britain before it became part of Canada". Similarly, the *Guardian* article seems to marginalise Quebec by indirectly contrasting the "*regional* Quebec government" with "*big* corporate transgressors" and "*celebrity* clientele". More specifically, the journalist discursively amalgamates "Anglophones", "ethnic communities", and "English-speaking entrepreneurs and businesses" in Quebec with "English voices in North America" more generally and contrasts this diverse and widespread group with "French-language advocates and Quebec separatists".

Alongside these other themes, there is also an emphasis on the importance of business. Although a focus on the Buonanotte restaurant and other restaurants, too, is unsurprising given the immediate context of Pastagate, most articles mention business more generally (e.g. "other businesses", "a business", "companies", "business owners", "business partner", "entrepreneurs and businesses", "small companies", and "corporate transgressors"). Additionally, both the *Globe and Mail* and the *National Post* cite De Courcy's statement about the negative impact of the story on "businesses, the Office personnel, the public and Quebec in general". The *Economist* and *National Post* mention the Quebec Premier's (unsuccessful) efforts to drum up "investor interest" and while the *Economist* notes that "English is the language of business", the *National Post* suggests that the international media coverage could have an impact on "business decisions".

In contrast, *control, negativity, international contexts,* and *business* are not dominant themes in the French news articles. The *Radio Canada* article discusses control to some extent, describing the use of foreign words on menus as "allowed" (*permis*) but they "must not" be dominant or replace the French (*ne doivent pas être prédominants ni remplacer les descriptions et explications en français*). Nevertheless, the majority of the article focuses on corrections and clarifications—that is, changes—being made to the OQLF procedures. For example, it is noted that the OQLF published a statement to "clarify" (*clarifier*) its position and to "admit" (*constater*) that the inspectors had been "overzealous". It also includes a statement from De Courcy, the Minister responsible for the Charter of the French Language, who stresses that "judgement and moderation" (*jugement et moderation*) must be what guide the OQLF and she is "confident" in the expertise and work of the institution (*j'ai raison de faire confiance à l'expertise et à la qualité du travail réalisé*).

Similarly, *Le Devoir* explains that the Marois government "changed tack" (*a donné coup de barre*) on the OQLF following the departure of Marchand, who left her post following the Pastagate controversy. The article continues to note "change" (*changement*) and "review" (*révision*) and the "creation" (*création*) of a new post dealing with OQLF service and quality. In *La Presse*, the actions of the OQLF are represented negatively as an "error" (*erreur*), but the focus of the article is mainly on subsequent changes to OQLF procedures. Similarly, *Huffington Post* thematises change, using verb tenses (e.g. past and future) and temporal markers (e.g. "until now"/*jusqu'ici*, "now"/*maintenant,* "from now on"/*à compter d'aujourd'hui*) to note developments in the OQLF. There is not, however, a contrast between negativity in the past and positivity for the future, because it is noted that historically the OQLF treated complaints "consistently and equally in the same way" (*de manière égale et uniforme*) and now out of a "concern for efficiency" (*souci d'efficacité*) the OQLF is developing a personal follow-up approach (*faire un suivi personnalisé auprès des personnes touchées*), addressing general and collective interests (*l'intérêt general ou collectif*), and improving the quality of services (*l'amélioration de la qualité de services*).

In contrast, the *Nouvel Observateur* is much more negative in its representation of events and it also thematises the international context. For example, the author notes that whereas the Pastagate scandal was a source of "amusement" and "derision" (*dérision*) for the international public, such issues "often preoccupy" francophones overseas (see Example 7.27)

Example 7.27 (*Nouvel Observateur*)

Dérive ou vrai débat ? Retour sur ces petites affaires qui animent beaucoup certains francophones outre-atlantique.

"Downward spiral or real debate? Returning to these little affairs that often preoccupy some francophones overseas."

The contrast between a marginalised "overseas" group and the international public represents francophones as isolated internationally. Furthermore, the journalist negatively evaluates the Quebec government as "poorly adapted" and "narrow-minded" within an international context of globalisation and migration (see Example 7.28).

Example 7.28 (*Nouvel Observateur*)

Ces pratiques bureaucratiques absurdes donnent plutôt l'image d'un gouvernement étroit d'esprit et inadapté à la mondialisation. Elles découragent l'intégration des immigrants plutôt que de la faciliter.

"These absurd bureaucratic practices instead give an image of a narrow-minded government that is poorly adapted for globalisation. They discourage immigrant integration rather than facilitating it."

The theme of control also figures in the journalist's account of a restaurant owner being required (*a dû*) to cover the English on his telephone and the PQ government believing it "must" (*il faut*) act to "brake" (*freiner*) the growth of English and "reinforce" (*renforcer*) the Charter of the French language. Thus, this article is rather distinct from the other French-language articles in its thematisation of control, internationalisation, and negativity.

The second step in the analysis was to establish how languages were being represented within the articles. In the English articles, the French language is discussed most frequently, whereas English and Italian occur less frequently. Language more generally, though, tends to be the topic of discussion (see Table 7.11).

In most cases (18 instances), "Italian" is used to describe the Buonanotte restaurant or the words or terms used on the menu (i.e. the words that were

Table 7.11 References to languages in English articles

	French (*French/ francophone/s*)	*Langue française/e francaise/e*	English (*English, anglophone/s*)	Language (*language/s, linguistic/s*)	Italian	Other
National Post	2	2	1	7	3	0
The Guardian	9	1	10	9	5	0
The Economist	9	1	6	7	2	0
National Public Radio	10	0	2	8	2	0
Fox News	2	2	0	2	5	0
Globe and Mail	5	1	4	10	1	0
Totals	**37**	**7**	**23**	**43**	**18**	**0**

objected to by the OQLF). Thus, there is no mention of Italian outside of restaurants and Italian speakers do not figure in the articles. The English language, which is discussed more frequently (23 occurrences), is represented as a humanised language. For example, there are six references to "anglophone/s" (in the *Guardian*, *Globe and Mail*, and *National Post*) and references to "English-speakers", "English-speaking" entrepreneurs and populations, and "English voices". Other references to "English" suggest the diverse contexts in which English is used (e.g. it is an international language: "in a world where English is the language of business" [*Economist*]). These examples suggest underlying instrumental language ideologies.

The English language articles discuss French speakers less frequently than English speakers: there are only five references to "francophones" and no references to "French speakers" or "French voices". There are two instances where people are described as "being" French (meaning, in these cases, French-speaking), but these in fact come from a restaurateur whose restaurant was targeted in OQLF investigations similar to those of Pastagate (see Example 7.29, emphasis added).

Example 7.29 (NPR)

"I love Quebec… but it's not getting any easier," David McMillan, owner of Montreal's Joe Beef, tells National Post. McMillan speaks both English and French. "*My wife is French, my business partner is French*, my children go to French school, but I just get so sad and depressed and wonder, what's wrong with *these people*?"

Although the restaurateur humanises the French language by using it as a descriptor of his wife and business partner, he then distinguishes them from other French speakers ("these people"), who reportedly have something "wrong" with them. In other words, the French language is not humanised in the same way as the English language is in the English articles.

Finally, references to LANGUAGE tend to be used to refer to language policies or institutions rather than to human or individual issues, and these tend to be negatively evaluated. The negative evaluation takes shape at the most basic level with the labelling employed by journalists: the *Globe and Mail* refers to the OQLF as the "language watchdog" (four instances) and all other articles use the label "language police" (eight instances). The *Economist* explains that OQLF inspectors are "known in English" as the "language police", but later the journalist uses the term "language police" without reference to the fact that this label is only meaningful to one linguistic community. Thus, the journalist (perhaps) unwittingly aligns with an English-speaking readership and perpetuates the negative representation of the OQLF as the "language police". All other uses of the label "language police" fail to indicate that this is a term used (predominantly) by English speakers (i.e. not French speakers). Indeed, the *Guardian* journalist uses the passive voice to contend that "[t]hey are known as the language police", without indicating *by whom* they are known. The negative connotations associated with this label are reinforced by depictions of their aggressive military-style actions (e.g. "deploys", "rein in", "take on", and "conduct spot checks"). The *Guardian* also describes OQLF inspectors as "zealots", and the negative fanaticism associated with this label is in keeping with representations in other articles. For example, *NPR* discusses "the government's efforts to *cleanse* [restaurants] of languages other than French" (emphasis added). Since "cleansing" pertains to purification, this description implies that other languages are perceived to be impure and even dirty by the government; indeed, in addition to cleaning and beauty regimes, "cleansing" also tends to be used within discussions of genocide (e.g. "ethnic cleansing"), thus, *NPR*'s use of "cleanse" is arguably part of an overall depiction of Quebec's language policy as extremist.

In the French articles, the languages most under discussion are French, Italian, and English, respectively (see Table 7.12).

Table 7.12 Frequencies of references to language(s)

	French (*français/e/s, francophone/s, franciser/ francisation*)	English (*anglais/e/s, anglophone/s, angliciser/ anglicisation*)	Language (*langue/s, linguistique/s*)	Italian (*italien/ ne/s*)	Other (*grec*)
Nouvel Observateur	16	6	6	6	0
La Presse	4	0	4	4	0
Radio Canada	10	0	7	4	2
Huffington Post	3	2	2	2	0
Le Devoir	3	1	5	2	0
Totals	**36**	**9**	**24**	**18**	**2**

The Italian language is the second most frequently discussed language, but most references to *italien* refer to the Buonanotte restaurant (e.g. *restaurant italien*) and "Italian words" (e.g. *mots italiens*) or the "use of Italian" (*l'usage de l'Italien*) on menus. As with the English articles, then, the language itself is not really represented outside of restaurants nor are speakers discussed. Similarly, there are notably few references to the English language in the articles. For example, the *La Presse* and *Radio Canada* articles do not contain any references to "English" or "Anglophones" and the *Le Devoir* article only contains one reference; this refers to the fact that the original complaint that sparked the OQLF investigations into Buonanotte pertained to the use of English—not Italian—on the restaurant menu. The relevance of this point is that it is English, and not Italian, that is seen as relevant to discussions of French.

Finally, most references to both *langue* and *française* tend to refer to the Office Québécois de la *langue française* and the Charte de la *langue française* (Quebec's *Charter of the French language*). In fact, 47 % (or 17 instances) of *français/e/s* and 75 % (or 19 instances) of *langue* refer to the Charter or the OQLF. Also, there are few references to francophones in the articles. Thus, similar to the English articles, there is a strong emphasis on Quebec language policy and less focus on French speakers. Nevertheless, there are also references to *francisation* ("to make more French"), which occur in the *Nouvel Observateur* and the *Le Devoir* articles. For example, the *Nouvel Observateur* discusses cases where restaurants were required to "become more French" through changes to menus and signage. Thus, the "objective of making more French", which is part and parcel of Quebec's language policy more generally, underpins descriptions of the actions and intentions of the OQLF and its requirements from the public. In other words, language policy seems to permeate the French articles not only in explicit ways (e.g. through references to the OQLF and the Charter), but also through the vocabulary used—and the fact that the act of "making things more French" (i.e. *franciser, francisation*) is used so unproblematically by the journalists in question.

7.3.3 News Commentary Findings

Following the analysis of the news articles, the news commentary was examined in order to determine if the journalists' representations were corroborated by reader comments. Notably, in English the articles that received the most comments were international publications: the *Guardian* (539 comments) and the *Economist* (19,860 words) (see Table 7.2). The high number of comments could be the result of the wider (and more active) readerships of these publications (see e.g. Marchi 2013), but the involvement of these audiences nevertheless indicates the international interest in and dissemination of the story.

The English commentary corpus contained 650 references to FRENCH and FRANCO* (FRANCOPHONE, 43, FRANCOPHONES, 41, FRANCAIS, 4, FRANÇAIS, 4, FRANÇAISE, 4, FRANCAISE, 3, and FRANCO, 3), 480 references to ENGLISH and ANGLO* (ANGLO, 36, ANGLOPHONE, 32, ANGLOPHONES, 32, and ANGLOS, 17), and only 53 references to ITALIAN/S. In other words, there is a much more concerted focus on French and English rather than Italian. The most frequent three-word clusters also indicate some of the dominant trends in the data (see Table 7.13).

The most frequent cluster (I DON[']T) indicates the personal and subjective nature of the discussions in this forum, with participants claiming they don't "understand" (2), "believe" (2), "see" (6), and "know" (7). Other clusters, such as "it's not", "it's a", "I'm not", "is not a" and "there is no" reveal the argumentative nature of this participant forum.

The second most frequent cluster is THE LANGUAGE NAZIS (39 occurrences) and the bigram LANGUAGE NAZI* is even more frequent

Table 7.13 Ten most frequent clusters in English commentary

Cluster	Frequency
I DON T	40
THE LANGUAGE NAZIS	39
IT S NOT	30
THE FRENCH LANGUAGE	30
THE REST OF	30
THE LANGUAGE POLICE	26
IT S A	24
I M NOT	21
IN THE WORLD	21
OF THE WORLD	19

(56 occurrences). Notably, 96 % (54) of these instances occur in comments on the *National Post* article and 93 % (50) of these instances can be attributed to a single user. The (perhaps) less contentious label "language police" (51 occurrences) is used in a broader range of news commentary: the *Economist* (24 instances), the *Guardian* (20 instances), the *National Post* (5 instances), and the *Globe and Mail* (2 instances). In some instances, commentators critique journalists' use of this label; in Example 7.30, the commentator argues that the *Economist* journalist should have avoided using such as "nasty slur".

Example 7.30 Contestation of the journalists' use of the term "language police"

It's a fun round-up, but I'm slightly appalled that a publication like The Economist thinks it's acceptable to dub the OQLF as the "language police"—a monicker coined and championed by the reactionary Quebecophobe right-wing press of the Rest of Canada. "Language police" isn't a neutral description of the OQLF, it's a nasty slur.

However, other participants support the use of this term, explaining that the OQLF inspectors "have been called [this] for decades" and "[f]rom a bilingual Anglophone living in Quebec, plain and simple; the OQLF is known as the language police".

Other notable clusters, such as THE REST OF (30), IN THE WORLD (21), OF THE WORLD (19), and REST OF CANADA (13)

suggest the extent to which the theme of internationalisation permeates this data set. Subsets of the cluster THE REST OF (30), which include THE REST OF CANADA (12), THE REST OF THE WORLD (7), and THE REST OF THE COUNTRY (2), suggest that Quebec is often explicitly contrasted against other national (Canadian) and international contexts. Many of these explicitly frame Quebec negatively in such comparisons, as in one comment on the *Globe and Mail,* which laments “A pity Mordecai Richler is no longer around to describe such nonsense to the rest of the world”. Also, FRENCH collocates with QUEBEC (57), QUÉBÉCOIS (22), QUEBECERS (8), QUÉBÉCOIS (5), and QUÉBEC (5) but it collocates far less frequently with FRANCE (13), CANADIAN (11), ITALIAN (10), CANADA (10), CANADIANS (9), and GERMAN (6). Thus, French is discursively linked to the Quebec context and much less so to general Canadian and international contexts, a finding similar to that uncovered in Chap. 5.

The most frequent cluster containing FRENCH is THE FRENCH LANGUAGE (30), which tends to be used to discuss policy and the rationale for French policy—that is, the need to “defend”, “protect”, and “promote” French. Similarly, the bigram FRENCH IS shows that a focus on—or debate over—French language endangerment preoccupies a number of participants, who discuss whether French is “safe”, “worth defending”, and “going the way of hundreds of other languages [towards a slow and steady demise]” (see Fig. 7.3).

The focus on the wider context of French language endangerment indicates the overall lack of consensus about the status and wellbeing of the French language, a finding also consistent with findings presented in Chap. 5.

In contrast, some of the most frequent lexical collocates of ENGLISH suggest that language use—and, in particular, speaking—is the most

the major neighboring languages.	**French is**	**safe** in Switzerland because it i
lar. Who cares if you think that	**French is**	**not worth defending**? The only fa
worse) need support to survive.	**French is**	**going the way of hundreds of oth**
y. **How is it possible** then, that	**french is**	**endangered in Quebec**. It boggles
ctant to step up when they **think**	**French is**	**being threatened**.) . That criter
end it is a sterile debate. Fact	**french is**	**being protected**, or english is d
it just strengthen the idea that	**French is**	**at risk** in Quebec. If (as that s
own. >> Much to Quebec's credit,	**French is**	**alive and well there**, even thoug

Fig. 7.3 Selected concordance lines with FRENCH IS

important concern for English commentators. Collocates such as SPEAKING (47 occurrences, MI 3.5), SPEAK (34 occurrences, MI 3), and SPEAKERS (24 occurrences, MI 3.7) all suggest the importance of fluency in English. This trend is also salient in the clusters, where THE ENGLISH SPEAKING (seven occurrences), TO SPEAK ENGLISH six occurrences) and EDUCATED IN ENGLISH (five occurrences) all indicate the relevance of fluency, which suggests underlying instrumental ideologies that privilege language use (see discussions in Sects. 1.1 and 4.2.2).

The language most under discussion in the French commentary is the French language, followed by English and then Italian (FRANÇAIS, 78; ANGLAIS, 29; ITALIEN, 25). The low frequencies of references to English and Italian mean that few patterns emerge from the data (e.g. there are no ANGLAIS or ITALIEN clusters). Most references to *anglais/e* occur within discussions of speaking (*parler*), writing (*écrire*), and "using" (*utilise/r*) English, suggesting, like in Chap. 4, that French speakers highlight the utilitarian value of speaking English (Oakes 2010). Discussions of Italian, like in the articles, refer to words and terms and the menu containing Italian. French, however, is more topical in the commentary data. Discussions of French tend to express concern over the protection of French and its role in society, indicating the presence of ideologies of language endangerment. Many commentators express embarrassment over the Pastagate context and condemn the actions of the OQLF. For example, OQLF inspectors are in some cases labelled "ayatollah[s]", "guardians" (*gardien*), "police", and "zealots" (*zélotes*) *de la langue*, and one commentator in *Le Devoir* says "good riddance" (*bon débarass*) to the exit of Louise Marchand. Nevertheless, many commentators argue that there is still a need to "defend" (*défendre*) French and the "protection of" (*protection de*) French is important. One comment on *Radio Canada* argues that French has "clearly regressed [...] in Montreal" (*le français a nettement régressé [...] à Montréal*).

There are also commentators who use the platform to lament the decline of "proper" French. The voicing of standard language ideologies occurred in both Canadian (e.g. *Radio Canada*) and international (e.g. *Nouvel Observateur*) news commentary. In Example 7.31, a commentator argues that more must be done to ensure the "quality of French".

Example 7.31 (*Radio Canada*)

De plus, au lieu de donner des leçons aux autres, nous ferions mieux de nous occuper de la QUALITÉ du français, dans nos écoles, nos entreprises. À voir des courriels qui circulent parfois, à faute échelle hierarchique, truffés de fautes d'amateurs, et des générations qui ne savent plus comment écrire une phrase correctement, pour moi c'est celà, le plus alarmant!

"Moreover, instead of giving lessons to others, we would be better off paying attention to the QUALITY of French in our schools, our businesses. Seeing emails that circulate sometimes, because of hierarchical scales, riddled with amateurish mistakes, and the generations that no longer know how to write a sentence correctly, for me that's more alarming!"

The same commentator goes on to argue that he would "rather hear English or Russian" than witness speakers of those languages destroying the French language (*J'aime mieux entendre les gens parler anglais ou russe que les entendre démolir la langue comme ça*). In the *Nouvel Observateur,* several commentators contest the journalist's negative account of Pastagate and argue that more must be done to speak and write French well (e.g. *il faut bien parler et écrire le français* [French must be spoken and written well]). Clearly, these indicate the underlying ideologies of standardised language that are impacting on the debates over French in this data set.

7.3.4 Twitter Findings

The final step in the analysis was to determine how the story was taken up and shared on Twitter. In English, it was found that the *Guardian* was the most retweeted, the *Economist* the second most retweeted, and *NPR* the third most retweeted article (247, 140, and 99 retweets, respectively). Notably, the Canadian publications are retweeted far less frequently than the international publications: the *Globe and Mail* article was retweeted only 31 times and the *National Post* article only 25 times (see Table 7.2).

The most frequently used hashtags (see Table 7.14) reveal that language issues (e.g. #LANGUAGE, #FRENCH, #ITALIAN, #LINGUISTICS)

Table 7.14 Most frequent hashtags in English corpus of retweets

Hashtag	Frequency
#LANGUAGE	29
#QUEBEC	29
#PASTAGATE	22
#NEWS	16
#CANADA	8
#FRENCH	5
#COOKING	4
#OQLF	4
#PASTA	4
#QCPOLI	4
#ASSNAT	3
#BILL101	3
#CDNPOLI	3
#DMCRSS	3
#ITALIAN	3
#LINGUISTICS	3
#MONTREAL	3
#POLQC	3
#BILL14	2
#BLOGS	2

and geography (e.g. #QUEBEC, #CANADA, #MONTREAL) are the most frequent. Another trend is a focus on Quebec politics (e.g. #OQLF, #QCPOLI, #ASSNAT, #BILL101, #CDNPOLI, #POLQC, #BILL14).

In addition to hashtags, many readers also expressed reactions to the story on Twitter by posting micro-comments asking questions (e.g. "Seriously?", "How ridiculous can one be?"), making exclamations (e.g. "That's embarrassing!"; "Hilarious!"), using repeated punctuation (e.g. "!!!!!", "?????????????????????????"), or combining these elements together (e.g. "LOL!! :-)", "Laugh or cry?!").

In French, the most frequently retweeted article is *La Presse,* followed by *Le Devoir* (44 and 21 retweets, respectively). Although these figures are lower than the English retweeting figures, notably, national publications have markedly higher retweeting figures than the international (French) publication (*Nouvel Observateur,* ten retweets). Unlike the English tweets, the most frequent hashtags in French tend not to be very revealing because they are not widely used: only 18 % of *La Presse,* 23 % of *Le Devoir*, 17 % of *Radio Canada*, and 20 % of *Nouvel*

Observateur retweets use hashtags. When hashtags are used, they mostly refer to Quebec politics (e.g. #ASSNAT, 6, #POLQC, 6, #MAROIS, 2, #QCPAYS, 2) or Quebec language politics more specifically (#OQLF, 8, #LOI101, 2, #OLF, 1). Although the *La Presse* retweets tend not to contain hashtags, they do contain the most freely worded commentary: 34 % of retweets include some freely worded commentary. Readers' comments tend to be negative and express embarrassment (e.g. "[it's] lucky that ridicule doesn't kill"; *Une chance que le ridicule ne tue pas!*), argue that the OQLF lacked judgement and wasted public funds (*une absence totale de jugement et un gaspillage de fonds publics*), and comment that the entire affair is "ridiculous" (*Tsé quand c'est ridicule…*).

7.4 Conclusions

To summarise the various elements of this study, let us return to the research questions. The first question asked how languages were represented in Pastagate corpus, articles, commentary, and retweets. Findings showed that in all cases the French language was discussed more than the English language and despite the relevance of Italian, it was hardly under discussion at all. Many French tweets in the Pastagate corpus discussed English only to establish the facts about the original complaint (i.e. English on the menu) whereas the English tweets focused on issues of using (e.g. speaking, learning, and writing), and preventing the use of (i.e. banning) English. In the English news articles, the English language is depicted as a humanised, international language necessary for business, but the French articles rarely discuss the English language. In the English commentary, collocates and clusters suggest the importance of fluency in English; although numbers were much lower in the French commentary and patterns less salient, most references to *anglais/e* also indicated the importance of fluency and language use.

In contrast, representations of French are rather different. In the Pastagate corpus, English tweets represent the French language as an overly policed language and question language endangerment. In contrast, French tweets often lament the declining quality of French and express concern over the future of the language, suggesting ideologies of language endangerment. In the English articles, French is again represented as an overly policed language and also a language that is marginalised in the international context. In the French articles, the language is not represented per se as most references to French pertained to the current and proposed changes to language policy in Quebec. In the comments, most English commentators argue that French is overly policed (this is especially notable through the frequent clusters THE LANGUAGE POLICE and THE LANGUAGE NAZIS) and question French language endangerment. In contrast, while French commentators often expressed embarrassment over the actions of the OQLF, there still seems to be a consensus that the French language needs to be protected—both from incursions from other languages and from a general linguistic decline from the "standard".

The fact that most English data foreground the importance of language *use* indicates the presence of instrumental language ideologies. The prevalence of these instrumental language ideologies rather than, for example, ideologies privileging identity and belonging, is in keeping with previous research on the English-speaking world and findings already discussed in this book (see Chaps. 4, 5, and 6). Rather than focusing on language use, many discussions of the French language in the French data represent the French language as needing protection, whether from incursions of other languages or from the general decline of the language. These examples suggest the presence of ideologies of language endangerment. Not only were ideologies of language endangerment not found in English data, the concept of language endangerment was linked to discrimination and was often questioned. Finally, some French tweets and comments suggested that attention should be paid to the quality of French in Quebec rather than the use of other languages. These examples could suggest evidence of standard language ideologies, which presuppose that there are "good" and "correct" ways of speaking that must be adhered to whereas "poor" and "incorrect" ways of speaking should be eliminated (see Milroy 2001). No standard language ideologies were found in the English tweets.

The second question asked if representations of languages differed according to the country of origin. While the anonymous nature of the Pastagate corpus means that it is not possible to assess such issues, findings from the other data sets revealed similarities across English language articles, comments, and retweets, suggesting a uniformity of opinion. More specifically, these texts are largely unanimous in their negative representation of the Pastagate affair and their focus on the international and business-related contexts. Also, articles published in UK obtained the most reader comments and the most retweets; one American publication (*NPR*) also obtained more retweets than its Canadian counterparts. In contrast, while there appeared to be consensus in French Canadian publications, these differed from the publication from France, which thematised issues in keeping with the English articles. Furthermore, there appeared to be less consensus between the journalists and the readers, with the latter expressing embarrassment and negativity. In addition, French Canadian publications did not obtain large numbers of comments or retweets, but the *Nouvel Observateur* obtained even fewer of both. These findings and statistics suggest that the English language may have facilitated the creation of the "moral panic" through the dissemination of the story to a wider, international audience and the concomitant marginalisation of representations that predominated in French-language media.

Finally, the third research question asked if representations of languages differed according to the linguistic medium. As already indicated, the English-language data were strongly cohesive in their representations of languages and the Pastagate affair more generally, and while these were somewhat similar to the article published in France, the French Canadian publications differed in that they did not focus on international contexts, business, or negativity. French commentators also expressed more negativity than their journalistic counterparts and they aired concerns about the decline of "standard" French, which was not an issue in French or English news articles. English articles were widely retweeted and hashtags tended to indicate a focus on language, geography, and Quebec politics; freely worded commentary tended to be more creative and expressed disbelief and ridicule about the reports. French articles were much less retweeted and contained far fewer hashtags and commentary; nonetheless, there were indications of negativity dominating the "sharing" of this news story.

In summary, findings suggest that languages are represented differently in English and French but the findings are largely coherent across news, commentary, and social media. While there is some discord between representations from France and from French-speaking Canada, there is much more unanimity in the English data. Together, these findings suggest that nation-states' ability to institute language policies and protect language rights might be curtailed by an international audience whose understandings of current affairs are driven by English-dominated news and social media.

References

Baker, P. (2006). *Using corpora in discourse analysis*. London/New York: Continuum.

Barbeau, G. B. (2013). *Le dossier* Maclean's *et le* Québec bashing *: Analyse socio-discursive d'une affaire médiatique controversée*. (Unpublished PhD Thesis). Université Laval, Québec.

Blommaert, J. (Ed.). (1999a). *Language ideological debates*. Berlin: Mouton de Gruyter.

Bouchard, C. (2002). *La langue et le nombril: Histoire d'une obsession québécoise*. Montreal: Fides.

Bourgault-Côté, G. (2013, 2 March). Buonanotte: la plainte originale ne portait pas sur l'italien. *Le Devoir*. http://www.ledevoir.com/politique/quebec/372332/buonanotte-la-plainte-originale-ne-portait-pas-sur-l-italien

Cameron, D. (1995). *Verbal hygiene*. London: Routledge.

CBC (Canadian Broadcasting Corporation). (2013a). Head of Quebec Language Office Resigns in Wake of Pastagate. 03.08.2013. Available http://www.cbc.ca/news/canada/montreal/head-of-quebec-language-office-resigns-in-wake-of-pastagate-1.1308461

CBC (Canadian Broadcasting Corporation). (2013b). 'Pastagate' Prompts Review at Quebec Language Office. 26.02.2013. Available http://www.cbc.ca/news/canada/montreal/pastagate-prompts-review-at-quebec-language-office-1.1305047

Cohen, S. (1972). *Folk devils and moral panics: The creation of the Mods and Rockers*. Oxford: Martin Robertson.

Cotter, C. (2010). *News talk: Investigating the language of journalism*. Cambridge: Cambridge University Press.

Fairclough, N. (2010). *Critical discourse analysis. The critical study of language* (2nd ed.). London: Pearson.

Fowler, R. (1994). Hysterical style in the press. In D. Graddol & O. Boyd-Barrett (Eds.), *Media texts: Authors and readers* (pp. 90–99). Clevedon: Multilingual Matters.

Heller, M. (1999a). Heated language in a cold climate. In J. Blommaert (Ed.), Language ideological debates (pp. 143–170). Berlin: Mouton de Gruyter.

Johnson, S. (1999). *From linguistic molehills to social mountains? Introducing moral panics about language* (Lancaster University Centre for Language in Social Life Working Papers Series 105). http://www.ling.lancs.ac.uk/pubs/clsl/clsl105.pdf. Accessed 4 Dec 2014.

Leppänen, S., & Häkkinen, A. (2012). Buffalaxed superdiversity: Representations of the other on YouTube. *Diversities, 14*(2), 17–33.

Marchi, A. (2013). *The guardian on journalism. A corpus-assisted discourse study of self-reflexivity* (PhD dissertation, Lancaster University).

Mediaobs. (2014). L'offre exclusive Mediaobs Culture. http://www.mediaobs.com/titre/nouvelobs_com. Accessed 4 Dec 2014.

Milroy, J. (2001). Language ideologies and the consequences of standardization. *Journal of Sociolinguistics, 5*(4), 530–555.

Newspapers Canada. (2013). *Daily newspaper circulation report.* http://www.newspaperscanada.ca/sites/default/files/2013%20Daily%20Newspapers%20Circulation%20Report%20FINAL.pdf. Accessed 7 Apr 2015.

Oakes, L. (2010). Lambs to the slaughter? Young francophones and the role of English in Quebec today. *Multilingua, 29*, 265–288.

OQLF (Office québécois de la langue française). (2013). L'Office québécois de la langue française modernise ses pratiques. Available http://www.oqlf.gouv.qc.ca/office/communiques/2013/20131018_modernisation.html

Schiffman, H. (2006). Language policy and linguistic culture. In T. Ricento (Ed.), *Introduction to language policy: Theory and method* (pp. 111–125). Hoboken: Wiley-Blackwell.

Teisceira-Lessard, P. (2013). "Pastagate": La présidente de l'OQLF démissionne. 08.03.2013. Available http://www.lapresse.ca/actualites/politique/politique-quebecoise/201303/08/01-4629080-pastagate-la-presidente-de-loqlf-demissionne.php

Wyatt, N. (2013, 26 February). Pastagate: Quebec to review language law violation policies after PR mess. *National post* Online edition. http://news.nationalpost.com/2013/02/26/quebecs-pastagate-pr-nightmare-story-gets-60-times-more-coverage-outside-province-than-marois-investment-trip/. Accessed 4 Dec 2014.

Zappavigna, M. (2011). Ambient affiliation: A linguistic perspective on Twitter. *New Media & Society, 13*(5), 708–806.

8

Conclusions

The past four chapters have explored case studies focusing on language ideologies and Canadian media, starting with more traditional news media and moving towards new and social media. In this chapter, we review some of the themes and commonalities across these chapters and, to do this, it is useful to return to the research questions posed in Chap. 1. Section 8.1 summarises the findings with relation to these research questions, and Sect. 8.2 discusses the implications of the findings with relation to Canadian language policy and planning; the book concludes with Sect. 8.3.

8.1 Summary of Findings

The first question asked how the French and English Canadian media discursively represent languages and language issues. The chapters have shown that only English and French, the official languages of Canada, tend to be discussed. Only in very rare cases are other languages discussed and even when other languages are relevant (e.g. the Italian language in the Pastagate context), these tend to serve as background against

R. Vessey, *Language and Canadian Media*,
DOI 10.1057/978-1-137-53001-1_8

which official language debates are played out. The prevalence of official languages suggests the banal nature of English and French in Canadian media. However, these languages are less banal when they figure in debates; as shown in Chaps. 5 and 7, when debates about languages arise in Canada, their roles are often hotly contested. Furthermore, language issues are arguably more commonplace discussion topics in French Canadian media. As shown in Chaps. 4 and 6, language issues—and especially those pertaining to French—tend to figure far more frequently in French newspapers and in French Twitter than in English newspapers and English Twitter. Furthermore, when English Canadian media do discuss language issues, these often focus on the French language rather than the English language, suggesting the extent to which the role of English is taken for granted. Similarly, it is the French language that is most often discussed in the French Canadian media, but here this suggests that its status cannot be taken for granted. Indeed, discussions of French often focus on the need to protect, promote, and defend it from linguistic decline.

This brings us to the second question, which asked which language ideologies predominate in English Canadian media and which predominate in French. Findings from across the chapters showed that language ideologies tend to be distinct in English and French Canadian media. More specifically, Chaps. 4 and 6 showed the extent to which the English language tends to be taken for granted in English Canadian media, suggesting the prevalence of monolingual ideologies. In Chap. 4, this was most evident through the low frequency of references to language in the English Canadian newspapers as compared to the French Canadian newspapers, as well as through discussions of immigration and the importance placed on fluency. Similarly, in Chap. 6, monolingual ideologies were evident through the lack of discussion of language issues in English Canadian Twitter, which was in direct contrast to the greater emphasis on language issues in the French Canadian Twitter. Furthermore, while French-language content was marked (e.g. through "et en français"), English-language content was unmarked and normative. Although monolingual ideologies were less salient in Chaps. 5 and 7, these are cases that focused on ideological debates, where subtlety evaporates and language ideologies become more explicit through metalanguage. Nevertheless, Chap.5

demonstrated monolingual ideologies in the articles and, in the commentary, through the fact that English commentators criticised linguistic "complaints" and "whining" while at the same time failing to recognise their own engagement in and complaints concerning this same language issue. More generally, monolingual ideologies were evident through the scarcity of code-mixing and code-switching in all case studies. Even in online spaces where there is less pressure to maintain a monolingual standard, English and French tended not to mix.

Another trend was for instrumental language ideologies to predominate in the English data. In Chap. 4, when languages (and not just English or French) were discussed, it was most often with reference to fluency and education in languages, or with reference to languages being used in international contexts. Similarly, in Chap. 6 the data sets showed the important incremental and functional uses of English in URLs, hashtags, and @replies, even when French alternatives were available. In Chap. 7, collocates and clusters in the English commentary suggest the importance of fluency in English and English tweets focused on issues of using (e.g. speaking, learning, writing) and preventing the use of (i.e. banning) English.

While monolingual and instrumental language ideologies predominated in English, these figured to some extent, too, in the French data, although in a very different way. For example, while monolingual ideologies tend to be unmarked and the importance of English presumed in English Canadian newspapers, in French Canadian newspapers, the importance of French is explicit, especially with reference to the province of Quebec; this was particularly clear in Chap. 4. Similarly, while there was some evidence of instrumental language ideologies in Chaps. 4, 6, and 7, these cases tended to refer only to the English language. In Chap. 4, this became salient through evaluations of fluency in English, whereas in Chaps. 6 and 7, this became evident through the incremental incursions of English into the French Twittersphere, and the fact that most references to *anglais/e* in the French Pastagate commentary occurred in discussions of fluency and language use. Thus, while monolingual and instrumental language ideologies did occur in the French data, instrumental language ideologies focused on the practical importance of English—not French—and monolingualism referred to

French (especially in Quebec) rather than English and was explicit rather than implicit.

Instead of foregrounding monolingualism and instrumentalism, the French data instead tended to foreground the importance of the French language as a core value. In Chap. 4, this took shape through discussions of "our" language and the positive characteristics attributed to the French language. Similarly, in Chap. 5 discussions of "us" and "them" were salient with reference to the language debate and in Chap. 6, French tweets frequently discussed French language issues, including endangerment, with one example calling for Quebecers to defend "their" language. In Chap. 7, the need to "make things more French" (*franciser*) underpins the descriptions of actions and intentions of the OQLF, and commentators decry the (perceived) decline in linguistic standards. Since the French language appears to have an intrinsic role for French-speaking Canadians, its decline—whether in standards or in frequency of use—poses real challenges. Here, a decline in linguistic standards will be discussed through ideologies of standardised language, and a decline in frequency of use will be discussed through ideologies of language endangerment.

Although ideologies of standardised language were not salient in Chaps. 4, 5, or 6, they surfaced in Chap. 7 with reference to the Pastagate debate. In this case, some French commentators suggested that attention should be paid to the quality of French in Quebec rather than the use of other languages. This finding was somewhat surprising, given the lack of evidence in other chapters. However, previous research (e.g. Bouchard 2002; Oakes and Warren 2007) has suggested that concerns over standard French are often a concern for French Canadians. The findings from these case studies suggest that ideologies of standardised language are predominantly issues raised by individual commentators rather than by journalists or individuals in positions of power. For this reason, standard language ideologies tend not to surface in discussions about language more generally, but may surface in language ideological debates such as in the Pastagate context.

In contrast, ideologies of language endangerment figured in most data sets. For example, in the French Canadian newspapers examined in Chap. 4, concerns of language endangerment were expressed in a diversity of explicit and implicit ways. The detailed examination of a downsampled article, in particular, showed how newsworthy language endangerment is for a French-speaking audience; moreover, its comparison with an English article showed just how differently the same stories can be reported to the public. Similarly, in Chap. 6 we saw that French Canadian Twitter users were more concerned with language endangerment than their English counterparts, using hashtags such as #LANGUESOFFICIELLES to call for action in the defence or promotion of French. In other chapters, the issue of language endangerment was at the crux of the issues under discussion, that is, the issue of sufficient or insufficient French in the Vancouver Olympics (Chap. 5) and the action taken to protect French in the case of Pastagate (Chap. 7). Indeed, in Chap. 7, while some French Twitter users expressed regret and embarrassment over the actions taken by the OQLF, many argued that French still needed to be defended.

This brings us to the third and final question, which asked about the extent to which the language ideologies that underpin traditional news media also exist in new and social media. The case studies examined here suggested many similarities across the different data types. Despite differences in terms of authorship (e.g. journalists vs. reader commentators), audience (e.g. subscribers vs. a virtually unlimited and anonymous public online), and national context (e.g. Canada vs. international), English language data consistently represented languages—and the English language in particular—as having instrumental value. In fact, there was little indication that language could have any value other than instrumental value. In contrast, while the French language data also manifested instrumental language ideologies (in particular with relation to English), ideologies of language as a core value were more prevalent across all cases through ideologies of standardised language and ideologies of language endangerment. This was especially clear in the Pastagate data, where news and social media data were compared and contrasted. There, it was found that English-medium representations were largely unanimous in their negative representations, regardless of the country of publication. In fact, international publications tended to obtain greater response from readers (e.g. through comments and retweeting) than national publications. In contrast, there were some differences between French Canadian articles and the article from France, but commentators were more unanimous in the calls for French-language standards to improve (or at least be maintained). Thus, while findings are not precisely parallel across the data sets, there are some important similarities suggesting that new and social media are not as distinct from news media as might have been predicted.

8.2 Discussion

Having explored the extent to which language ideologies differ in English and French Canadian media, it remains to be seen how these can be managed within Canada's existing—and evolving—language policy. In Chap. 1, it was argued that language ideologies contribute to discourses about and the uptake of language policies; this is particularly true in the Canadian context, where language issues are directly intertwined with nationalism. The case studies examined here suggest that similarities in language ideologies across news and social media may present challenges to the Canadian government which, while successful in effecting linguistic change in offline environments, has a rather hands-off approach for online spaces (Vipond 2012: 92). Indeed, although the Canadian Standing Senate Committee on Official Languages (2012) and the Commissioner of Official Languages (Office of the Commissioner of Official Languages 2015) have both recommended that action be taken to respect language rights in the online world, the impact that these recommendations realistically have on the ground is questionable. As more and more of the offline world develops an online presence, the lack of mechanisms to enforce language policies online and the continued dominance of English in online spaces pose real challenges to the future of Canadian language policy.

Even when language policies are enforced, it is often only with the aim of effecting linguistic change—that is, increasing language use or ensuring the equivalence of provisions in both official languages. While these are certainly important issues, a focus on language use reinforces the notion that *use* is what matters for language rights to be respected (which, as we have seen, is a predominant belief in English Canadian media). Also, a policy emphasis on language use marginalises the importance that should also be placed on explicit and implicit linguistic representations (that is, language ideologies) and their relevance to language rights. "Discourse planning"

(Lo Bianco 2005) could perhaps contribute to the formulation and reformulation of language ideologies such that they could become more conducive to language policymakers' aims and objectives. However, the rise of user-generated media and Web 2.0 pose important challenges to language planning even in its more traditional forms (Wright 2013); therefore, the plausibility of discourse planning in this era is uncertain.

As we have seen, language planners and policymakers no longer function within nation-state contexts in isolation and must contend with international and internationalised notions about language that, as we saw with Pastagate, can have a real bearing on the nation-state context. Policymakers increasingly need to take into account global perspectives and the linguistic norms and values of the international community in order to avoid backlash similar to that seen with "Pastagate". This tenuous balance between the global and the local is crucial for the future of language policy and planning, especially as language issues are reported in news and social media.

That being said, the relevance of the globalised context and its majority and market-driven trends (cf. Kelly-Holmes 2010) suggest why language planning and policymaking are arguably more important than ever. Without policies in place, the international media system can become a means of catering to and favouring groups with access to particular communication channels for specific linguistic communities (e.g. English) (see discussions in e.g. Mac Síthigh 2015; Tagg 2015: 47). Indeed, a flawed policy-free "benign neglect" approach to language (i.e. the belief that individuals' language choices should be unrestricted and ungoverned, Kymlicka and Patten 2003: 10) seems to underpin many English-medium examples that disparage language protectionism while prioritising language use. Pressure is intensifying for minoritised groups to translate their linguistic cultures into English and globalised, market-driven contexts. As we saw with Pastagate, the ability to institute language policies and protect language rights is to some extent being curtailed by an international audience whose understandings of current affairs are driven by English-dominated news and social media wherein languages appear to be viewed predominantly through an instrumental lens. However, languages are not just tools to be used; they also have intrinsic value and serve as core values for communities. It is the fundamental intrinsic value of language that underpins ideologies of standardised language and ideologies of language endangerment. Indeed, it is the core or "intrinsic" value of language that has played a role in the preservation of some languages against the odds. For example, French Canadians' historic struggle for French-medium education was premised on the right for intergenerational cultural transmission (see e.g. Hayday 2005; Heller 1999).

If language is understood *only* or *predominantly* as a tool to be used—and its usefulness is determined only by the extent to which communication can be achieved—then the preservation of language (either from perceived decline in standards or from incursions from other languages) might be impossible to understand. Why, we might ask, should language be *used* if it is not *useful*? Why preserve its current standards if the speakers who *use* it choose to change these standards? And why protect a language from other languages if those other languages are more widely *used* and (therefore) more *useful*? All of these hypothetical questions overlook the other reasons why languages are still in existence. Accordingly, if Canadian language policy continues to stress the importance of language use to the detriment of the intrinsic value of languages (e.g. as markers of cultural heritage, as badges of belonging), then it privileges English speakers' language ideologies and ultimately provides little rationale for language protection.

Importantly, the differences between English and French speakers' language ideologies are not new phenomena: Haque (2012: 161) notes that the Commissioners of the B&B Commission in the 1960s found that anglophones were complacent about language maintenance and had little understanding of the role of language in intergenerational cultural transmission. Furthermore, the Commission's recommendations for Canada's bilingualism and multiculturalism policies were premised on the instrumental value of languages as commodities (Haque 2012: 204–207). However, Ricento (2005: 355) notes that seeing languages as functional tools may reduce individuals' capacity to comprehend other cultures' integrative attachment to their language. The instrumental/intrinsic divide in English- and French-speaking Canada may thus be a primary feature in the perpetuation of Canada's "two solitudes".

However, Canada's language policies ideally should help to surmount the linguistically marked social divide through the respect of language rights on both sides. Certainly, most Canadians are familiar with the argument that the national language policies are in place to respect the equal role of the two founding "nations" (English speakers and French speakers). While the premise of this argument is that the two languages have cultural value for Canadian national identity, it has consistently been problematised by the huge number of Canadians—not least of which the First Nations—who have contributed to the building of Canada as we know it (see e.g. Haque 2012). As noted in Chap. 5, since most Canadians (83 %) are not French–English bilingual and many do not have English or French heritage, the identity of the nation as "bilingual" does not necessarily map onto the national identity of individuals. The link between language and national identity has caused important tensions between Canada's official (bilingual, multicultural) identity and the identity of individual Canadians. As a result, Canadians who question the value or relevance of French may simply be trying to justify their identity as an "unhyphenated" (i.e. authentic) Canadian. The language ideological debates that ensue could very well pertain to the diverse understandings of Canadian national identity and, perhaps, a desire to belong.

Since belonging is often predicated on an ability to communicate with others, and this is crucially facilitated by the media, it would seem that Canada's dual-media system functions to perpetuate the two solitudes. The nature of a media system is for it to report news that is relevant to the community—and with a country as large and multilingual as Canada, this is difficult to achieve on a national scale. Although previous research (e.g. Elkin 1975; Fletcher 1998; Halford et al. 1983; Hayday 2005: 60; Kariel and Rosenvall 1983; Raboy 1991; Robinson 1998; Siegel 1979; Taras 1993) has shown that English and French Canadian media report different news *topics* and other research (e.g. Pritchard and Sauvageau 1999; Pritchard et al. 2005) has suggested that English and French Canadian journalists conceptualise their roles somewhat differently, this book has helped to show that differences also exist in terms of language ideologies. Thus, a diverse body of research continues to show the manifold ways in which the two solitudes exist and become manifested in Canadian daily life. If Canada is to be a united country with a more unified national discourse, then the media have an important role to play.

The theoretical lens of language ideologies has proven to be useful for exploring language politics and the two solitudes in Canada. As discussed in earlier chapters, language ideologies do not refer to facts about languages, nor about "truth". No language ideology is real or unreal, "right" or "wrong", "true" or "false"—ideology refers to lived experience and the commonplace understandings that help individuals operate within their environment without questioning all aspects of the world around them. In other words, the differences between the language ideologies in English and French Canadian media suggest some of the differences in the lived experiences of English- and French-speaking Canadians. For example, since monolingual ideologies and instrumental language ideologies predominate in English, this simply suggests the fact that most English speakers live in a world where the English language has an unquestioned role—and this is reflected in the media. However, when languages are discussed in English-speaking Canada, they are perhaps perceived within a context where English is ubiquitous and therefore useful in all domains; understandably, it might be difficult to understand what role other languages could serve when faced with the hegemony of English. Accordingly, a focus on use—the instrumental value of languages—is perhaps the perspective most readily available to those accustomed to understanding languages as having comprehensive, universal functions.

However, French-speaking Canadians have a rather different lived experience and this, too, is reflected in the media. Unlike English-speaking Canadians and despite the efforts of language policymakers (especially in Quebec), most French speakers do not live in a world where French serves as an unquestioned role and is useful or ubiquitous in all domains. Therefore, it is manifestly more topical in discourse, including media discourse. The range of ways in which discussions emerge pertains to the reality of the lived experience of French Canadians themselves, where the dominance of English and its incursions in daily life may indicate to some that the language is endangered. While the exploration "truth" of French language endangerment is not within the remit of this study (for further discussion, see e.g. Castonguay 1979, 1999, 2002), beliefs in endangerment and the decline of standards relate to the very real lived experience of French speakers themselves who value the French language and are witness to important changes to its status and role in society, especially in comparison with English.

Given French speakers' concern with the status and future of the French language, it is curious, perhaps, that there is still demonstrable interest in and valuing of the English language. However, this finding is in line with that uncovered by other researchers (e.g. Cardinal 2008: 69; Oakes 2010), who have noted that many francophones want to improve their fluency in English because of the important role it plays in Canadian society—and internationally. This supports Garvin's (1993) conceptual framework of language standardisation (see Sect. 1.1), which posited that when a language has predominantly instrumental value, individual fluency in a standard language is highly prized.

Given the fact that the role of English is uncontested and ubiquitous in most areas of life in Canada, it is also rather unsurprising that English speakers express some consternation at the need to respect French speakers' language rights when the same rules do not (need to) apply both ways. However, as Pinto (2014) explains, the respect of minority language rights almost always requires some infringement on majority language rights; this infringement, though, is arguably reasonable given the much larger infringement on minority rights if minority language speakers were forced to forego their language and adopt the majority language in all domains. This interpretation of language rights helps to explain why English speakers often express resentment towards the enforced role of French in Canada: in many cases, the role of French infringes on the role of English, thus compromising English speakers' own language rights. For example, English speakers' contestations of the Official Languages Commissioner's conclusion that federal ministers should tweet in both official languages could perhaps be explained by the fact that English Twitter users need not be confronted with other languages in their socially mediated lives (as we saw in Chap. 6). The enforcement of French on Twitter could seem like a deliberate incursion on English speakers' freedom to produce and consume exclusively English-medium material. However, since French Canadians' Twittersphere undergoes incursions from English in nearly all respects with regular occurrence (as we also saw in Chap. 6), this infringement of rights on the part of English Twitter users seems a rather small price to pay.

8.3 Summary

The chapters of this book have suggested that language ideologies differ between English and French Canadian media, and these differences have important implications for language policy and planning in Canada. These differences were consistent across different media types, and the role of English was particularly important because of the ease with which it served to propagate language ideological debates from the local to the national and international contexts.

Certainly, there are many limitations to the findings of this book, where only four case studies are covered and some of the data sets are rather limited (especially by corpus linguistics standards). Also, there is little indication of change over time, since data sets were not charted diachronically. In some instances, it might have been insightful to have more data on the participants in the debates or about the journalists or authors in question. Furthermore, it is impossible to know if English tweets come from "English speakers" and French tweets from "French speakers"—or if these categories have any meaning in online spaces. Accordingly, findings from these tweets cannot really be generalised from these communities of "ambient affiliation" to offline language communities.

Another limitation to this study is the oversimplified categorisation of Canadians into an "English" and "French" binary. Indeed, while the focus here has primarily been on French in Quebec, there are important characteristics of the Quebec context that differ markedly from other French-speaking areas of Canada. There has been little space for discussion of Franco-Ontarians and Acadians, and even less for considerations of smaller French-speaking communities. In a similar way, English speakers in Canada have not been accorded the detail that is their due; this group comprises great ethnic, religious, historic, and cultural diversity that is inadequately accounted for by a common language. It would be useful for a future project to compare case studies of individual groups' language ideologies so that the similarities and differences between these can be explored at a more local level.

Perhaps more significantly, there has been no discussion of the First Nations or minority groups, and little mention of languages besides English and French. While English and French are the dominant groups in the country, other demographics are not insignificant. With a decline in francophone birth rate and a surge in aboriginal birth rate (Statistics Canada 2006: 17), increased immigration, and one in five Canadians a visible minority (Statistics Canada 2011: 3), the Canadian demographic is changing. These changes are reflected in the 2011 Census results, in which Statistics Canada opted to not use the traditional categories "anglophone", "francophone", and "allophone", since these apparently no longer reflect the complex linguistic reality of Canada today (see Scott 2012). Although Canada has never been a country consisting only of English speakers and French speakers, the terms "francophone", "anglophone", and "allophone" have been used since the B&B Commission as labels that enabled the people of Canada to be categorised according to their place in a society that was designed to be French–English bilingual. These labels served to reify the role of these languages in the country, with individuals identifying themselves or being identified according to these categories. While the decision by Statistics Canada, a federal government agency, to alter the terminology certainly reflects the broader changes in Canadian society, the replacement of essentialist group labels also indicates a change in frames of reference in the country. New frames of reference may lead to the gradual devolution of the bilingualism model on which Canada was based in the 1960s and 1970s. With this changing environment, there is considerable room for future research on the relevance of languages and nationalism in Canada.

In terms of methodology, a number of challenges were posed to the corpus linguistic methods (and especially frequency) by the "superdiverse" nature of the social media data. Although frequency counts revealed some findings, frequencies were affected by, for example, the high concentration of retweeting, the nature of the multilingual data, and abbreviations and misspellings. These all impacted the analysis to the extent that salience based on frequency was rather difficult to establish. In other words, frequency was less useful here than in other data sets that contain less verbatim repetition (e.g. retweets), less multilingualism, and more "standard" language. Since superdiverse online environments are increasingly part of offline daily life, the ability for corpus linguistics to address these challenges will be essential in short order. As concerns the discourse analysis, not all features of the discourse were accounted for. For example, not all "hypertext" (e.g. URLs) was investigated, and yet this comprises an important site of meaning-making, especially on Twitter where the retweeting of stories from external sites is so common.

Despite these limitations, the findings across all chapters were remarkably consistent, suggesting some of the fundamental differences between the ways in which language issues are represented in English and French Canadian media. These media arguably reproduce discourse that takes place in society more generally and, accordingly, the language ideological systems and power hierarchies that exist there (Page 2012, 181–182). More specifically, since English predominates in the offline world, so too does it predominate in the online world. Its hegemony not only privileges monolingualism but also seems to privilege and foreground specific language ideologies. So long as English predominates in online spaces, ideologies of instrumental language that predominate in English-speaking contexts (cf. Garvin 1993) may be imported online, where language policies and the protection of minorities have little relevance, and "democratic" participation in the negotiation of meanings (Small 2011; Zappavigna 2011) is contingent on the use of the dominant language—English. Although French is an international language, French perspectives on issues were comparatively marginalised within the data sets examined here, and the English-dominant representations seemed to have greater impact. Thus, this book finds that dominant, transnational language ideologies produced and reproduced through the media can have rather direct implications for linguistic minorities, their rights, and the policies protecting them in the offline world of nation-states.

The findings uncovered in this book also suggest the relevance of language ideologies within studies of multilingual data. It would be difficult to assess the impact of English if data in other languages were not examined as well. It seems that more cross-linguistic work on language ideologies is required in order to better understand how, to paraphrase McLuhan (1964), the language is not only the medium but also the message. In other words, unless we have access to multiple languages, it is difficult to understand the nuanced differences between discussions taking place in other languages. In Canada, where most citizens are not French–English bilingual, Canadians tend to not have access to ideologies of the other language group. Without exposure to one another, the "two solitudes" of Canada may persist well into the future.

References

Bouchard, C. (2002). *La langue et le nombril: Histoire d'une obsession québécoise*. Montreal: Fides.

Canadian Standing Senate Committee on Official Languages. (2012). *Internet, new media and social media: Respect for language rights!* Available http://www.parl.gc.ca/Content/SEN/Committee/411/OLLO/rep/rep05oct12-e.pdf

Cardinal, L. (2008). Linguistic peace: A time to take stock. *Inroads, 23*, 62–70.

Castonguay, C. (1979). Why hide the facts? The federalist approach to the language crisis in Canada. *Canadian Public Policy, 5*(1), 4–15.

Castonguay, C. (1999). Getting the facts straight on French: Reflections following the 1996 Census. *Inroads, 8*, 59–78.

Castonguay, C. (2002). Assimilation linguistique et remplacement des générations francophones et anglophones au Québec et au Canada. *Recherches sociographiques, 43*(1), 149–182.

Elkin, F. (1975). Communications media and identity formation in Canada. In B. D. Singer (Ed.), *Communications in Canadian society* (2nd ed., pp. 229–243). Vancouver: Copp Clark Publishing.

Fletcher, F. J. (1998). Media and political identity: Canada and Quebec in the era of globalization. *Canadian Journal of Communication, 23*(3). Retrieved from http://www.cjc-online.ca/index.php/journal/article/view/1049/955

Garvin, P. (1993). A conceptual framework for the study of language standardization. *International Journal of the Sociology of Language, 100*(101), 37–54.

Halford, P. W., van den Hoven, A., Romanow, W. I., & Soderlund, W. C. (1983). A media tale of two cities: Quebec referendum coverage in Montreal and Toronto. *Canadian Journal of Communication, 9*(4), 1–31.

Haque, E. (2012). *Multiculturalism within a bilingual framework: Language, race, and belonging in Canada*. Toronto: University of Toronto Press.

Hayday, M. (2005). *Bilingual today, united tomorrow: Official languages in education and Canadian federalism*. Montreal/Kingston: McGill-Queen's University Press.

Heller, M. (1999). *Linguistic minorities and modernity: A sociolinguistic ethnography*. London: Longman.

Kariel, H. G., & Rosenvall, L. A. (1983). Cultural affinity displayed in Canadian daily newspapers. *Journalism Quarterly, 60*(3), 431–436.

Kelly-Holmes, H. (2010). Rethinking the macro-micro relationship: Some insights from the marketing domain. *International Journal of the Sociology of Language, 202*, 25–39.

Kymlicka, W., & Patten, A. (2003). Language rights and political theory. *Annual Review of Applied Linguistics, 23*, 3–21.

Lo Bianco, J. (2005). Including discourse in language planning theory. In P. Bruthiaux, W. Atkinson, W. Eggington, & V. Ramanathan (Eds.), *Directions in applied linguistics* (pp. 255–263). Clevedon: Multilingual Matters.

Mac Síthigh, D. (2015). Because the computer speaks English? Language rights and digital media. *Journal of Media Law.* Vol 7, issue 1, pp. 65-84

McLuhan, M. (1964). Understanding Media: The Extensions of Man. New York: McGraw-Hill.

Oakes, L. (2010). Lambs to the slaughter? Young francophones and the role of English in Quebec today. *Multilingua, 29*, 265–288.

Oakes, L., & Warren, J. (2007). *Language, citizenship and identity in Quebec.* Basingstoke/England/New York: Palgrave Macmillan.

Office of the Commissioner of Official Languages. (2015). *Statement from the Commissioner of Official Languages about ministers' Twitter use.* Available http://www.officiallanguages.gc.ca/en/news/releases/2015/2015-02-20

Page, R. (2012). The linguistics of self-branding and micro-celebrity in Twitter: The role of hashtags. *Discourse & Communication, 6*(2), 181–201.

Pinto, M. (2014). Taking language rights seriously. *King's Law Journal, 25*, 231–254.

Pritchard, D., & Sauvageau, F. (1999). English and French and Generation X: The professional values of Canadian journalists. In H. Lazar & T. McIntosh (Eds.), *How Canadians connect* (pp. 283–306). Montreal/Kingston: McGill-Queen's University Press.

Pritchard, D., Brewer, P. R., & Sauvageau, F. (2005). Changes in Canadian journalists' views about social and political roles of the news media: A panel study, 1996–2003. *Canadian Journal of Political Science, 38*(2), 287–306.

Raboy, M. (1991). Canadian broadcasting, Canadian nationhood: Two concepts, two solitudes and great expectations. *Electronic Journal of Communication, 1*(2). Retrieved from http://www.cios.org/EJCPUBLIC/001/2/00123.HTML

Ricento, T. (2005). Problems with the 'language-as-resource' discourse in the promotion of heritage languages in the U.S.A. *Journal of Sociolinguistics, 9*(3), 348–368.

Robinson, G. (1998). *Constructing the Quebec referendum: French and English media voices.* Toronto: University of Toronto Press.

Scott, M. (2012, 26 October). Census 2011: StatsCan does away with 'francophone', 'anglophone' and 'allophone'. *The Gazette*. Available http://www.montrealgazette.com/news/Census+2011+StatsCan+does+away+with+francophone/7439307/story.html

Siegel, A. (1979). French and English broadcasting in Canada—A political evaluation. *Canadian Journal of Communication, 5*(3), 1–17.

Small, T. A. (2011). What the hashtag? A content analysis of Canadian politics on Twitter. *Information, Communication & Society, 14*(6), 872–895.

Statistics Canada. (2006). *Population projections by aboriginal identity in Canada: 2006–2031.* Available http://www.statcan.gc.ca/pub/91-552-x/91-552-x2011001-eng.pdf

Statistics Canada. (2011). *Canada at a glance.* Available http://www.statcan.gc.ca/pub/12-581-x/12-581-x2012000-eng.pdf

Tagg, C. (2015). *Exploring digital communication: Language in action.* Abingdon: Routledge.

Taras, D. (1993). The mass media and political crisis: Reporting Canada's constitutional struggles. *Canadian Journal of Communication, 18*(2), 131–148.

Vipond, M. (2012). *The mass media in Canada* (4th ed.). Toronto: James Lorimer and Company.

Wright, S. (2013). Status planning. In C. A. Chapelle (Ed.), *The encyclopedia of applied linguistics* (pp. 1–6). London: Blackwell.

Zappavigna, M. (2011). Ambient affiliation: A linguistic perspective on Twitter. *New Media & Society, 13*(5), 708–806.

Index

R. Vessey, *Language and Canadian Media*,
DOI 10.1057/978-1-137-53001-1